Because I Was Flesh

By Edward Dahlberg

Because I Was Flesh

The Autobiography of Edward Dahlberg

New Directions

. . . because I was flesh, and a breath that passeth away and cometh not again.

Psalms

Why weepest thou, Hagar? Arise, take the child, and hold him in thine hand; for God hath heard thy voice, and hath seen the child." And she opened her eyes, and she saw a well of water, and she went and filled her bottle with water, and she gave the child to drink, and she arose and went toward the wilderness of Paran.

Book of Jubilees

ACKNOWLEDGMENTS

Portions of this book first appeared in *Best American Short Stories of 1962, Big Table, First Person, The Massachusetts Review, Prairie Schooner, Sewanee Review* and *The Texas Quarterly*, to whose Editors my gratitude is offered, as to the National Institute of Arts and Letters and the Longview Foundation for grants which enabled me to complete it.

For My Wife Rlene

Because I Was Flesh

I

"What moved you to 't?"
"Why, flesh and blood, my lord;
What should move men unto a
woman else?"

Tourneur

Kansas City is a vast inland city, and its marvelous river, the Missouri, heats the senses; the maple, alder, elm and cherry trees with which the town abounds are songs of desire, and only the almonds of ancient Palestine can awaken the hungry pores more deeply. It is a wild, concupiscent city, and few there are troubled about death until they age or are sick. Only those who know the ocean ponder death as they behold it, whereas those bound closely to the ground are more sensual.

Kansas City was my Tarsus; the Kaw and the Missouri Rivers were the washpots of joyous Dianas from St. Joseph and Joplin. It was a young, seminal town and the seed of its men was strong. Homer sang of many sacred towns in Hellas which were no better than Kansas City, as hilly as Eteonus and as stony as Aulis. The city wore a coat of rocks and grass. The bosom of this town nursed men, mules and horses as famous as the asses of Arcadia and the steeds of Diomedes. The cicadas sang in the valleys beneath Cliff Drive. Who could grow weary of the livery stables off McGee Street or the ewes of Laban in the stockyards?

Let the bard from Smyrna catalogue Harma, the ledges and caves of Ithaca, the milk-fed damsels of Achaia, pigeon-flocked Thisbe or the woods of Onchestus, I sing of Oak, Walnut, Chestnut, Maple and Elm Streets. Phthia was a bin of corn, Kansas City a buxom grange of wheat. Could the strumpets from the stews of Corinth, Ephesus or Tarsus fetch a groan or sigh more quickly than the dimpled thighs of lasses from St. Joseph or Topeka?

Kansas City was the city of my youth and the burial ground of my poor mother's hopes; her blood, like Abel's, cries out to me from every cobblestone, building, flat and street.

My mother and I were luckless souls. She strove fiercely for her angels and was wretched most of her days in the earth. Moreover, if she failed, who hasn't? If she prayed for what she thought was her good, and none heeded her, that had to be too. Each one carries his own sack of woe on his back, and though he supplicate heaven to ease him, who hears him except his own sepulchre? Night covers the acts of man; could he lay his follies on the ground and in the light of the sun as he committed them, he would shriek like the owls for his tomb. We know nothing and understand nothing, and this is no boast. The trees are tender and the voices of the many rivers are pleasant, yet our bones quake every day.

She never desired to be miserable, and neither did I, but it is just as important to be unfortunate as it is to be happy. She sighed as often for the wheat as she pined for the chaff, not knowing one from the other. "Many cry in trouble and are not heard, but to their salvation," declares St. Augustine.

My mother had two miserable afflictions, neither of which was she ever to overcome: her flesh—which is my own—and the world, that cursed both of us. "Let me, O Lord, be most ungrateful to the world," comes from the mouth of Teresa, the Jewess of Avila.

There was no angel in Beersheba to comfort my mother or to take pity on her unquenchable thirst for the living waters: "What aileth thee, Hagar?" Nobody heard her tears; the heart is a fountain of weeping water which makes no noise in the world. The Kabbalists claimed that when man cries out, his voice pervades the Kosmos; stones are sentient and tremble for us when we are heavy with trouble, and the ground is our brother and keeper though man is not.

A tintype taken of my mother in her early twenties showed a long oval face with burning brown eyes and hair of the same color. She did not have thick features, and her hands had the soul of the pentagram, which Plato considered the geometric figure of goodness. There was much feeling in the appearance of her mouth, although most of her teeth had been removed by a quack dentist of Rivington Street in New York. Perhaps no more than four feet ten inches in height, health was her beauty. Lucian affirms that "there are some who will be admired for their Beauty; whom you must call Adonis and Hyacinthus, though they have a nose a cubit long." My mother's long nose sorely vexed me. I don't believe I ever forgave her for that, and when her hair grew perilously thin, showing the vulgar henna dye, I thought I was the unluckiest son in the world. I doted on the short up-turned gentile nose and imagined myself the singular victim of nature in having a mother with a nose that was a social misfortune. Aside from her unchristian nose, what troubled me enormously was her untidiness. She slopped about the rooms in greasy aprons and dressed more like a rag raker or a chimney sweep. I was ashamed when we walked together in the streets, and when she showed a parcel of her winter drawers as she sat I suffered discomfiture.

This book is a burden of Tyre in my soul. It is a song of the skin; for I was born incontinent. Everything has been created out of lust, and He who made us lusts no less than flesh, for God and Nature are young and seminal, and rage all day long. I shall sing as Tyre, according to the Prophet Isaiah, like a harlot, and for seventy years.

It is a great pain to divulge the life of a mother, and wicked to betray her faults. Why then do I do it? I have nothing better to do with my life than to write a book and perhaps nothing worse. Besides, it is a delusion to believe that one has a choice. If this book is a great defect, then let it be; for I have come to that time in my life when it is absolutely important to compose a good memoir although it is also a negligible thing if I should fail. Fame, when not purchased, is an epitaph which the rains and the birds peck until the letters on the headstone are illegible.

Would to God that my mother had not been a leaf scattered everywhere and as the wind listeth. Would to heaven that I could compose a different account of her flesh. Should I seem to mock that *mater dolorosa* of rags and grief, know that all my laughter lies in her grave. *Mea culpa* is the cry of all bones. I have always blamed myself for everything except when I was idle and had the time to find fault with others. Our errors, I pray, save us from being dullards; what other salvation have I since I am gross, vile, licentious, stupid, and withal am so peevish that when I lose a pin I suppose I am dropping my blood and sweat in Gethsemane.

Should I err against her dear relics or trouble her sleep, may no one imagine that she has not always been for me the three Marys of the New Testament. Moreover, whatever I imagine I know is taken from my mother's body, and this is the memoir of her body.

My mother was utterly separated from the whole race

of mankind save when she was concupiscent. This woman suffered immensely from solitude—and what eases the lonely so much as sexual pleasure? Unlike Hamlet, I cannot accuse the womb that begat me; however, I am his bondservant when he sobs, "Mother, mother, mother!" for this is Christian grief.

My mother's family came from outside Warsaw, and there were as many Catholics as Jews among my ancestors. I have high Slavic cheekbones, and I am sure my mother and I have Polish blood. How I came by the name of Dahlberg, which is Swedish, I do not know. Often Jews assumed the name of the district or province where they dwelt; they also sometimes took the appellation of a neighboring prince or burgher. The predatory Swedish hordes overran Europe and they came to Novgorod as traders as early as the eleventh century. My maternal grandfather's name was written Dalberg and my mother used this spelling, which was printed in black letters on the cash register of the Star Lady Barbershop in Kansas City, though later through error I added an "h." I always thought this name was apocryphal and from the time I was a child of eight I was sure that my mother had no parents. When I heard a boy speak of his brother or sister, I ran back to my mother and wept: "Mother, have I no uncle, aunt or cousin? Are you an orphan, mother?"

On rare occasions she mentioned a deceased one and whispered in German, "*Selige Mutter*," and I could not believe that she spoke the truth. When she said that her father had been educated and rich I was certain that she only wanted to comfort both of us.

I had lost even my name, and was as much a pauper in this as those exiled Jews who were not entitled to engage in the occupations of their forefathers because the Prophet could not find their names in Ezra's register.

The Jew is a confusion of tongues and peoples, and though once his language was referred to as the "lip of

Canaan," the Jews were separated from their alphabet, which is a tragedy to a nation as well as to a family of two. My mother's family spoke and wrote Polish and German; she used both languages and muttered Hebrew in the synagogue on high holy days: but I doubt that she understood her prayers.

My grandfather was a timber merchant who traveled back and forth between Warsaw and London to do business and to visit relations who had lived and flourished in London. He also wished to avoid his wife, who was an unleavened mass of Jewish orthodox shibboleths. Many years later I saw an oil painting of my grandfather; he resembled Robert Browning. There was a tintype of my grandmother, whose solid dour jaw dominated her physiognomy. My great-grandmother was a matriarch who locked the pantry and never relinquished the key lest any of the nine surviving grandchildren should filch the black bread. Ordinary aliments were imprisoned and hoarded as much as love. My mother, Lizzie, and her fair-haired sister, abhorring such parsimonious fury, fled to Warsaw and found refuge in a Catholic nunnery. Their father brought them back from the convent, but both refused to remain any longer under such a loveless roof.

There had been fourteen children. Alexander, the eldest brother, killed a Pole over a woman and, after my grandfather secured his freedom by bribing the local authorities, he married a Polish farmer's daughter and reared Catholic sons and daughters in that land. The sister who fled with my mother took a Polish officer for a husband, and two of their sons were Polish aviators in the first World War.

Solomon, who had a tender consumptive face, came to America with my mother when she was fifteen. Herman, another brother, who had mattress factories and sundry properties, and was at one time the wealthiest man in Toledo, Ohio, was supposed to provide for her. He had an evil miserly skull and placed Solomon in one of his sweat shops but did nothing for my mother, who found employment in a button factory in the New York ghetto. Still another brother, vastly inferior in pecuniary importance to Herman, was a chemist in Toledo. He read many books—which makes a man lickerish—and was never able to keep his hands from the hunkers of any chambermaid that happened to be near him. He died of a cancerous prostate at the age of seventy-seven, the reward of countless bawdy thoughts and acts. One of his daughters was given in wedlock to a professor at the University of Moscow, where she went to live.

My uncle Herman, anxious to be rid of his sister, but still moved by some niggish filial feeling, came to New York to see whether he could peddle her flesh. He found a stocky fur operator who was eager to wed her. This man's only virtue was that he had no conspicuous vices. My mother would have preferred to make buttons than to lie in such an arid marriage bed; though she was only sixteen she knew that he could provide her with food but not with fuel. Nevertheless, she obeyed her brother and married the man. Jacob, according to Philo Judaeus, means the performer, which my mother knew before she married him could not be the name of the fur operator.

There were three sons by him, three feeble seminal accidents. In the Kabbala it is said that when a woman has conceived, the Angel of Night, Lailah, carries the sperm before God. But does God see all human semen?

She disliked his nose and thought he grubbed up his soup with it because he kept it so close to his plate. Her days were larded with tedium, and her body was like the salamander, which cannot live unless it burns.

My mother always carried her head high to raise her hopes and to show that she had no reason to be ashamed of her life. After the death of one of her infants, she took to passing a barbershop on Rivington Street, which was on her way to the carts loaded with vegetables, goose feathers for

7

pillows, cotton chemises and corsets. One day she noticed a man leaning against the red and white striped barber pole. He had the soft, crooked locks of Absalom and vain white teeth which he showed her; he wore a dude's vest the color of deep brown eider and patent-leather shoes. He carried a gold watch and chain in his showy vest pocket. She had never seen a sport before; he had a quick, teasing manner, clever and nimble rather than jolly. Wholly deprived by a lubber in bed, she could not resist Saul the barber. He was not that Saul who was king in Israel, or the other of Tarsus, but she had not been born to gratify a monarch or tempt a saint.

She abandoned her two sons and fled to Boston. There she bore a child in Charity Hospital. She had been lying in a cheap rooming house where her bastard would have been born had not her groans attracted the attention of a neighbor. She gave me her father's name to hide the fact that I was as illegitimate as the pismire, the moth or a prince.

When I was six months old she sailed steerage for London. An uncle of hers had died there who was far richer than Herman. She expected—without any reason at all—that there would be a handsome legacy for her. True, securities, much cash and blocks of properties had been left—but to one of the Protestant churches. Penniless and with an infant in her arms, she found work as a scrubwoman and then as a parlormaid, and when she had enough money to secure passage on a ship she returned to the United States.

Then Saul and she went to Dallas, Texas, where they opened a small barbershop in a clapboard shack. There were two barber chairs in front, and in the back of the shop was a pallet and one chair. The customers had to stand and wait for their turn.

Saul taught her how to trim hair, hone a razor and strop it, how to stand with her feet together as she waited for a cowpuncher or a rancher, and how to speak: "Good morning, sir; you're next. Will you have a close shave, a light trim, or a feather-edged haircut? Don't you think a good massage would ease the strain of the day?" The customers were big, fleshy men—joshers, triflers and mashers who ran livery stables or shipped horses and mules to Omaha, Kansas City or Chicago. She knew how to keep her place and give a customer a chin-scrape without using too much alum to staunch a wound from a razor or the hair clippers. She had stout, thewy fingers and could give a drowsy cattleman a vigorous scalp treatment and deftly dust his red corrugated neck with talcum powder. It was a pleasure to have a lady barber wait on the Dallas trade, and a man would rather have her cut his throat than sit in Saul's chair. Some stood waiting for an hour on hot horsefly afternoons, chewing tobacco and spitting in the cuspidor to pass the time. No matter how full the shop, Saul's chair was nearly always empty. After working hours he told her that she was a nobody, without even a diploma from a barber college.

Lizzie liked being with the public and listening to the easy drawl about the swapping of a mare or shipments of stallions, geldings and cows to Topeka, Sedalia or St. Joseph. Still hankering for some other kind of life, she thought she would go from town to town as an itinerant hairdresser, give beauty treatments, clip toenails and do a little manicuring. Sometimes a horsedealer would drop by the shop and offer to take her out for a buggy ride. But she had no time for man foolishness; she wanted to make money and establish herself in some city where the men were good spenders and she could bring up her son.

She kept the cash taken in for the day in a cigar box; Saul would take the money and spend it on sporting women in the Dallas red-light district. When he came back he would sit in the barber chair, wax his mustache, brush his curly hair and show her his white foxy teeth. He had all the arrogant airs of a Spanish conquistador who kept his privities in a calabash of gold. After she had saved more money, he stole it and left town with a chippy from Galveston. When he returned she reproached him for spending the money and in a rage he attempted to slap the infant. She placed her strong, short arms around the child, and Saul broke her small finger, which was crooked after that.

She ran away to Memphis, taking the boy with her. She went from house to house selling hair switches, giving body massages and paring the toenails of women. The boy was always at her side, dressed in a Buster Brown suit and collar and carrying a dummy book which a photographer had given him after he had taken his picture. This made a good impression upon customers.

She would go from house to house and when a door was opened Lizzie would deliver a speech that she had patched together from newspaper articles and advertisements: "Good morning, madam, and health to you. I'm a high-tone hairdresser and beauty specialist. What lovely hair you have, but you look down in the dumps; I hope no man has deceived or swindled you. I'm a hard-working widow myself and know sorrow and disappointment, and here is my only son. I restore hair, give enemas and remove soul-grieving calluses. May I step in and give you a demonstration? It's free of charge."

Memphis was a fast town. Soon she had regular clients in what appeared to be a high-class neighborhood. They lived in solid red brick houses, which gave her stamina. She pared their corns, bathed them, and rubbed lotions on their bodies, which relieved them of all their aches. She was very proud of her strength which flowed so easily from her to them. They wore stylish satins and taffeta gowns; they gave her corsets, stockings and gold hairpins and cockered the boy.

She learned that these ladies had a trade not too dissimilar from her own—they relieved the aches of men. But she was too nervous to look down on anybody. When she told them she had to leave town, they wept and each one took the child in her arms. She thought she would do something wrong by remaining and she was worried about her good name. Although she did not know anybody in Memphis except her customers, she was afraid people would talk about her.

Then Saul blew into town. They went to New Orleans and started another barber business there. If Saul were cutting hair or scraping a man's chin and he saw a fourteen-year-old girl pass by, he would drop his scissors and comb, or shut his razor, and hurry out of the shop after her. The sight of a skirt made his blood run mad. Whatever Lizzie earned with her ten hard-working fingers Saul spent chasing hussies. Though she had the tender, full paps of the Ephesian Diana, no woman or town could keep Saul. He vanished again.

Lizzie and the boy went to Louisville, as rich in blue-grass as Homer's Coronea and stocked with the mares of Pelops. After that they moved on to Denver, where she said the people were spitting and hawking from morning until night. The Rocky Mountain city of consumptives gave her a fear of rot and worms that lay upon her dreams and fogged all her days.

In 1905 they came to Kansas City; it was a wide-open town; there were more sporting houses and saloons than churches. The stews were as far out as Troost Avenue. When a bachelor or a stale codger was in sore need of easing himself, he looked about for a sign in the window which said: *Transient Rooms* or *Light Housekeeping*. A brakeman on the M-K-T knew where he could get a glass of beer for a nickel, which also entitled him to a free lunch of hard-boiled eggs with pretzels and Heinz ketchup. The streets were cobblestoned hills, and their names were April songs of feeling: Walnut, Locust, Cherry, Maple, Spruce and Oak.

The town was not a senseless Babel: the wholesale distillers were on Wyandotte, the commission houses stood on lower Walnut, hustlers for a dollar an hour were on 12th and pimps loitered in the penny arcades between 8th and 5th on Main Street. If one had a sudden inclination for religion he could locate a preacher in a tented tabernacle of Shem beneath the 8th Street viaduct, and if he grew weary of the sermons, there was a man a few yards away who sold Arkansas diamonds, solid gold cuff links, dice, and did card tricks. Everybody said that vice was good for business, except the Christian Scientists and the dry Sunday phantoms who lived on the other side of the Kaw River in Kansas City, Kansas.

The great Missouri River on which Kansas City, Missouri, lay, once known as the *Concepción* in honor of the Virgin Mary, was as dissolute as the inhabitants. There was a lusty steamboat trade on the Missouri, and freighters plied between St. Louis, Kansas City and New Orleans. Country boys from Topeka and Armourdale came to Kansas City to get work in the stockyards and in the Armour and Swift packing houses; and chicks, with rosy, jocular rumps, arrived in hordes from Roanoke and Joplin.

One could take a nickel streetcar ride to Swope or Fairmount Parks; on an Indian summer evening, when the crickets sang in the tall, speared grass or in the oak branches, workmen in trade-union denims and overalls sat on the porches to take the air and say hello to a switchman or an acquaintance who had a job in the West Bottoms.

When business was dead and the Dog Star had parched the melons, dried up the heifers and the white leghorns, and prices were high, many blamed William Howard Taft. In the Teddy Roosevelt days butter had been eighteen cents a pound, milk was five cents a quart and eggs were ten cents a dozen.

When Lizzie came to Kansas City there was one lady barbershop on Walnut which was three doors from the ticket office of the Burlington Railroad. The proprietor of the place was a round-shouldered, cranky man barber who had an interest in the barber college located on Delaware Street. After six weeks of training at the barber college a green farm girl would be hired as an apprentice; she received no wages for the first three months and had to depend upon tips from customers. Usually no more than seventeen years of age, she attracted a great deal of trade. A stockman or a smart drummer from out of town would rather get a manicure from a lady barber than go to the Orpheum for an evening of big-time vaudeville. The odor of witch hazel, hair tonic and face powder, and the motions of the girls, who wore tight corsets, inflamed an old rounder. When a railroader got into the chair of a country trollop, he felt that he would perish from pleasure when she removed the lather from his jaw with her small finger.

These farm girls were as wild as Semiramis; but if they found out that they had a clumsy simpleton on their hands or an indefatigable curmudgeon who had already used up a wife with a hanging udder and five children, they would make him cough up a few hundred dollars. They did not care very much about an ordinary masher or a codger but they would support a curly-haired Adonis who knew how to chew Spearmint gum and smoke Turkish Hassan cigarettes with the air of one who had had enough amours to have set Ilium on fire.

No lecher was so intolerable as a skinflint. A lady barber took the greatest delight in being courted although she had no thought of a wedding. She liked to go to a good show, say to the Gillis Theatre for a wild West performance; if she craved refinement she preferred *Beverly of Graustark* or a swell burlesque at the Grand Opera House. Supper at an oyster house and a night at Electric Park were exciting; when a city alderman or the owner of a big livery stable took a girl out to Cliff Drive for a buggy ride, she talked about it for a whole week.

It was the time when women went to law for heart balm, and when breach-of-promise suits were exceedingly popular. A lady in sound health, who had locked all her hopes of marriage in her breast, had no hesitation in divulging them in court if she felt a man had been so low and rotten as to deceive her. There was hardly a judge sitting on the bench who was so callous as not to have considerable feeling for the delicacy of her heart. If a bachelor was foolhardy enough to be seen with a woman in public, or worse, to take an embittered spinster of thirty to Swope Park, and after that denied he was engaged to her, he was undone. He was sure to be seethed in the marriage-pot, and should he prove too tough for boiling except in some illicit hotel room, he was compelled to pay for the honor of the woman he had never desecrated. A good many such triflers, or just dead beats who had gotten into woman trouble of this sort, vanished or crossed the state line and found employment in Kansas City, Kansas, so that their wages could not be garnisheed. Fast women, and ladies with the subtlest principles, preferred to speculate in men rather than risk their savings in wildcat oil or second mortgages.

There were six barber chairs in the shop on Walnut Street; a cuspidor, shaped like an Etruscan amphora, stood within reach of a man in a barber chair who wanted to spit the brown juice of his chewing tobacco into it. A shave was five cents and a haircut a dime; a good tipper gave a girl an extra ten cents for a close shave.

Lizzie was given the last chair because she had a long, Jewish nose; turned-up gentile noses were very much in style, and a dapper man who wore suspenders and was as neat as a pin and had a fine position in a meat-packing house or at the Union Depot would go mad over a barber girl with a snub nose. Quite a few embezzlers would skip town with a warm, Grecian-nosed trull from Joplin. The prettiest chits were put up front to draw in transients who happened to pass by and who had never heard of a lady barber.

The shop opened at seven in the morning to catch railroaders on their way to the yards or big loafy-faced men who auctioned off horses and mules in livery stables near the stockyards. The girls rushed to their chairs when a locomotive engineer dropped in; anybody who worked for the Santa Fe or the Burlington was rumored to be a good spender.

The barbershop was an emporium for talk, easy, warm joshing, and expectorating in the brass spittoons. Lizzie knew how to keep a customer in his place, and on occasion cut a man with her razor or dug her scissors into his ear because he had his hand on her thigh instead of underneath the haircloth.

Often the shop did not close till nine o'clock at night. She took the boy to a Catholic parochial school to learn German because she wanted him to be cultured. The school did not let out till late and that kept him off the streets.

She had to work on a commission basis, and her wages, including tips, were seven to eight dollars a week. Cutting hair and shaving cowhands, grouches and town loafers for fourteen hours was no picnic, she told her boy. Most of the time she had to stand on her feet. The man barber would not allow the help to sit, even when the place was empty on dull, rainy days. A woman seated in her chair with crossed legs or lounging on the mahogany settee looked bad and attracted the wrong kind of trade. He was particularly strict in July and August, which he claimed were the two worst months for temptation; a man was teased more in summer than in any other season. He warned the barber girls not to spit, wriggle in their bustles as they stood by their chairs and called out: "You're next, sir," or make squeaking, sensual noises with their patent-leather shoes when they stepped over to the basin to soak a towel in hot water. Smoking was positively forbidden; sporting women were easily recognized because they smoked Sweet Caporals. He cautioned the girls not to chew gum and make loud, clucking sounds with their tongues, and he would not keep a lady barber who went to the water closet too often;

he said that flushing the toilet during business hours raised disorderly feelings in the customers.

He expected a barber girl to keep occupied all the time. When no one was in her chair, she had to cut the *Kansas City Star* into small square sheets on which the lather was wiped. She had to sharpen her razor on a hone and then ply it to and fro on the leather strop. There were the shaving mugs and the hairbrushes to be washed out in boiling water and the combs to be disinfected in Lysol.

Some proprietors of the genteel barbershops on Baltimore Street were thinking of raising prices because the cheaper chin-scrapers were giving the trade a bad name. People said that barber tools were dirty and carried such contagious diseases as dandruff, scarlet fever, barber's itch, boils, pimples and water on the knee. Horse swappers and common teamsters who sat on empty fruit crates in the big livery stables and swore and guffawed all afternoon claimed that one could get the pox or the clap from an unsanitary hair clipper, eyebrow tweezer or hairbrush. This kind of loose chatter could start a panic, and the owner of the place on Walnut was so uneasy that he changed the name of it to The Sanitary Barbershop.

The girls were flighty and easily discouraged, and if a lady barber thought she could not please the trade she took off her apron and quit. A lady barber was in the dumps all day if a customer had been short-tempered with her. She liked to coo into the ear of the man in her chair: "Sir, do you part your hair in the middle, or on the side? What a lady-killer's pompadour you have! How about some tonic? Or let me rub pomade into your scalp and give you a stiff hair brushing." But if he gave her a short answer: "Just leave it dry, lady, I'm in a hurry," she wept or took the afternoon off.

Lizzie rented a furnished bedchamber in a rock-ribbed house on McGee near Admiral Boulevard. McGee was a poor humble street, lined with elms, maples and oaks—what bread and meat there is in the sight of a living, green tree. There were many yards and vacant lots covered with tangled grass and rough, acrid sunflowers, and the latticed porches and sun-fed wooden steps were a comfort to people.

On her feet all day, except for a few minutes to take a quick bite or when the owner ran out for a bowl of chili, she would sink into the oak rocker as soon as she returned to the lodginghouse. She unlaced her high-top shoes, worked herself out of the corset, and removed her beige cotton stockings.

The child slept, graved in the large double bed. When she was so worn out she wondered how she would make ends meet, and then she looked about to find something to do so that she could banish such weak thoughts. She hunted for her pince-nez glasses, which she had laid on the floor, picked up a curling iron or tried to mend the yellowing corset cover.

At least she had gotten rid of Saul, and after she had muttered a curse in German, "*Verdammter Saul,*" she repeated "*Selige Vater*" several times. She never used bad language or swore and she feared that if she cursed somebody she might raise some unexpected grief and wrath from out of the past. She wrung her hands when she remembered how she had sweated her shame in Saul's foul bed.

In the shop and with the public she seldom lost control of herself. At times she had been made to feel that she was a lady-barber Magdalene, and though she had many misgivings about her trade, she liked working hard. Hands engaged in good, honest work are seldom mediocre. Was there not something else in her life besides eating, sleeping and the foolish mandrake apples? Her hopes, which she could not bridle and which were as forceful as her blood, redeemed her. Always believing that she would accomplish something, she was almost invariably duped—and he who is deceived often is never ordinary. She was everybody's gull.

There were days when Lizzie assuaged the weariness of

men by easing their dry, sour nerves and massaging their faces; this was as important to her as it was to that Mary who poured the ointment on the head of Christ. It was only when she doubted that she would have that frugal reward from her efforts that her courage flagged. She prayed every day, but still there were the alms that she required for herself and the child. Saint Teresa has said: "For those who pray, God himself defrays the charges." But how many afflicted ones have wept by the waters of Babylon and to what avail? And what profit had they of their tears save the joy of shedding them? Who hears sorrow, disease and indigence?

She offered her petition to the Lord; she rose from the rocking chair, regarding the washbowl and the crockery pitcher that were as empty as the pots at Cana. She was as impotent as the water hen that stands by the marsh and considers its blighted feathers. She cried out, "O Lord God, I quake before everybody, I am such a nervous woman. I'm not greedy, and I beg Thee only for bread and hope; You know my purse is stuffed with sorrow and when I open it all my poverty falls out of it. It is easier for Thee, O God, to shake the wilderness of Beersheba than for a widow to show her need."

She was afraid of the unmercied space around her, and even her bed was a pit. We go to a room to hide grief and shame as though they could be mewed up in walls, and the sleep we take therein to cover our lives bursts into dreams which paint our sins. Hard, deep sleep would have comforted her did she not dream. Dreams came before there was earth, grass, fish or any other living creature. Sometimes she awakened and found that she had wet the bedclothes, and she sobbed because she had a weak bladder, and all that she recollected of her sleep was water.

One sticky July afternoon, when a pair of flies dozed on the wattled throat of a farmer slouched in one of the barber chairs, the boy, returning from school, asked the owner of the shop for a glass of water, and was chased into the street. This was the child of her belly and sorrows, and there was nothing between her and the winds that always soughed the same refrain through her head: "I am alone in the world. Give Thy servant bread and water, and, yea, for my only infant Ishmael, lest we perish."

She saw her child fall on the pavement, but waited for the proprietor to step out for a Bromo Seltzer. She had laid aside a little money to open up a barbershop of her own and she talked to the girls about her plans. Though they called her a Sheeney when they had a poor day and she a good one, they hated the man barber. All the girls packed their tools and quit.

There was a wholesale barber-supply house on lower Delaware. She needed credit but she was afraid to approach the owners. She knew they were two brothers of German origin. Very nervous, she prepared a cultured speech. When she entered this barber's temple, she gazed at the long show-case filled with scissors made of the best Sheffield steel, hair clippers and combs of bone; on the shelves were jars of face creams and bottles with the necks of geese filled with refined hair tonics. One of the Haeckel brothers was standing in front of her. She closed her eyes and commenced her recital: "I imagine I have the honor of speaking to Mr. Haeckel. I'm Lizzie Dalberg, a hard-working widow with a child to support. My family spoke an educated German, God bless them. There's a dandy location on 7th opposite the high-tone Grand Opera House; I'm going into the barber business for myself. You can have a hundred dollars spot cash if you will let me have three up-to-date barber chairs, razors, hair clippers, hones, scissors, brass cuspidors . . . well, everything."

She removed her pince-nez glasses and wiped her eyes with the one lace handkerchief she owned, and continued: "I don't need charity, just a little time. Believe me, I'm reliable, and besides, I wouldn't harm you for the world."

Then she adjusted her shirtwaist to call his attention to the solid-gold watch that was pinned to it, so that he could plainly see that she was no pauper. She wore no powder or rouge, which only chippies painted on their lips.

He asked her to take a seat and brought her a small glass of brandy, which she refused. She believed that only sporting women drank between meals. Making a well-disciplined laugh, she thanked him and said, "No better tonic, Mr. Haeckel, mein Herr, for good health than a hard day's work."

Haeckel took the hundred dollars and asked her whether it would be too hard for her to pay twenty-five a month. He called her Miss Dalberg as a mark of esteem for a respectable widow with a child, for he regarded a woman, married or not, as a maid, if he thought her morals were sound.

She walked up and down in front of The Sanitary Barbershop, handing out cards which read: Lizzie Dalberg, New High Tone Barbershop, 7th and Walnut Streets, COURTESY IS OUR MOTTO.

Business was good for Lizzie and she associated this with the strength of her body. She took a cold bath morning and night, in winter or summer, and after rubbing her stout thighs and solid buttocks with a rough turkish towel she was confident that she would overcome any obstacle. She kept her bowels open and every morning, before she had gotten into a kimono, she held a small gilded mirror in her hand and put out her tongue to see whether it was pink or not. She then raised both arms and bent her face to smell her armpits before dusting them with talcum powder. How often the girls sweated and just threw powder on their flesh. It was ignorant to smell bad when water and soap were cheap and one could take an enema for nothing.

After a year on 7th Street she thought she could afford to move to a better location. A brand-new building had just been put up at the corner of 8th and Walnut. But when she heard that the rent was sixty-five dollars a month and that a five-year lease was required, she was afraid to take the risk. Suppose she failed, what would become of her and the child who was so sallow and sickly?

Nevertheless, Lizzie took the shop on the hilly part of 8th Street; it was underneath the viaduct over which the streetcar ran to the Union Depot in the West Bottoms. On the door she put a sign: OPEN FOR BUSINESS, and on the plate-glass window in heavy, enameled white letters was: STAR LADY BARBERSHOP: 16 East 8 Street. She had bought a round barber pole with peppermint stripes on it which stood in front outside. A fine metal cash register sat on a pine table, and when she regarded her name, Lizzie Dalberg, printed on it, she had no doubt that she would catch the rush viaduct trade. There were five Haeckel Brothers' barber chairs and two mahogany settees for the customers who sat and read the *Kansas City Star* while waiting for their turn. Up front Lizzie had a glass showcase in which she kept five- and ten-cent cigars and a box of Wrigley's chewing gum. On a rubber mat that covered a part of the showcase was a leather cup containing five Indian dice. She was particularly proud of the two electric fans that hung from the ceiling, and when she observed the brass cuspidors, she knew she had a high-class place.

There was a rumor going around town that the Union Depot, a remarkable red-brick building, a fine example of the old-time tradition of honesty, would soon be torn down and that a fifty-million-dollar railroad temple was to be built a little beyond the outskirts of the business district at 15th and Main. Gossips in the saloons and dry-goods stores were saying that Walnut was a tumble-down street and would look abandoned were it not for the Grand Opera House, the commission houses and Jenkins' Cigar Store, where a Stutz or a Buick was raffled every Saturday night.

When Lizzie heard this kind of loose talk she quaked; she had already signed a five-year lease and thought that her landlord, Mr. Wolforth, had taken advantage of her. Whenever she believed she had been misled by someone she ran into the small room at the rear of the shop, took off her glasses and rubbed her eyes on the soiled haircloth. She was easily duped for she had strong, heady blood. Had she had a more dry and shrewd nature, she would have had fewer disappointments—but less hope. Those who pray God for good luck should also beseech Him to deceive them!

If the boy pestered her for pennies, after she was perspiry from shaving too many bristly chins and cutting hair all day, she would become so nervous that she would weep: "Son, you know I've only got ten miserable fingers and that I can make just so much out of them. Do you think I find money in the streets? If I don't work, who'll help me?"

"But mother," answered the boy, "why don't you invest in real estate? You can buy a small lot around 15th and Grand and open up a beauty parlor there, or become a swell optician and get out of the dirty, rotten barber trade."

When a steady customer gave her a big job and then played Indian dice with her and she won a quarter, or when she coaxed him into going up to the corner to buy her a sack of fruit, she was jolly the whole day. She enjoyed shaking dice with a cattleman who had just come in from Oklahoma City. If the stockman won a Havana cigar, he put it up to his nostrils and as he smelled it with genuine satisfaction his craw shook a little. A cattle dealer always relished any game of chance, and playing a game of dice with a woman was, next to horse swapping, the best of sports.

"You start, Miss Lizzie, I'll shake you for a dime Havana," he would say, winking at her as though he knew beforehand she would win.

"Now, don't be a piker, Mr. Bob. Look at that fortune in ponies and jackasses you're carrying in your hip pocket. How about shaking for a quarter? You sure can afford it."

If she picked up the leather cup and threw three aces, she clapped her chubby hands together; her eyes would fill with so much wet glee that she'd have to wipe them on her white barber apron. The man would watch her every movement, taking out a bandanna handkerchief that was a foot square to dry his rugose neck and the dewlap hanging from his throat.

Lizzie was proud of the trade; solid and well-established people began to patronize the Star Lady Barbershop. There was Max Stedna who owned the livery stable; it was built in gothic fashion of roughhewn rock. Besides the viaduct transients, the Star Lady Barbershop was patronized by well-to-do merchants. One named Cromwell had a commission house on Walnut and sold grain and imported bananas and peanuts from South America. He had been a city alderman and everybody looked up to him. He was a spare, gray man who wore eyeglasses and sat in Lizzie's chair every morning at 7:15. He gave her half a dollar for a shave, and she took the greatest pains with him, powdering his face with talcum, seeing that both business sideburns were neat and equal; and if the colored porter were late or had quit, she took a dirty barber towel and wiped his black shoes. His closest friend was Hagen, a wholesaler in eggs and butter, who wore the latest octagonal spectacles with solid gold rims and parted his hair in the middle. Cromwell and Hagen had two bonds that united them: Cromwell looked hungry, while Hagen, jolly and fat, always appeared as if he had just eaten a big meal. Friends nourish one another, and a bald man enjoys the company of one who has a great deal of hair. Both were most loyal Democrats and fell out only when Hagen voted for Teddy Roosevelt.

Experienced lady barbers were now available. Often down and out, they came to Lizzie for work, and she would lend them money and take them in as free lodgers until they were on their feet. Among these was Gladys, who had Indian blood and a large bun of chestnut hair. She was a great drawing card for the shop. Emma Moneysmith, a Mormon with legs that quivered like a drawn bow, had the second chair; her boy, Marion, took violin lessons. The third was Miss Taylor's, whose son, Noah, had the sexual habits of Ham. He claimed that Tisha, the daughter of the prostitute who kept light-housekeeping rooms above Basket's Lunchroom, had put a love potion in his cup of coffee. Sally Muhlebach, a good hairdresser but too seedy to bait trade, served the fourth chair. Her nine-year-old girl, Gizella, had ballooned, dropsical legs and once when she and Lizzie's boy were at the flat together, she told him some of the dark secrets of pleasure while fingering the keys on the Bach upright piano in the parlor so that none of the girl roomers could hear her. The fifth chair was Mrs. Harney's. She had come to relieve a chippy who had left for Seltzer Springs to take the mineral waters. Claiming to be thirty-four, Mrs. Harney had the blowsy, sapless complexion of a woman who has reached her autumn. She had the dry, average lips of one who had been used rather than loved and she smiled only to gain an advantage over somebody else, opening her wide, sour mouth when she wanted a cheap chin-scrape to crawl into her chair. Whenever Mrs. Harney had finished honing her two razors she sat with *Science and Health* in her lap. The girls remarked that she would not even cross her legs just to show a customer a little courtesy.

Lizzie gave little thought to recreation; if she happened to shut the shop somewhat early on a weekday, she walked back to the flat. She doted on the elms and maples as she sauntered up 8th Street on an Indian summer evening. Stopping at the corner to buy a few apples, she was overflowing with emotion when the Italian fruit dealer graciously saluted her. What health there was in a few pleasant words exchanged between acquaintances. The boy at her side was silent, rejoicing in the Pleiades that hung over the Troost Avenue streetcar as it babbled along the tracks.

He carried his mother's straw basket filled with homemade jellies, some ragged morsels of rye bread with caraway seeds, and grapes and apples. Holding a Winesap in the palm of her hand, she broke it into several pieces between her stout thumb and fingers and spat out the peelings while breathing deeply to exercise her lungs in order that she would have a long life.

When business was dull, or if she had lost money investing in a wildcat oil company, the habits of the girls became a trial to her. They were not hygienic. Lizzie insisted that they scour their armpits, and when she was alone in the back of the shop she would say in a low voice, "My God, they smell like a water closet." She told them that bad odors had an adverse effect upon the trade and tried to persuade them not to wear the same sweaty pumps each day. However, there was always a cruddled voluptuary who was excited by their smelly shoes.

Their profligacy also got on her nerves; she did not care to think about sensual entertainments, which disgusted her. Who can bear somebody else's seminal sheets or tolerate his own turpitudes in another person? God had not endowed these carnal chits with a desire to be ascetic. What is the oldest vice in the world? Itching. Had not Adam scratched himself he would never have thought about pleasure.

Lizzie believed it more sensible to work than to consider the lilies that toil not. Not base by nature, she had sufficient deprivations to ennoble her. Up till now she had not been poisoned by that drudgery which produces the gall on which the larvae of all our living feelings feed.

What worried Lizzie was that the barber girls would give her place a bad name, and that she would lose her lease. How could she guard her bread and roof?

One Sunday morning when Lizzie was obsessed by those motions of night which are the contemplative exercises of great angelic birds, she screamed, bursting the seams of her sleep, "O Lord, I have died, and I have no roof over my head except a terrible dream." The boy crawled up to her damp pillow, his nose nuzzling her neck, and kissed her shaking, obdurate arm, but she thrust him aside and turned her back to him so that she could nurse her bitterness.

How many times she wished she had taken a location on 11th Street, hard by the Bank of Commerce, which was a stately pantheon of lucre. Such thoughts came to her mind when a boozer tottered in from the saloon next door. Lizzie did not care to have a drunk in her chair and would let one of the trulls take him. Good for a two-dollar job, he would not know what had happened to him even after he had crept out of the chair. Each girl wanted the drunk's money and two or three of them would rush forward to help him into her chair, and often they quarreled over him. Lizzie disappeared in the back room to drop a piece of stewing meat into a charred pot so as not to be involved in the dispute. A quarrel upset her stomach, and if someone insulted her, she could not put a morsel of bread into her mouth for a whole day. She would allow the meanest sloven to spit on her and call her a Jew rather than answer one word.

By the time an old sot had sobered up in the chair he would have had the whole bill of fare: a shave, a light trim, raw-egg shampoo, massage, every hair tonic in the shop and a manicure. The colored porter, who mopped up the linoleum, washed the spittoons and helped customers into their coats, would have shined his shoes several times. Unsteady on his feet, the drunk paid his bill and found his way back to the saloon.

The Star Lady Barbershop, though not a Bible house, was no den of atheism either. The girls were spiritualists, revivalists, Christian Scientists, and whenever a preacher set up a tent as the Lord's tabernacle beneath the 8th Street viaduct, one or two of the girls would be absent. If a girl was having her period, or an intrigue was at low tide, she

was sure to have a religious seizure. By now Lizzie knew
the symptoms: all of a sudden a girl became a dowd; her
hair was no longer spun fine and silken, and her shift was
frowsy and showed beneath her sanitary white apron.
Lizzie kept a bottle of carbolic acid handy to revive a girl
who had slumped to the floor—and who seldom awoke
without groaning for Jesus Christ.

Only a man cankered by his own zeal would crimp
Scripture in order to call a lady barber a disorderly Magdala.
When the time came she would be a steadfast wife and provide a husband who cherished her with a jolly, bawdy bed
and fat gammons. She would look just as legal and righteous
as any other female householder. Love restores the blind,
the palsied and the virgin, and even if a lady barber smeared
her bridal sheet with Heinz ketchup, no bridegroom should
be so foolish as to examine it. A man who scrutinizes everything that he does—or someone else does to him—will die
swearing or live to run mad in the streets with no other
cover for his nude soul but a syllogism. Besides, a woman
is a marvelous chameleon creature, for she can cheat, lie
and copulate, and still be the tenderest pullet.

A hustler in the shop had to put up with a great deal
to earn her onerous piece of bread. She was besieged all
day long by rounders. A steady customer was no better
than an out-of-town drummer or the transient viaduct
trade; he would never say one word out of the way, keeping his true motives in huggermugger for months until he
was ready to take his prey. Hardly a month went by that
a girl did not receive a marriage proposal or the promise
of an oil well in Tulsa. Even Emma Moneysmith did not
know how to handle these lickerish strategists. Just as she
was beginning to wax warm over a stockman or brakeman,
imagining that he chewed a quid of tobacco as if he had
the moral cud of St. Luke in his mouth, she would find
out that he had a wife and six children on a heavily mort-
gaged poultry ranch in Roanoke. Emma had no other

teacher but her mistakes. We never learn anything, but simply call old errors by new names. A strict Mormon, she knew that when the body had to be relieved, it did not care a rush for Brigham Young.

When business was dragging, the girls pushed the Star Lady Barber hair restorer. This was one of the specialties of the shop, and although each bottle bore the label: Dr. Ignatius Waxman's Excelsior, Vienna, Oklahoma, Lizzie was the author of this nostrum.

Lizzie had clandestine yearnings to be a physician; she thought herself better than an orthopedist at paring a callus, dissolving a corn or prescribing for aching feet. She prized her brass mortar and pestle, which she had bought from the Haeckel brothers. When a girl was too often cozened, Lizzie made a preparation of diuretics, concocted of dandelions and other pissabeds, to rinse out her kidneys and wash out her stupidity. In addition, she had a more astringent catholicon for pregnancy.

She attributed most of the ills of the lady barbers to excessive indulgence in the ecstasies of Venus. An absent barber had usually lost all her strength in bed; on occasion a girl failed to appear for work for several days, and when she was asked why she had not come, she replied that she had forgotten. For persons with such weak memories Lizzie took sunflowers from the back yard, levigated them and when she had soaked them in whisky gave them to the patient. The sunflower, a foe of frankincense, the Arabian spice of love, is an antaphrodisiac.

Lizzie also had a sample case of lenses and a paper sack filled with frames. When a myopic brakeman handed her a ten-dollar bill and told her to keep the change, she gently led him to the settee as if he were carrying a tin cup and a cane, and after he was seated she let him know the mistake he had made. She then advised him either to stand on the corner of Walnut and 8th and give his wages away every Saturday or get a pair of eyeglasses. After trying on several pairs of spectacles, he selected one because he liked its appearance. As he was a steady customer, she gave him a discount and charged him nine dollars for the glasses. However, if a regular client had had hard luck, if somebody had taken his wallet out of his hip pocket while he was riding on the trolley, Lizzie would give him a face massage and trim his sideburns free of charge. She had, like everyone else, a homemade conscience.

The circulation of money in the Star Lady Barbershop was sound though corrupt; currency was always in good health there because it was never stagnant. The lady barbers stole from Lizzie, and she took what she could from them —plus a bit of interest to which she felt she was entitled. One has to have indignation to steal with virtue. When Lizzie thought she could not make her expenses, she took what she could because she believed that if she had to close the shop the girls would not have a job; she had to see to it that they were not cast into the streets. The lady barbers had their fingers in the cash register whenever Lizzie was in the back of the shop. They also robbed one another.

The girls worked on a commission basis, the barber receiving sixty per cent of her earnings and Lizzie forty. Each girl kept checks either in her apron-pocket or in an empty shaving mug; on these Lizzie marked down the amount she had gotten from each customer. If a beau arrived to take a girl out for a plate of chili or clam chowder, she removed her apron and hung it on a peg, often forgetting to put the checks in her purse. Soon as she was seen passing the plate-glass window and waving to the others sprawled in their chairs, the lady barbers ran to get their hands into the pocket of the apron. When Lizzie witnessed such doings, she reproved the girls very sharply. Mrs. Harney was sorely tempted but she preferred to be more dignified and furtive, and only stole another girl's checks when no one was around.

Should the colored porter be snoring on his shoeshine box, Lizzie would wash the clippers and combs, and if she came upon a shaving mug filled with checks she might put some of them in her pocket. On occasion this did not bother her; were she examining a pair of scissors or wiping the mirror, and at the same time denouncing the girls for not keeping their tools clean, she felt indignant enough to take their checks without moral anxiety. At other times she would suddenly awaken from her soporific routine, part of which was pocketing what checks she could lay hands on, and catch herself stealing. This had a very unpleasant effect upon her blood, and she frequently had long arguments with herself, justifying her deed. But all reasons are so useless that even when we are not guilty we cannot prove it to ourselves.

A balding codger had little chance of getting out of Emma Moneysmith's chair without trying Dr. Ignatius Waxman's Excelsior. Had he intended to spend no more than what a chin-scrape costs, he was mistaken. Emma took pains to show him how dirty his scalp was; she took a filthy towel from the wire basket, rubbed it on the floor and showed it to him. If he was obdurate, she took a handful of hair from the haircloth that had just been removed from a customer of another girl and exhibited that to him. She ran one hand through his hair, holding a heavy clump of shorn locks in the other, and then told him that if he did not do something about the condition of his scalp, he would be absolutely bald before the equinoctial rains. That the hair she clenched in her hands did not match that of her customer never seemed to matter. Had he been told that he had just lost his nose, and been shown somebody else's, he would not have recognized the beak as not his own. One must be very thoughtful to know his own face or body.

Lizzie's remedy for all ailments was a purgative, an emetic or a diuretic. When a customer's hair was falling out, or he had bad breath, she advised irrigation. Pythagoras held that no one could be free of sickness or viscid visions at night unless he had been purged. A balding client received a bottle of Dr. Ignatius Waxman's Excelsior with instructions to take an enema every night. The bottles contained a mixture of horehound, ordinary tar soap, Twenty Mule Team Borax, brandy and geraniums that had been brayed in Lizzie's mortar. She thought that a scant man with a dry hip joint should be purged upwards, but that a corpulent patient given to lickerish phantasms, and who belched solely for pleasure, ought to have a far more puissant curative.

Spite of Lizzie's activities as a Galen, she could sometimes hardly pay the rent for the shop; her roomers often quit and left town without paying for their lodgings or repaying the money she had lent them. Though she continued to get a dime for a haircut, she could not understand that the value of ten cents had fallen. What's in a dollar? It has no skin, veins, gut or heart, and though it is said to circulate, it has no blood either. Even the greediest blackguard, who would eat his neighbor or an absolute stranger, would not thrust a dollar down his gullet.

Lizzie could not charge her girls money for her medical labors. She knew when one of them was in man-trouble. She had gotten into the habit of looking over her glasses to observe a girl who ran frantically back and forth to the water closet. When a jillflirt had lost a Pinkerton detective to another woman or when she was dosing herself with castor oil, Lizzie could not stop a smile from glimmering down the flanks of her steep nose. She did not have the cold, hard ability to revenge herself on a girl who had called her a Jew, but it could not be denied that such misfortunes gave her small rills of pleasure.

Gullible persons are the most suspicious; it is not that they are so mistrustful as that they have so little control over themselves that they confide in everybody. Whenever Lizzie lost anything, she suspected everybody; of course, she did not speak out since she was afraid of altercations. But after misplacing her pince-nez glasses, she would often give one of the girls a severe, sly look, imagining that this was a piece of spite work on her part. She would ransack her steamer trunk, searching for her brooch, diamond ring or the gold watch she wore appended by a gold pin to her bosom. If something was missing, there was no doubt in her mind that one of the lady barbers had pilfered it; much of the time she had one or more of the girls living with her. Her glasses sometimes fell off when she looked in every corner of the flat for the missing object. Then she spent several hours trying to find them. She became so upset that her face broke into many rivers of sorrow and, sitting down on the mahogany piano stool, she wept, saying that she was blind, and that there was no woman so unfortunate as she. Why could not God give somebody else a bit of her bad luck? There was no equitable distribution of sorrow or of money.

If one of the lady barbers had been stealing constantly from the cash register, Lizzie imagined that she bore her an immense grudge—until the girl needed her. Then her kindness, which was a parcel of her nervous disorder, was boundless. But we often love our enemies far more than our friends; we are compelled to observe our foes continually, and there springs up such an intimacy between two hostile people that neither wishes to see the venom abate. When Jesus cries, "Smite me on the other cheek," he is not averse to the joy of pain. Like all solitary figures, he would rather be lacerated and touched than avoided. It is the untouchable who is deprived of everyday raptures.

Of all the lady barbers Lizzie liked Emma the best; she had no respect for the giddy heads who wore their skirts stuck up behind them as hens their feathers, but she envied Emma. Miss Moneysmith had thick, auburn tresses, while Lizzie's hair was beginning to fail. When she held up her glass she imagined her hair was nervous and would revive when she was feeling better. The lines around her mouth were also temporary and were caused by worry. These harrowing thoughts came upon her when she was not at the shop. Every workday was a blessing when one could hear the wheels rattling against the cobblestones and listen to the peddler chanting, "Watermelon, pears, lettuce, potatoes." For six days the streets sang in her blood; every weekday was Walnut, Grand, Oak, Cherry, Locust and Holmes Streets, but on Sunday Kansas City died.

Lizzie knew that Emma had been keeping company with a stockman. She could see him scrabbling about to draw up his puling hams from the barber chair as if he were crippled, or worse, impotent. Emma knew how to work a dewlapped horse trader who was a good sixty-five. It was sport on both sides. An elderly, bowlegged, slouchy stockman who forgot to button his pants was simply reminiscing. So long as he had nothing else to do but cough up a few hundred dollars for Emma he had the foretaste of happiness without going through the ordeal of proving whether he could take it. Emma knew this type of rancher who only wanted to whinny and snort since he had put his pair of senile stallions out to pasture in order that they could run with the mares and still imagine they were in the game. A man likes the company of a woman though he is past the time he can enjoy her; he can groan for her just as loudly as the mandrake does when it is wrenched from the ground, though he has nothing else for his labor and delight but the shriek.

Lizzie knew that Emma was a two-timer; while she was taking money from the cattleman she was also having an intrigue with a curly-haired rakehell from 12th Street. When Emma told the rancher that she thought she was pregnant he left for Seattle.

Emma never confided in the common petticoats on the first and second chairs. She did not trust Mrs. Harney's gold-toothed grin either. Emma thought that Bible-reading at the Star Lady Barbershop would hurt business and attract impecunious celibates or chaplains from the Helping Hand Society. Emma did not think she could afford to have any principles. She was good as she could be, and were she to try to be any better, she would be worse. A very pretty woman, she saw no reason why she had to be a dissembler. She refused to smile when she was peevish and showed the teeth of the fox when it was necessary instead of putting on the face of the lamb. Emma would have believed in virtue had she found anybody else who used it. Lying, cheating, stealing, fornication and fleecing were contagious diseases she had caught from the most respectable folk who patronized the shop.

Emma was positive she was in the family way. A fearless woman, she did not know to whom to turn; and she dreaded nothing except to be stabbed in the back by a simper. She had considered her flesh and knew that she was unlucky during the dog days. Among the very few adages in her bosom was: shun pleasure when the flies copulate. The drowsy, opiate months were insidious and underhanded; it was best to avoid any connection with a man from the time of the summer solstice until the season of the Pleiades. She believed she should have smeared sunflowers on her skin, and upon the rim of her secret parts, before indulging in her fevers. She was still wondering whom she could confide in; she did not trust anybody except herself—until she realized that she was just as treacherous a person as anybody else.

But she knew that Lizzie was no gadder or chatterbox and finally turned to her. As soon as Emma opened her mind to her, Lizzie examined her nipples, which were as erect as the cedars of Lebanon. Seeing that there was no time to be lost, she went straightway to her mortar and pestle, gathering together her glass jars filled with pickled melon rinds and orange peelings, which she took as cathartics. She made

Emma swallow these laxative conserves and gave her two dozen cups of hot tea with senna leaves. The two of them were alone at the flat; the boy was playing on Admiral Boulevard, and the girl roomers were either at Electric Park or spooning on the Troost Avenue trolley.

Lizzie shared the opinion of sacred Hippocrates that to open the matrix one has to free the bowels. She had learned of a Haitian resin, a brown, woody substance that in pre-Columbian times was used by the natives as an antidote for snakebite and which was later exported to Oklahoma and there used as a cure for rheumatism. This indigenous American gum had since acquired an underground and illicit fame as an abortive, though it was kept in almost every family cabinet along with Grandpa's Tar Soap, Smith Brothers' Cough Drops, Sloan's Liniment, Argyrol, Unguentine, Twenty Mule Team Borax, castor oil and barley water. Midwestern folk suffering from strangury, constipation, sciatica, neuralgia, the vapors or ordinary household impotence were their own physicians, and if their condition was aggravated by one nostrum, they tried another—which was all that Galen could do.

Moreover, what reason was there to doubt that a resin which could cure the stings from a scorpion was not forceful enough to bring on a woman's flux? It is said by olden rabbin that when Adam lay with Eve, she bit him.

Lizzie took this Haitian remedy guaiacum and put it into the brass mortar, and dropping in anise seed, garlic, horse-radish, geraniums and the pippins of quince, she brayed them with the pestle. After she had made a thick compost, she poured a pint of whisky into a saucepan and lighted a fire under it; she waited for it to simmer, then put the hot whisky and the pharmaceutical conserve together into a large bottle and gave Emma two tablespoonfuls of it every three hours. The blood ran out of Emma's face, and she looked so green the Lizzie thought she had purged her upwards.

Lizzie then went to work on Emma's body; she separated one thigh from another, pulling them as wide apart as she could, as if each leg were a stalk that had to be plucked up by the roots. After that she kneaded the small of her back with her short, healing fingers, next proceeding to the cerebellum. Could she persuade the head to react to the lower spine, just as the mind gasps and dies a little in the moment of orgasm, she could then relax the uterus. She laid Emma on the kitchen table and beat her hypochondrium, where all her stubborn spleens lay, and turning her over gave her great loud thwacks on her fundament until she broke wind, hiccoughed and coughed.

The two women were so wrapped up in this ecstatic treatment that when Lizzie looked at her patient and saw an ichorous discharge coming from Emma she was elated—until she realized that it was only her nose that was running. Lizzie looked upon the expulsion of sweat, mucus, urine or feces as an encouraging symptom. She listened to Emma's abdomen, putting her ear on it until she heard her ululant intestines, an Atlean borborygmus, after which she gave her more guaiacum.

For three days Lizzie fed Emma the resin, and made her take six hot baths a day. She did not go to work, asking Mrs. Harney to open the shop and shut it at night. She knew that when she returned the girls would tell her that they had done nothing but scrape chins since she was away. Whenever Mrs. Harney went to the cash register, wondering whether she should ring up *No Sale* or not, she remembered the line out of Mary Baker Eddy: "There is nothing either good or bad, but thinking makes it so."

When it became apparent that Lizzie could not open Emma's matrix, both women wept. What a woe was the uterus—a great sea trough through which four edenic rivers flow, one of milk, the second of honey, the third of balsam and the last of urine. Both women lamented their uterine ills, and when Lizzie picked up a pair of old man's drawers

36

as a clout to wipe the perspiration from Emma's face and saw the immoral stains, she threw the cloth back into one of the girls' rooms where she had found it. Lizzie told Emma of her own prolapsus; her womb had been torn at childbirth, and now there were days when she dragged herself about as if she were yoked to some heavy disappointment from which she could not loose herself.

Emma had dire cramps; she said her body tasted of salt, bowels and sin. She told Lizzie that there was no sweeter physic to the soul than self-denial. After a long seizure of indigestion, preceded by large plates of mutton and yards of beef and venison longer than the intestinal tract, even the glutton abhors all animal flesh and imagines that nothing will ever content him more than pulse and water. The maggot always comes after surfeit; since lovemaking has emasculated the race, we are as foolhardy as the domesticated caterpillar in the mulberry tree who devours the base of the leaf on which he is standing.

After Emma was sure that she would have no need of the menstruous cloth, she had her period. She tried to persuade Lizzie to take money, but all that Lizzie wanted was thanks—a word very few can evacuate.

II

In the middle of the journey of our life I came to myself within a dark wood where the straight way was lost.

Dante

Luck is a vast energy, but Lizzie feared that her days of fanged penury and misfortune had not come to an end. The Aztecs set aside five barren days in the year, and every man, woman and child took care not to do anything imprudent in that time and was on guard against the bat and the coyote until these hours would pass and flowers and incense were his portion. Lizzie wished that she and the child were back in the rooming house on McGee Street where they had been as content as Shem in his tents.

By 1907 McGee Street was in the poor shambles of Kansas City but was not evil in aspect. Most of the houses were built of roughhewn rock. The street was of hilly cobblestone and was mapled and aldered. There were plenty of porches overgrown with high, ragged grass.

She now had a refined suitor, a bald, sallow Major in the

U.S. Army. He was such an easy mark that the lady barbers said she ought to sue him for breach of promise even though he had not proposed to her. On Christmas he had given her a purse with a fifty-dollar bill in it and he bought two new mahogany settees for the shop. It was then that she thought she could afford to purchase the upright piano, on which she always played "Tell me something, tell me true, dear, tell me why you went away." She was wondering whether she could ever move up to Rockhill or somewhere out near Swope Park, where she could have a few cherry trees in the back yard. She would like to get out of the barbershop, though work meant being with jolly men and was a kind of social ecstasy for her. With the Major she could have all the refined things of life—cut glass, solid oak rocking chairs and a front lawn. He was such a gentleman of principles—which were splendid for the daytime.

He asked for her hand in marriage. He would retire in a few years, and she could give up the barbering for good. He said she was a very upright widow, and she could not help appreciating such a gentleman who had never laid an ill-bred hand on her. She refused his proposal.

Some doom hovered uneasily over her; how quickly the bad angels, who carry misfortune in their pinions, succeed the bearers of felicitous news. Nobody can endure his own happiness; besides, what weakens human character so much as a long spasm of agreeable events? Good and bad luck follow one another just as regularly as a long summer heat comes after heavy spring rains. There is nothing in the universe that is not affected by glaciers, tides, winds and the Water Star Arcturus. Each person has his own singular weather, and there is no stone which is not influenced by pests and ill-hap and which does not sorrow and rejoice as much as flesh does. But darkness covers all life; stones show their lights more clearly at night. What illumination is there in the night of the soul save when the white breakers and the Evening Star beat upon it?

Lizzie began to stay even later in the barbershop; the porter had quit, and often she was on her knees scrubbing the linoleum with filthy rags. Sometimes she did not shut up the shop until she had just time to walk to the corner of 8th and Walnut to catch the midnight-owl streetcar.

She had become morose; was there an evil agent that harmed some persons more than others? In the prime of her years who had wronged her complexion? She never bathed her face in hot water and she was certain that she could remove any wrinkle with her lotions and creams. But had not a pittance of her mouth vanished? Lord, we die all day long, and come closer to the grave each time we have an experience. Lately, she had been almost insensible because nothing either good or bad was happening to her.

She sought refuge in prayer whenever she thought of it. She prayed in the back room of the shop while waiting for pasty cereal or potatoes to boil, and when a lady barber rushed in to go to the water closet or to primp, she pretended that she was reckoning her expenses. She would as soon be caught in a shameful act as in her orisons. At the flat she retired to a corner of the alcove and beseeched heaven for a few pennies of good luck so that she could meet her bills. But aside from the hope her prayers gave her she had no other reward.

When she imagined that she could not overcome her life, she complained that fate was persecuting her. Many who have not toiled so hard as she or reaped such a famine from incessant labors scorn those who pity their own condition. Well could this Jewess, not of Avila but of Kansas City, cry out: "I am the Cross, for I am a weariness." However, not a soul said "Come unto me, and I shall feed and succor you."

She did not know what to do with her life or with her feelings. She toiled because she was afraid to starve, and because she had nothing else to do; but her will was too sick to love the child of her lust. He was so skinny and yellow that his nose seemed to cover his face; and all the obduracy that was in her short, round neck had passed over to him. If he saw a speck on the wall, he imagined that it was the ordure of flies. When he looked at the greasy, rotten oil-cloth on the table, he would not touch his scummy soup. His mind gave him intolerable pain when he thought of the back alley that lay between 8th and 7th where he had seen gross rodents. On occasion, when he heard the chirruping of rats in the basement of the building or in the rear of the shop, his face grew more peaked and rancid, and he buried his head in his arms and retched. Lizzie was unable to com-prehend his nausea, for like most people of her class in the Midwest she found a certain amount of rapture in look-ing at vermin. Often the lady barbers spoke at great length about loathsome creatures, and the boy listened and could not leave off hearing what made him green and sick for weeks.

All that Lizzie could understand was that the child of her profligacy vomited and that he would grow up ugly. Sometimes she would whip him in an endeavor to force him to take food; but the act of eating, and thinking about what his teeth did, made him irreparably ill. Who can consider the carcasses he puts into his mouth? Filthy animals had wounded his childhood, and he would never be able to exorcise those abominable phantasms from his imagination.

She did not know what to do with herself or with him. She had reached the zero point in her freezing heart, and now the rain, the snow and the sleet could fall upon her—it did not matter, for she was dead, and the tomb is not trou-bled by the weather.

Late one evening she heard a customer enter and with-out looking up she called out, "You're never too late for a haircut or a shave, sir; we aim to please." In the doorway stood a dandy in a vest that was the color of a rusty robin; he wore a gold watch and fob which he displayed by put-ting his thumb foppishly into a buttonhole of his jacket. He had the dude's waxed mustache of the day and showed his clever, magnetic teeth. Saul had come back from a bed of lust in Salt Lake City.

The faintest symptoms of rot were beginning to show in Saul's face, which now lacked a great deal of its former self-confidence. His crooked locks were not so crisp, his teeth no longer glowed as before and he was unable to produce the smile that had been such a threat to a trollop. He had been canvassing small hamlets, looking for farm girls. He doted on a farm diet—a country chit or virgin—if he could have it in the city. Only a city could slake Saul's venery. He had grown afraid of large rooms and high cold ceilings, and felt old and worn-out in stupid towns and imbecilic villages. The sight of a decayed Main Street or of a dry-goods store diminished his manhood; he was worthless on holidays and absolutely impotent on Sunday and the Fourth of July. When he found himself on a vacant, shut street he regarded himself as dead.

Saul only cared for low-class women; a waitress in an apron and wearing crude black cotton stockings gave him the most acute erotical anguish. His blood smarted and boiled as he watched a chambermaid in a hotel toss the sheets, spank the pillows and empty the night pot.

Saul resolved to become Lizzie's partner again. As there was no chair for him in the shop, he lay around with sporting women on 12th Street or stewed in rooming houses beneath the 8th Street viaduct. The light-housekeeping rooms were filled with transients or farmers who lived in the dour state of Kansas and who crossed the Kaw River to come to wide-open Kansas City where they could smoke, drink a tin pail of beer and ease themselves. The city wore its wanton summer apparel, and the air was wild; the sluggish August flies spent their lechery on the plate-glass windows of the Electric Oyster House and on the free-lunch counter of the saloon next to the barbershop.

Saul wanted money to hire pleasure, and Lizzie gave

him that as well as her body. Carnal expression was as necessary for her health as it was rot to his blood. "None can be continent unless Thou givest it," says St. Augustine—and He obviously never meant her or Saul to be abstemious.

Lizzie had no compassion for Saul and she never tried to comprehend him. It takes a long time to misunderstand people, and whatever we know about others is only what we are able to understand about ourselves. Nobody can pass beyond the boundaries of himself. We fall more quickly under the spell of snakes than we do of friends. Besides, Saul could not imagine that he had any imperfections. Even when a man avows that he is a monster, he imagines that he is being outrageously charming. Saul was quick-witted and unusually sensitive about himself. He possessed all the sensibilities of a man who would have been a thinker if he had had any feeling. Lizzie was guided by the laws of her body and the fear of any excesses that might curtail her days on the earth; Saul did not care how long he lived so long as he lived virile.

There is a Buddhist saying that it is wicked to change the course of a river; it is just as evil to endeavor to alter the character of a bad person. Besides, it is best for Herod to show his face. When we struggle against our defects, it is an artistic delusion which is necessary to our souls. The truth is that we can only perfect our vices, for we die with all our sins entire, and every wrong thought or dream or vision in the child matures in the man. However, the moral combat against our flinty hearts must be waged; otherwise we eat ourselves in disgust and do nothing but feed and gender. There is nothing more important than this incessant warfare with our hard demons which makes men better thinkers but not better men. The only comfort that God can take in His Creation, after He has grown weary with the winds, India, the Cordilleras of the Andes, an earthquake or a tornado is that man is a reflective beast. God caused men

43

to die because He wanted them to think; our first parents ate of the tree of knowledge of good and evil though they knew it would cause them to die. All wisdom is sensual since it comes from the body.

Whatever Saul was not even Saul knew; he was born corrupt, and what he did was natural to him. What was bad for others was good for him. A kind or charitable act on his part would have been gross deceit. He fobbed women when he desired to lie with them—which is nature. This is not hypocrisy because it is the way the world is made. Saul was some baleful seminal drop of a depraved rotting forefather; he lived solely to discharge his sperm.

The lady barbers decided to help Lizzie get rid of Saul. He grumbled that the girls were lazy chippies, and when they saw him go to the cash register and steal Lizzie's money, they were so outraged that they forgot that they themselves cheated Lizzie whenever they had the chance. The girls who had concealed their checks from Lizzie so that she would not take them, now hid them in order that Saul would think that business was poor. For a while the lady barbers gave over slandering one another. Emma kept all the money taken in for the day, and everybody was ecstatically honest.

When Saul came in at about seven o'clock to go over the cash, the lady barbers told him that trade was so bad they intended to quit that Jew Lizzie and take chairs in a high-tone barber shop that had opened up on Holmes and 11th opposite the cultured public library and the hotel where the Kansas City ballplayers stayed. Lizzie said she would have to close up the place as there was not enough money to be earned to support either Saul or the boy. After a week Saul found that he could not get enough money out of her to pay a single fast woman. He claimed that he still owned half of the business which they had started together in Dallas, and he decided to sell his share to her and go back to Salt Lake City. Lizzie had to pay him off or remain the prey of his uncontrolled ill temper.

For the first year or so Lizzie had been an easy mark—but poverty instructs the gullible. She was too nervous to be a self-confident cheat. However, when she had to run to the back of the shop to relieve herself, she did this in a hurry and rushed to the front again to be sure the lady barbers were not swindling her. After Saul disappeared, the girls fell back into their easy, amiable thievery, and every week they used a different hiding place for their checks.

She ate in the back room which was near the water closet, and, though she bolted her sirloin steak and beer, she always paused to go out and keep an eye on the girls who allowed too many liberties to a masher who was a big spender.

Lizzie herself began to overcharge drunkards who lay in her barber chair to sleep off the fumes of a stupor. She cozened the apprentices who came to her from the barber college before they learned to steal from her. Everybody in the shop was the most artful cutpurse. This did not prevent them from becoming the warmest friends, although they never lost an opportunity to slander a girl who was out of town, in bed with a customer or pregnant. The lady barbers preferred excitement to work and when they had had a good day, they cooed into one another's ears. These girls had such little schooling they hardly knew how to count, and it might be said they had genuine integrity because they ✓ were too illiterate to violate good principles. In spite of all the skulduggery, no girl could say with any self-assurance that she had more or less money than she had earned. Even when a lady barber quit in a great huff, she never said that Lizzie had stolen any money from her, for the simple reason that she was under the impression that she was the thief and not Lizzie. The girls had the compassion that goes with boiling venery; only a cold-hearted person has the skill to harm others with deliberation. They had just enough scruples to blush if there were an occasion for it. Jean Jacques Rousseau was no different from the lady barbers, saying: "I learned to covet, dissemble, lie, and at length, to steal, a propensity I never felt the least of before, though since that time I have never been able entirely to divest myself of it."

Lizzie's misgivings were tentative; her blood was strong enough to pump into her heart that ass's milk which is the fountainhead of hope. However, the long hours she kept, standing under the bare electric lights, were extremely hard on her eyes. The perspiration flowed over her glasses so that she would hurry to the faucet and throw cold water on her face before finishing a customer's sideburns or shaving his neck.

When she closed up before midnight, she trudged home very slowly, as she did not want to spend a nickel for streetcar fare. She took deep breaths of the evening air and was overcome with a beating, upsurging confidence. As long as her lungs and heart were sound, she knew her future would be right. Her landlord, Wolforth, believed in her noble traits—since she always paid her rent on time. As she gazed at the maples along the street, she let out a sigh like that which had saved desponding Hagar in the wilderness.

Late in the evening, when every bone in her body ached, she would sometimes stop in a dark hallway to relieve herself; while she squatted there she told herself that she was the most miserable woman on earth. The boy walked a few paces ahead so as not to see her and also to watch for anybody who might be passing by. When he looked at the Milky Way, he would lift up his voice to the stars that were the lambs and stones of heaven, and heave a prayer out of his mouth to God, beseeching Him to give his mother a firm bladder so that she would not let out water in doorways, which he could not help hearing. Feeling easier, she walked up 8th Street to the flat, and when she heard a trolley on the tracks her courage came back to her.

Had she not had such a strong body, Lizzie would not have been so easily deceived; sickly people seldom suffer from optimism. She took so much pride in her vigor that she never thought it unnatural to rub her back and nude loins in front of her child after taking her cold bath; she stood before him naked until she had dried herself with a rough bath towel. Criminal imaginings come from the perverted head and not from physical strength. She rejoiced because her breath was fragrant as the cows of Job.

At the flat she dissolved her solitude by putting up glass jars of marmalade and counting the laundry that she sent out to a Negro washerwoman. She watered the geraniums on the back porch, which was three stories above a yard overgrown with massive weeds and sunflowers. On Sundays she dusted the cut glass and fetched a dirty cloth to polish the mahogany piano and clean the postcards on a tin rack against the wallpaper in the parlor. There were artistic pictures of Swope Park, Seltzer Hot Springs, Cliff Drive, the Fidelity Trust Company and one of the Woolf Brothers' fancy bakery where she bought rye bread with caraway seeds. She always admired a fine likeness of the Major in uniform. The postcards and the music sheets she kept inside the mahogany piano stool were evidence of her genteel breeding, and they were a source of intractable elation. When she was dejected, she would search for a piece of music and play a semi-classical tune, singing in a tenuous treble:

I was jealous and hurt
When your lips kissed a rose,
Or your eyes from my own chanced to stray.
I have tried all in vain
Many times to propose
But at last I've found courage to say. . . .

About this time Lizzie had a serious operation. Surgery became almost a pastime for her when she grew discouraged and felt that she had no future. We owe everything to nature, even our desire to annihilate ourselves. She had fallen under the evil star of Dr. Minerva Evelyn, a female physician who made a handsome income from lady barbers, milliners and dressmakers. In return for the clients Lizzie brought her, Dr. Evelyn gave her special prices for operations she did not need. A year earlier she had had her appendix removed—though it had never troubled her. Now again she was in the throes of her aridities and hoped that if she could convalesce in Dr. Evelyn's private sanitorium her fortune would change.

It never occurred to Lizzie that Dr. Evelyn might kill her; she was certain that she would not die—and that the Kosmos does not lie to flesh. Lizzie placed Emma Moneysmith in charge of the shop while she lay in a room in Dr. Evelyn's house. Emma was a Hecuba with the unbridled girls; she was so disgusted with their venery that she became exceedingly circumspect herself while Lizzie was away.

These wenches seldom married until they were frowsy flowers. After they had deteriorated into marriageable drabs, they did not cease to be a benefit to the race since they knew how to gratify a spouse. Their amorous experiences kept them vibrant and sensual until they were old women. According to Buffon, those who rarely employ their organs suffer most from fatigue. Besides, these wanton fillies had seasoned an entire generation of men in the arts of love. It was as natural for these women to gull men as it was for the men to spill their sperm. There was hardly a ripe semi-tart from Hannibal or a pelting Kansas town who did not later become a steadfast wife. She had enjoyed her lawless flesh to the full, and then slowly and wisely savored her legal bed.

Emma Moneysmith was greatly concerned over herself and her son Marion. How long could she excite a voluptuary from the West Bottoms? And who would provide for her when she was middle aged? Casanova said that in Paris in his time a woman of fifty-six was no longer considered to be among the living.

It took Lizzie a year to overcome the ineptitude of Dr.

Evelyn's knife. During her long convalescence the boy was put in a Catholic home; all he could later remember about the place was that if a child said one word at the table in the refectory he could not go to the urinal without passing a nun who hit the talker on his hands with a thick ferrule. When Lizzie was able, she came to the Catholic institution, and the boy threw his face into her lap and sobbed during her entire visit.

When she took him out of the Catholic home he was almost eight and ran in the streets, either visiting Stedna's livery stable or playing with Tisha, whose mother ran the brothel above Basket's lunchroom. He ate only whenever Lizzie could get away from her chair. She hurried to the rear of the barbershop and prepared his soup without removing her apron; sometimes the haircloth she had taken off the last customer was still hanging over her shoulder. It would have been as hard to count the hairs in his food as to reckon the number on the head of Abraham.

It had not occurred to the child that he had a stomach or a throat until he heard the flushing of the barbershop toilet and saw the vestiges of vermin in the back room of the shop. He learned anatomy by being sick.

There were scarcely any good objects for the boy to behold; he pleaded with his mother to quit barbering so that he would not see what he saw or hear what he had to hear in the shop. God made the Seven Pleiades, and He brooded upon the face of the waters—but who made vermin? All the abominable creatures that make our dreams a sepulchre of horrors were in that back room or in the alley behind it.

Lizzie was beside herself; the boy was skin and bones and given to infernal vomiting spells. She learned from a stockman about an Indian herb doctor in Oklahoma who could cure piles overnight and a consumption in two weeks. Lizzie sent for the herbs, but what effect could they have against the disease of the imagination?

Nobody ever overcomes the phantasms of his childhood. The man is the corrupt dream of the child, and since there is only decay, and no time, what we call days and evenings are the false angels of our existence. There is nothing except sleep and the moon between the boy and the man; dogs dream and bay the moon, who is the mother of the unconscious. Sorrow and pleasure are the stuff of dreams and the energies of myriads of planets. What is the space between the boy and the man? Did the child who is now the man ever live? Did Christ exist and was Brutus at Philippi? The centuries that divide one from Jesus and Brutus contain no time. We still hear the tinkling of the sheep bells at Mamre, and Abraham continues to sleep beneath the terebinths just as Saul sits and broods underneath a tamarisk—but all these are "thoughts of the visions of the night."

At about this time Lizzie had an attack of brain fever, and her hair began to fall out. What comforted her was Emma's tender but heavy braid. Lizzie touched up her hair where the gray was showing.

Emma now had a splendid breach-of-promise suit against a flatiron salesman. She intended to make him pay for her small flaring nostrils, which had dilated his own narrow life, and for her amorous chestnut-brown tresses.

Nobody had ever jilted Emma. But if a woman felt she had been sinned against there was no man in that golden age of unreluctant wenches who would be so ungallant as to question the veracity of her charges. The girls were incensed; they removed their white sanitary aprons and rushed to the courthouse to be character witnesses for Emma. Lizzie closed the shop as she hated a trifler no less than a cheapskate. She went to her landlord, to the proprietor of the Electric Oyster House and to Philip Schier, a gentlemanly whisky wholesaler on Delaware Street, to secure letters attesting their faith in her as a noble hard-working widow.

When the Star Lady barbers cast their eyes upon a man so warped as to contest a woman's lawsuit, the flatiron drummer cringed. The judge was visibly impressed by their indignation—which cannot be mimicked, as it falleth out of the heart. We are confused matter, and the kindred of every wind; and who can withstand the fair daughters of the Moabite? What effect had the law of Moses upon the lusts of Ba'al Pe'or? Was a judge in Kansas City any different from King Solomon in Jerusalem? The legal question was simple: Solomon had advised men not to give their strength to women—which good counsel neither Solomon nor the flatiron salesman ever took, for which reason it was only just for the latter to pay. Moreover, nobody ever gets a single experience for nothing; we pay just as much for being cast down into the dust as we do for gendering. If a woman sues a man she is in her element, but when a man enters into a litigation with a female, he pisseth against the wind.

Lizzie came into the courtroom with a satchel filled with paid rent receipts and the highest personal references. She dumped the rent receipts and the character testimonials upon the magistrate's desk, but not without giving him an exceedingly low bow. Then, removing her glasses and wiping the tears from her eyes, she said, "Your Honor, nobody can speak against my good name," whereupon she handed him one of her business cards, which the judge took and read: "Star Lady Barbershop . . . 16 East 8 Street . . . Courtesy is our motto." The judge awarded Emma Moneysmith a thousand dollars as heart balm and promised to come to the shop for his next haircut. The girls rushed over to embrace Lizzie and told her that, though she was a Jew, she was the truest Christian they had ever met. Emma kissed her and told her never to forget that she was one of God's chosen people.

Emma, though proud of her victory, saw that she had to be more vigilant with the race of males who would take advantage of any helpless woman; she resolved that no man was going to taste the sweet body that the Lord had given her without buying her an expensive wardrobe and helping to educate Marion and continue his violin lessons. But soon she met a cowboy from Fargo, North Dakota, and went off to Seltzer Springs with him. Lizzie was in the dumps. She was too weak for another operation and was now thinking of investing money in an oil company about which the saloonkeeper had told her. Whenever business flagged, she became inordinately tired. There was an economic colic because William Howard Taft had become President, and everybody said the plush spending of the spirited Teddy Roosevelt days was over. Lizzie was sorely depleted for reasons she could not understand—but comprehension does not depend upon reason at all.

Emma had told Lizzie she would get what money she could out of the cowboy and come right back. After Emma had left, Lizzie stumbled about the flat, misplacing her keys, diamond ring and pince-nez glasses more frequently. She counted on the health of the women who worked for her. A tough hen like Mrs. Harney, or Birdie, a skinny bantling, deprived her of confidence. When she observed the dry pile of chaff on Harney's head, she was sere and flaccid herself. Birdie was so thin that when Lizzie looked at her she felt unsteady on her own pins.

Birdie had dugs void of *milke and cruddles;* who could junket there? Lizzie had to give her the second chair, and Mrs. Harney took the first. Ruby du Parr, who had astonishing buttocks, promised to work in the shop but did not appear. Another newcomer was Catholic Mary, a doubtful quantum of force. How such a prude had ever become a lady barber was an enigma to everybody. Now the Salvation Army people began to drop by with their collection plates; nuns came in selling religious pamphlets and crucifixes. On Saturday nights Salvation Army lassies wearing black stockings, which were a sexual novelty to the viaduct mashers, stood in front of the Star Lady Barbershop singing hymns and warning the bystanders not to go into the light-housekeeping rooms. Lizzie thought she had pews instead of barber chairs, and after looking over the scrawny poultry in the shop, who seemed to have the pip, she was sure they would drive away all the customers.

However, every trifler got into Mary's chair; near-sighted old-timers wore their spectacles, hoping to see what was behind her woollens and cottons. Was there a pair of rosy-nosed sows rooting underneath her starched shirt-waists? She wore such high collars that it took a customer a half hour to sober up after he had observed a tittle of her naked neck. Like Harney, Mary had not revealed an ankle since she had commenced barbering. Even the steady joshers wondered whether there could be any sport in those booted feet. What Theban towers could her narrow, correct bodice sink?

Oklahoma Indian Gladys had returned to Tulsa, and Noah Taylor's mother, who had superior legs, had vanished. Business was slow, and though formerly Lizzie was out of her wits because the girls were strumpets, she now feared her business might fail as the temperature in the shop had dropped to zero.

She had fallen into an infamous desolation; an empty shop reflected a vacant universe. Dostoevski admitted that after contemplating Holbein's corpse of Christ, which is impermeably lifeless, one could become an atheist. It is a painting of changeless rest and indissoluble death, which could only be true did time exist. But nothing is dead— neither Christ, nor the widow Lizzie. Nor will the Star Lady Barbershop ever expire—because there is no time, and nothing really changes. Jesus and the little place at 16 East 8th Street will always exist somewhere in the planets Venus and Jupiter, or in a galaxy of constellations we have not yet discovered.

Lizzie, carrying a heavier truss of grief than others, thought that God was a just almoner who distributed mis-chance and good hap without prejudice, and that it was now time for her to receive her pittance of charity before the tares choked her wheat, just as it was right that those who were puffed up and rich should be brought down.

Then there came a season of vitality in the barbershop. Mr. Hagen, the wholesaler of butter and eggs, was drawn to skinny Birdie because he imagined there were fewer sins in less flesh, and Birdie was overjoyed at the thought of attracting a heavy man. When Hagen placed an amiable, fat-trousered leg on the foot of Birdie's chair and sang to her: "By the light of the silv'ry moon," everybody in the shop was jubilant and certain that she would be his mistress. Hagen was married, which did not trouble Birdie or Hagen, who did everything he could for his wife so that he would not have to lie with her. They occupied the same pew every Sunday, which made it unnecessary for them to share the same bed.

If there were only a customer or two in the shop, the lady barbers would say to Hagen, when he was arranging his fleshy shirt and putting on a bow tie: "Come on, Mr. Hagen, give us a courteous tune," and Hagen would oblige by singing to Birdie with a morbid amorous passion. He never said one disrespectful word to Birdie, which had a bad effect upon her.

In January, when Mrs. Harney had increased her Christian Science reading to placate her throbbing appendix, Harry Cohen became a regular customer. A baker on Independence Avenue, the Jewish ghetto, this Cohen was a bowlegged, red Edomite with brutal hair. He had a deep gut on each side of his raw, rough mouth and a hinder gold tooth that he thought quite modish and regarded as an amative fang. The girls snickered whenever he showed this false, mandrake tooth.

Harry Cohen became very frank with Lizzie, asserting that he had been unusually handsome as a youth and that he still looked far younger than she. There is no affront so cruel as this, for each one loves his own bones until he is told they are worthless and old. Lizzie was so unnerved by this remark that she cut his chin, saying, "Hold still, Mister, if you don't wish me to slice your throat with the razor." She observed the blotchy, vulgar hands of the Edomite which lay upon the haircloth and covered his face with a scalding towel, which made him start up from the chair. She let him burn while she went to the back room and wiped her sweaty eyes.

Cohen dropped by every day after his bakery oven was cold and, dressed in a brown woollen shirt and loud tan brogues, he considered himself the sport of the town. He spoke of the big profits to be made in huckstering cantaloupes, watermelons, apricots, apples, cherries and vegetables. There was a wagon and a team of pinto ponies on sale at Max Stedna's stable on McGee. She could be his silent partner and make an enormous amount of money without lifting a finger, if she would lend him the cash.

Lizzie could withstand almost anything except the promise or assurance of a windfall. No matter how absurd the scheme, she was ready to believe in it, and this looked like a sound business investment. Euripides held that Apollo was always about to come to the aid of man, but is too busy ever to do it, and Aristophanes prays: "Do not cheat me of my coming hope, O Jove."

Lizzie hesitated after she heard the tittering of the girls, as Harry Cohen stood on the first step showing the tooth that represented his animal strength. Her heart fell down in the dust. The boy attached himself to any man who was interested in his mother and he winced when he heard the cheap raillery of the lady barbers; they were so merry over Cohen that they bawled into their aprons. Life had become embarrassing to the child. Though he did not understand that malice is the most entertaining pastime of the human race, he knew that people laughed at a crookback or guffawed at a hearse passing by. Tears came to his eyes when he saw somebody fall in the street; it wounded him to see a human body humbled.

Lizzie did not want to be involved with such a low man, but Cohen mentioned marriage—and this always baited her.

After Lizzie had paid for the wagon and the team of horses, the boy no longer slept at the side of his mother on the brass bed in the alcove which gave onto the front porch facing 8th Street. He now occupied the sofa in the parlor. The child missed the comfort of her strong back. When he held her stubby arm in his fingers, or pressed his lips against her elbow, she pushed him away.

She was engaged in a war for her life, and the cold months had all of a sudden come upon her. She believed that she was starving, and no less than the horse in a boreal climate she scraped away the snow for whatever lean herbage there was beneath it.

Were she and the child alone on Sundays, the mother would promise to take him out for a long streetcar ride to Swope Park. The preparations for this excursion usually took so much time that it would be too late for them to go. She had to have her cold bath and get into the one white lace dress she wore for parlor visitors or for rides to the parks. She could never find her hairpins, or she broke the laces of her corset and complained that standing beneath the electric bulbs cutting hair had blinded her so that she could not mend them. After that there was the wild search for her gold watch. Lizzie rested on the settee, trying to push her switch into the spot where her hair was hollow, and then she looked for her keys, and by the time she had ransacked the bedclothes she had misplaced her glasses, and then, seating herself on the piano stool, she wept.

The boy was already the miserable prey of Eros. Ruby du Parr's posteriors had moved his whole soul. When he heard the sighing undergarments of Blanche Beasley, a roomer who had come to work for Lizzie lately, he suffered sexual agonies. What delights in Eden were locked in that room where she lay with O'Rourke, who worked at the

56

Kansas City Journal? About nine each evening she came out carrying a towel and soap, and as she shuffled in her slippers toward the bathroom, he saw her revolving naked thighs as they pushed open the kimono. Women cindered his imagination though he had no knowledge of bodies.

The child was as gross in his desires as the man who grew out of him. The greed for voluptuous sensations is a disease. Who invented the torments of the testicles? Had he the nature for it, he would have renounced the lunacy called sensuality. Pleasure is the tickling of the maggots that ravin upon the bones. Who has not experienced that inexpressible sadness that comes after copulation? This is the sorrow of every particle of energy which has been momentarily diminished and which is the result of the sport of the worms.

Once, at daybreak he suddenly awakened, hearing his mother let out a cry of pain. Harry Cohen was covering her, and he knew that the cause of her outcry was carnal. The baker was of the issue of those giants who, in the Ethiopic *Book of Enoch*, were said to have had the monstrous privy members of horses.

We inherit our songs of lust from angels. The heavens are defiled, and God makes nothing that is not corrupt. The angel 'Azazel taught men the uses of lechery; everything that lives is incontinent. Are not the seas, the earth and the firmament round and sensual?

Harry Cohen insured the pair of ponies against fire, drowning, pests and tornadoes, and made himself the beneficiary should the horses perish. He told Lizzie that it would spoil her reputation if he put her name on the policy.

Harry lived a block and a half from the stable, which was opposite a Negro baseball park on Independence Avenue. He was in the habit of stopping by the shanty to see whether the team was safe, and on occasion, with a nosebag across his shoulder, he met the horse and mule dealer, Stedna, who had a genuine affection for the western pintos he had sold Harry Cohen, and who appreciated his concern for them.

One early morning Harry Cohen saw smoke piling up over the roof of the feed store which was in front of the stable. He ran down Independence Avenue, bawling, "Fire! Help! Police!" and when he entered the small yard littered with hay, oats, turnips, lumps of sugar, wisps of grass and gunny sacks, he filled a tin pail with water which he threw on the flames. By the time two fire engines arrived, Harry Cohen was smudged with smoke and water, and those red orbs of Esau were swollen with tears. He had covered his head with dust and lay there sobbing: "Oh, my pinto pets, my infants!"

After he had collected the five hundred dollars from the insurance company for his dead, charred horses, he did not return to the barbershop. There was a rumor that he and an Independence Avenue whore had opened up a house of ill fame.

Now a number of accidents occurred, as though mishaps were just as gregarious and average as people. Cromwell and Hagen had fallen out over politics. Hagen supported a Republican candidate for mayor, and this grieved the commission-house gentleman. A lonely, halved man, Cromwell continued to come in for his 7:15 morning shave; too kind and circumspect to chatter about his friend, he expressed, without talking about it, concern for Hagen. Lizzie knew that Hagen was a big skirt-chaser, a fleshy, sensual laugher who could not stay away from women. He was now trifling with a motorman's wife, taking her out for long buggy rides beyond the city limits. Cromwell went over one day to Hagen and Company, Wholesalers of Eggs and Butter, and beseeched his friend to renounce this imprudent pastime; when Hagen gave him a few short words, Cromwell turned his back to him so that Hagen could not look into his eyes that were hurt.

Shortly afterwards there was a front-page picture of

a carriage riddled with the bullets from a streetcar motorman's rifle. Hagen was lying in the hospital, and while Cromwell held his hand, Hagen, knowing that he was dying, sang: "Jesus is mine, Jesus is mine."

Within two weeks a thunderbolt had struck 16 East 8th Street. The *Kansas City Star* reported another shooting. About to quit a hotel room with a suitcase and a cowboy's money belt, Emma Moneysmith was killed by bullets from a pistol.

The death of Emma bruised Lizzie for a long time.

One day there was a photograph in the paper of a deceased seer who resembled a great bag of holy relics; each feature was canonized by contemplation. The boy, poring over the picture, studied the gray-white, feathered beard, the shaggy, jealous underlip and the wild potato nose. The dead author's name was Count Leo Tolstoi, and the boy was so pierced by the death of this savant, of whom he had never heard before, that he wondered and asked: "Who was Leo Tolstoi?"

Lizzie was still smarting from the infamous connection with Harry Cohen when a man named Popkin, who had a partnership in a jewelry store on Main Street, commenced to patronize her chair. He wore neat cloth suits to match the brown-red hair which fringed his dapper neck. He looked trim and spruce as a bald man; were there more hair on his head, people would have mistaken it for a toupee. Popkin had a wife from whom he was estranged. He planned, he told Lizzie, to buy diamonds in Palestine and smuggle them into the United States—with a small investment he could be a rich man. Popkin, unlike Harry Cohen, was a straight, principled man; he asked her to be his wife, and she accepted him. After he got a divorce they were married and took a spacious apartment at Fountain Place, which was beyond Forest Street, where Stedna lived in a rambling, monied clapboard house.

Popkin's former wife pestered him for money, and he

advised Lizzie that he ought to go to Jerusalem straightway. He was sure this would discourage his first wife, so that by the time he returned she would no longer interfere with them. Lizzie gave him her entire savings and even sold her diamond ring and brooch to raise more cash for him.

Popkin was aware that he was a simpleton with women and was resolved to be shrewd; so he signed over his half of the jewelry business to his partner, a man who had never cheated him. He employed an attorney to draw up a document so astutely worded that neither Lizzie nor his former wife could claim his share of the business while he was absent.

Lizzie received no letters from Popkin for six months; when he returned he brought her two bedspreads embroidered with gold, pillowcases to match, a lace dress and a Jerusalem parrot that spoke three Hebrew words, after which he called Popkin by name: "Aleph, beth, gimel . . . Popkin!"

When he called on his partner at the jewelry store, Popkin was ordered to quit the premises at once or be arrested by the police. After this misfortune, he resumed his life with his former spouse and became a salesman in a secondhand clothing establishment. Lizzie could have gone to law and attached his wages, but she considered Popkin a weak rather than an evil man; however, a steadfast foe is always more reliable than a timid friend, and far less dangerous.

She divorced him and again announced that she was a noble hard-working widow who could hold her head high wherever she went. Everybody respected a widow; for since her husband was presumably dead, she was regarded as both unfortunate and chaste. What's in a name, every poet has asked? Everything.

Lizzie, embittered and ill, deemed this incident another lesson in experience. She imagined that some day, after she had been thoroughly instructed by woeful experiences, she would know how to handle trouble. With at least half of her mind she decided to relinquish all thoughts of felicity. What else was there for her but bread, butter and reverence? Could one be noble cutting hair and removing the whiskers of men? Nietzsche, who had no more chagrins to count than Lizzie, made a similar covenant with his own mountainous soul: "I no longer strive for my happiness, I only strive for my work."

Lizzie sought refuge in the asceticism of everyday toil, but there was still the adhesive child. He was a burden of Tyre to himself. He had all the disgusts of his environment in him without any of the health of place. What he needed was a long respite from erotical symbols. Lately, Mrs. Hickman had taken one of the barber chairs, and her daughter, Venus, had overwhelmed him. Her silk dresses harmed his entire nervous system. Heine has disclosed that when he was a boy he fainted because a ten-year-old girl entered the classroom while he was reciting a poem.

One evening the lady barbers had gone home and Lizzie was pouring fresh water into the tobacco-stained spittoons when she heard the door open and someone enquiring: "Too late?"

"It's never too late for business; you're next."

Her customer was a short, fat josher with flat blond hair and river-gray-blue eyes. He was the captain of the *Chester*, a freighter that plied between St. Louis, Kansas City and New Orleans. He explained the anatomy of the Missouri, its shoals and sandbars, while she trimmed his hair, and she could scarcely believe that it was possible to have so much knowledge of a body of water.

Lizzie put her scissors away and laid her hone and hair clipper inside her tool kit while Captain Henry Smith loitered on the settee. Then they strolled up 8th Street and had an ice-cream soda at Jenkins' cigar store.

The captain came to town about every third or fourth week. He earned two hundred and fifty dollars a month, in addition to his cabin, meals and laundry—which was a fabulous wage—and he had property in Louisville and houses in St. Louis. As a young man he had played small-time vaudeville—jigging, strumming the mandolin and singing early ragtime. Stout, but not flabby, he sweated copiously; when his pants stuck to the settee in the shop, and the boy leaned on him, Captain Henry Smith grew quite testy and asked the boy to try standing by himself. Most of Captain Smith's delight in calling on Lizzie was annihilated by the boy, who stepped on his polished shoes, hung on his coat sleeves or just leaned. Had he not used Henry Smith's fleshy, perspiry shoulders as a bastion, the boy's whole life would have been different.

The captain was jolly company for Lizzie; he liked a rib steak and dill pickles, with a bottle of beer. He did everything in a round, fat manner; he had a heavy orotund gait and long, snorting, orbed slumbers.

Lizzie had gone back to the 8th Street flat after divorcing Popkin, and when the *Chester* was moored to the wharf in Kansas City, Captain Smith lodged with her. She cooked for him, washed his socks and drawers—and waited for his proposal of marriage. Meantime, when she was indignant and moody, she composed a brief, rancorous declamation that she intended to recite to him. He had become her star boarder, but aside from buying a few bags of fruit and several ice-cream sodas, he never paid her anything. She hated to humiliate him by pointing out that she was supporting him, while he had no wish to be chagrined and so said nothing about it either. But he could discern the oration on her lips, could even hear the words: "See here, Captain, what is your proposition? Am I your kitchen mechanic and washerwoman? Don't you think, sir, I'm entitled to a little courtesy? Don't be two-faced with me. I respect a plain, straight heart."

When he saw her rigid mouth and understood her mind, he would nudge her ribs and go to the piano, which he

played by ear, and sing one of his foolish, sensual ditties to
her:

> That last kiss was sure some winner, honey,
> Much too good for a beginner, honey;
> Someone's been 'round here
> Since I've been gone . . .

Too late, she had discovered that Captain Henry Smith
was exceedingly stingy. How could she have fallen into
another trap? My God, does one experience yield nothing
except the appetite for another disappointment—which we
would like to think, to save our self-esteem, is different from
the preceding one?

Had she dolled up for him, that might have altered his
inclination; but Lizzie thought she did enough for a man
when she undressed for him. Her natural strength was her
fetching apparel; one of the seven deadly sins is clothes.
Besides, any woman who can satisfy a man is a beauty.

The steamboat business on the Missouri was rapidly
failing, and the *Chester* was put in dry dock. Captain Smith,
now more or less retired, did little but shuffle from the bedroom to the kitchen. Sometimes he didn't even bother to
carry the light basket of food from the grocery to the flat.
Lizzie complained that she could lift nothing, and when she
was tired and raised her arms it was hard on her bladder. He
pretended that he had not heard her chiding; moreover, as
a matter of fact, he was rather deaf in one ear and always
walked with that side next to her.

Although her life was an uninterrupted humiliation she
did not know how to deliver her piece of elocution on
marriage, or how to manage the captain's deceit and cir-
cumlocutions. He had intimated that if she could get the
boy out of the way—so that he could lean somewhere else—
they might make plans together. At thirty-eight, she was

positive that if Henry Smith did not marry her, she was as good as dead.

Philip Schier, a wholesaler of whisky on Delaware Street, had once mentioned that he was a trustee of an orphanage in Cleveland. Following a long conversation with Mr. Schier, she decided the boy had to be removed from the bad streets.

At the train her face was a thousand grieving rivers; she jostled the crowds waiting on the platform, turning and twisting as though she were trussed up by her nerves. She was nearly ill because she feared that the boy would not have a seat in the railway coach. He pressed his face against the window and saw her worn-out skin. She was his only cruse of water and morsel of bread—the immaterial food we need when we are a wilderness. Like St. Jerome the mother smote her breast with a rock. It had never occurred to her that her son would be separated from her. Sending him off was another way she had of taking up her heavy life, as Sisyphus lifted the stone in order to push it up the mountain side to the top, although he knew it would roll down again. What else could she do with the boy, her life or the rock?

III

For nothing is more easy to be found than be barking Scyllas, ravening Celaenos, and Laestrygons, devourers of people, and suchlike great and incredible monsters. But to find citizens ruled by good and wholesome laws, that is an exceedingly rare and hard thing.

Sir Thomas More

In April 1912, when he was eleven, the boy became an inmate of the Jewish Orphan Asylum in Cleveland, the Forest City. No Spartan ordinances could have been more austere than the rules for the orphans. The regimen was martial; Scipio, who compelled his troops to eat uncooked food standing up, would have been satisfied with these waifs who rose every morning at 5:30 as though they were making ready for a forced march.

There was a dormitory for the boys on one side of the shambly four-story brick building, and the other opposite was for the girls. The long hall that lay between the two dormitories was guarded by monitors so that the two sexes would be rigidly separated.

The main edifice had been built in the classical style typical of the almshouses, reform schools and charitable penal institutions of the late Edwardian period. There was a separate school building of the same kind of brick with a kabbalistical stairway leading up to an attic above the third floor where the boys played basketball. Two infirmaries were close to the hinder side of the main building. One was for general disorders, pleurisy, rickets, consumption, coughing, appendicitis, impotent intelligence—and dying. The other was a spital house for contagious diseases. Besides that, there was a steam laundry adjacent to the engine room, and behind that a green-house where turnips, kale and kohlrabi were grown; there were no flowers, since these were regarded as the petticoats among the plants and were banished from the sight of the children.

The playgrounds in back resembled Milton's sooty flag of Acheron. They extended to the brow of the stiff, cindered gully that bent sheer downwards toward a boggy Tophet overrun with humpback bushes and skinny, sour berries. Beyond the bushes was a pond close by a row of freight cars on a siding near the Standard Oil tanks. All this was as sacred to the children as Thoreau's Merrimac or Winnipiseogee rivers.

Some of the children were admitted to the orphanage when they were two and a half years of age. These were known as the little pissers and they slept in a much smaller hall; their mattresses were covered with rubber sheets. Miss Price was the head of this dormitory for little boys. She said she could tell as soon as a newcomer arrived whether he was a bed-wetter or not.

At daybreak a governor rushed about the dormitory, followed by a pair of monitors, shouting, "All up now!" They came by the cots and threw back the bedclothes. Nobody wanted to air his bare buttocks on January mornings at 5:30, and often a monitor dumped a boy out of his cot to encourage him. In the washroom were two long soapstone troughs. Each boy, naked to the navel, his blue shirt, drawers and suspenders hanging, stood in front of a faucet, washed his face and body in icy water and scrubbed his teeth with Ivory soap. Adjoining the washroom were the water closets, separated from each other by wooden panels —which had been made without doors to discourage orphans from indulging in self-abuse or sitting too long and getting piles.

After making up their beds and combing their hair, the orphans ran down to the basement. This was the playroom; there were long, rough wooden benches with boxes under the seat. Each box had a number—which became the boy's identity for his whole life in the orphanage. If the boy were talking or giggling, the governor or monitor cried out: "Number 92, quiet now, all in order!" In these boxes the orphans kept shoe polish—and marbles, ball bearings and stale Washington pies or doughnuts stolen from Becker's Bakery on Woodland Avenue. In the morning the boys would get out their daubers, spit on them and dig them into a tin of shoe polish. When a nearsighted 5th-grader, or a soft-witted half-orphan who wore glasses, spat on his own shirt or the pants of the boy next to him, someone would guffaw and a fight would start.

Everybody wore the orphan asylum mouse-gray jacket, lank, straight pants that fell as far as the knees and woollen stockings with thick ridges. They had no overcoats or caps and often ran out to the playground in their shirts, returning, when their ears were blue, to sit on the hot radiator pipes. There were iron bars on all the windows, and two monitors guarded the door so that nobody could leave the playroom except to march to the schoolhouse, or to play for an hour outdoors after 4 o'clock. The grounds were surrounded by a high wooden fence; in front of the brick ramshackle was a fine lawn and a fountain which made a good impression on passers-by; however, this was *verboten* grass, and the orphans were only allowed to walk on it on first and second picnics in summer. Anybody caught going over the fence got a hundred demerits and was kept indoors for a week. If an orphan were good all year and had received no demerits, two dollars was his award, which he could spend on first and second picnics or on the one occasion when they had a day at Euclid Beach.

At 6:30 an 8th-grader read the Hebrew prayers and each boy, standing at the bench in front of his numbered box, chanted aloud the orison. Some said *Baruch atah Adonai Elohenu,* and others muttered any words that came into their heads; two governors ran up and down to discover who was being profane and garbling the Lord's prayers. At 6:40 they marched in double file up the stairs to the refectory; two girls, dining-room help, opened the doors, and they went in and took chairs at long tables which resembled the planks of a house painter. The boys said they were convict tables. Two hundred girls sat at one end of the vast hall, and three hundred boys at the other. There were four governors assigned to rule the boys, but only two for the girls, who were not considered bona fide orphans anyway, because they were good, quiet and were dining-room helpers. No boy could get near the dining hall except for mess, and they had the greatest scorn for those female hypocrites on the far side of the orphanage who received an extra apple or a meat sandwich from Christine, the Polish cook.

The orphan asylum traditions were severely observed, and any boy caught talking to a girl was taken down the gully, or into the basement when the governors were at their meals, and beaten. This had been a custom for seventy-five years, and no older boy was going to allow laxity of this sort; how could they be tough enough to fight the Irish Micks if boys were permitted to hang around girls?

Breakfast began with a short prayer; then there was a tumultuous scraping of chairs, the rattle of five hundred tin plates and cups, or the rancor of somebody who thought he had been fleeced: "Hey, don't go changing mush plates with me, you crook." The children abhorred the breakfast gruel which was served without milk or sugar in chipped, enameled tin plates; they called it mush. A boy who puked at the table was regarded as a menace because they said the mush looked like vomit anyway. The coffee was a slop of stale ground beans and hot water, and also contained no milk or sugar. Each child was given a slice or crust of dead rye bread which was thinly swabbed with oleomargarine. A tin cup of milk was reserved for boys who looked tubercular. It took the orphans about three minutes to finish their meal; then they grew restless and threw bread rolled into hard pellets from one table to another, or, if one were moody, or just starved, he pushed the boy next to him and said, "Meet me in the playroom; I challenge you to a fight."

When Lizzie's boy, Number 92, had arrived, wearing a pink shirt, a Panama straw hat and tan stockings, the 7th- and 8th-graders said that if the trustees had no more sense than to spend their money and ruin the annual budget to support a nut like that, they might as well admit their defeat and close the J.O.A.

Brutality was also an orphanage fetish; the smaller children were bullied by the older boys. They had no manual skill in affections and were sore afraid of touching another except to harm or punish. The hand is a greater revelation than the face, which is always an enigma. The outward countenance can resemble Jacob but the inward one may be Esau. Lizzie's boy was a greenhorn with his fists and was intimidated by the orphanage dialect. Even the names of the inmates seemed as esoteric to him as the *Pirke Aboth:* Mugsy, Prunes, Shrimp, Bah, Mooty, Spunk, Pummy, Bonehead Balaam, Moses Mush Tate, Phineas Watermelonhead, Mushmelonhead, Sachemhead. . . .

Number 92 wrote his mother, begging her to take him back to Kansas City where he could run in the streets, hear the cicadas singing on Indian summer evenings or listen to the Troost Avenue streetcar making soft water-sounds against the tracks as it passed over a trestle twined with weeds and sunflowers. Later in life, Number 92 came to understand Kierkegaard's "The crowd is untruth," for at eleven he had been a spindly, puking weanling in the midst of a fell herd. He pined to be close to his mother. He was no stoic and wept, because he had no choice, and at the age of eleven one of the few illusions that he still had was that one could do what one wanted to do.

Letter-writing day was once a week. Then an orphan could write to an uncle or aunt in Milwaukee, or a cousin in St. Paul, but there were many who had been in the Home since kindergarten and had not a soul on the earth to claim them. The letters received were opened by the Superintendent to see whether they contained a dime or a quarter— which was promptly confiscated. The contents of all epistles were read and censored; if an inmate said that the *weisenhaus* was a reform school, the words were scratched out, and the turncoat who had reviled the Superintendent, the trustees or the meals was given fifty to a hundred demerits. If the offense was repeated, he was deprived of first picnic and lost the privilege of "going out walking," the traditional reference to a day at Euclid Beach with a philanthropic dowager from Shaker Heights or Chagrin Falls.

The commons were always the same: Monday was a goulash day; for Tuesday there was a stringy, tepid stew with a piece of fat as old as Methuselah's toe. Every other Wednesday they got biscuits with raisins in them. This was a dietary blessing and also the cause of much strife among the orphans. Reliable and honest feeders finished their buns and raisins right away, but there were some table-misers who slowly dug the raisins out of the biscuits and piled them at the side of their plates; then they broke the biscuits into tiny morsels to make them last until everybody marched down to the playroom. A meal snudge was in ill repute.

Twice a month a pair of sausages was served to each boy; these were later vended in the basement for a penny each. During the war years they were sold for three cents apiece, which caused a great deal of argument about unjust war prices. On Thursday they got green-pea hash. By Thursday everybody was starving, but one's appetite was always ruined; either it was goulash or green-pea hash day or some boy puked on the table right after the orphans had asked the Lord's blessing. The easiest way to commence a brawl was to dump goulash or green-pea hash into another boy's plate.

Everybody looked forward to Friday evening *kuchen*. A first-grader could buy the protection of a bully for a coffee *kuchen*. There were *kuchen*-hoarders too who walked about the playroom tearing the coffeecake to pieces while the others roller-skated, braided a horsehair chain while sitting on the window sill or counted the days until confirmation, just to forget they were hungry. On Sundays, when there were stewed prunes for supper, all a downcast orphan had to say to his neighbor at the table was, "Think you're much? Do you know you're living?" and there was a prune fight.

The food was boiled, or rather thrown into vast iron vats. Christine, the head cook, was blamed for all the sorrows of their gullets. Nobody would touch the noonday tomato soup because one orphan swore he had seen Christine cut her finger with a kitchen knife and then let it bleed into the tub.

Eggs were served once a year on the Passover. The Pesaḥ eggs, biscuits and *kuchen* were hawked or bartered for special favors from the door-monitors or the good will of an older boy. After sundown of Yom Kippur, the Day of Atonement and a fast day, each inmate got a small piece of chicken. Though Saturn could not have offered them a dearer bounty, the orphans abhorred the high holy day. The ancient Jews went to the wailing wall of Jerusalem to ease

71

their misery; the boys, forced to keep to their benches or sit in the prayer hall, ran in and out of the toilets. It was sacrilegious to drink water, but no one had asserted that it was unorthodox to pass it. Saturday was as obnoxious as Yom Kippur; that morning they marched to chapel, which spoiled a good day. What had the orphans to pray for? For what had they to thank God? For Christine's rotten food, or not having a kin in the earth? Were they always to be kinless and to have dwarfed hearts?

When they were told to open their hymn books to page 98, the boys in the front seats screamed, "God humbles the proud," and when they came to the second line, "and the lowly he raises," Mugsy, Bah, Pummy and Mooty stuck safety pins through the cracks in the chairs, and into the buttocks of religious maniacs like Bucket De Groot and Pinkie the door-monitor until there was a terrible uproar. Doc put his hand on his ailing heart, and Simon Wolkes, the Assistant Superintendent, shouted that he would expel the whole orphan asylum. The girls on the opposite side of the chapel started to snivel. Blanche Reinitz, who was good in composition, called them atheists, and the boys in high disgust said, "Aw, shut up."

The fighters, Max Lewis, Mugsy, Prunes, Hans, and even Pinkie, who had read *Silas Marner*, would sneak out at night when the governors were at their meals, crawl over the transom of the bread-room and steal bread and apples. A rural delicacy was a crust of rye with large holes in it, known as *gimmels*, filled with molasses. They would break into the kitchen and stuff a gunny sack with raw potatoes, which they took down to the gully where they roasted them. Such an excursion was a jubilee, for every nook of the ravine was holy ground.

For the first lustrum after they had been confirmed, former inmates would return to visit the orphanage, and what a pain was in their eyes because the hill, the gully where they had roasted potatoes and the bend that led to the gut of water that lay close to the cabooses on the siding and the Standard Oil tanks had diminished so much in size. Was their childhood so niggard? Why does everything dwindle as we grow into men?

Before returning to the dormitory each one removed the burrs from his uniform; the boys called them "Doc spies." When the governors or the Superintendent discovered these burrs stuck to the pants or stockings of an orphan, he was taken off the honor roll, which meant that he lost his two dollars spending money and had to stay in the basement during first or second picnics. Besides that, he could not "go out walking."

If an orphan were caught too many times with "Doc spies" on his uniform, he was expelled and sent back to Newport, Minneapolis, Wichita or Kansas City, to join a distant relative, or simply returned to a blank, kinless city. The asylum grounds, its cinders, its junky buildings, the *verboten* grass and muted water fountain out front, were in their ruined infant roots. It bruised their deformed minds when they thought of a separation from the Home. An outcast would never cease hearing the governor blow his whistle and bawl out, "All quiet now!" while Bucket De Groot jumped from one wooden bench to another to escape from Bah, Mugsy or Pummy, yelling, "You stop that now or I'll report you." They would never forget the governor's second warning: "All in order now!" as each one took his seat where his number was, folded his hands and tried not to sprawl.

It was an ineradicable infamy to be expelled. From the time they were 5th-graders they began to count the days until confirmation; yet none wept more by the waters of Babylon than an orphan who was about to be banished. Born to be exiled, he would not get his blue serge long pants and stand together with his classmates in front of the Torah and intone the reverential confirmation song: "Father, see Thy suppliant children."

When he was confirmed and had quit the orphanage would that not too be a phantasm? Or was his suffering so pitiless that a whole numb experience had expunged what we call the corporeal? All acute moments are the same. When pain is absolute, or unbearable, it is similar to the most heightened pleasure. But nothing really exists, for nobody can handle his memories, or take hold of a single sensation, no matter how immense it was when he had it.

Each boy cut his name or initials into wooden benches, painted them on the galvanized refuse cans, on the toilet panels and seats, or carved them on the gardener's wagon. Ulysses in his dotage pined no less for a noble tomb than these pariahs did to leave their imperishable names in the laundry, on schoolhouse desks or around the basketball court of the Jewish Orphan Asylum.

When a boy had been expelled, others helped him pack his agates, marbles, ball bearings, a shoelace, a horseshoe and a stale Washington pie, into a bandanna handkerchief or a paper bag. The outcast sobbed or, utterly silent, asked God to pardon him and to bless Watermelonhead, Prunes, Monkey Bergman, Moses Mush Tate, Bonehead Balaam, Shrimp, Bah, Pummy, Mooty, Bucket De Groot and Frank Lewis. They were all beggars but as immortal as Caleb, Gideon and Deborah the prophetess, who came out with the timbrel and sang before the ark.

Nor was it possible for these "gal-haters" to exclude the petticoat snivelers in woollen drawers, crude, ridged stockings and prison blue cottons who resembled the descendants of the wrinkled, squinting daughters of Thersites. How few had a bosom; would not Solomon have said of them: "We have a little sister and she has no breasts." The girls' dormitory was the clandestine Valhalla of the orphan boys. Suppose a male inmate were exiled to St. Paul or Fargo, North Dakota, how could he endure the world without one of these *weisenhaus* Venuses? No girl would marry one who had been expelled. He would always be in disgrace with

74

Gizella, Mary Brown from North Yakima, Washington, Ida Lewis from Detroit, Blanche Reinitz, the pretty Mann sisters and Beulah Bull, whose quick, bleating paps once lay in the hands of Harry Kato, who was caught by Simon Wolkes, the next Superintendent after Doc, and sent back to Los Angeles.

The J.O.A. boys often climbed over the eight-foot fence to go to Becker's Bakery on Woodland Avenue, which they called Pushcart Boulevard. Five stale doughnuts cost two cents, a Washington pie, three days old, was a penny, and a half dozen day-before-yesterday's jelly rolls were three pennies. Sometimes seven orphans would come into the bakeshop at a time and while two of them pretended that they were at a stationer's or a candy store, and asked for lead pencils, a copy book, ice-cream cones or jawbreakers, in order to exasperate old man Becker, the others would run out with a tray of cakes.

Some of the boys had huge boils on their necks, cheeks and chins and impostumes—which were called "Becker's boils"—on their heads. For years many had sore heads which were smeared with Unguentine and bandaged with white gauze. Lice were a common affliction, and the two nurses at the orphanage infirmary were kept busy with their fine combs. A continual discharge of mucus flowed from the noses of spindly 3rd-graders. Had Gabriel, Michael, Raphael and Uriel forgotten them? Why was Abraham, who saw the angels as he slept beneath the oaks at Mamre, more blessed than these helpless oafs? Howl, O Heshbon, for ʿAi is spoiled; run to and fro in the hedges. I chant the song of the fungus. I am clay, dust and maggots, but I shall not forget thee, O ye who wore bog moss and hunger, until I forget my own crying flesh.

They were a separate race of stunted children who were clad in famine. Swollen heads lay on top of ashy uniformed orphans. Some had oval or oblong skulls; others gigantic watery occiputs that resembled the Cynecephali described by Hesiod and Pliny. The palsied and the lame were cured in the pool of Bethesda, but who had enough human spittle to heal the orphans' sore eyes and granulated lids? How little love, or hot sperm, had gone into the making of their gray-maimed bodies? The ancient Jews, who ate dove's dung in the time of dearth in Samaria, were as hungered as these waifs. Nobody can even see another without abundant affection. Whatever grace and virtue we give to others comes from our own fell needs. We pray for the face we need and call this intellectual perception. Without the feeling we are willing to give to others, the Kosmos is vacant and utterly peopleless.

Though all day long nothing was in the ailing minds of the orphan-asylum Ishmaels but the cry for food, what these mutes asked for was never given. O Pharisee, when will you learn that we never came to your table for the gudgeons and the barley loaves?

Whenever Doc walked through the back yard, a covey of small oafs took hold of his scriptural sleeves and fingered the sacred buttons of them as though they were lipping the rood. The lucky ones who took hold of the hands of this Elohim of the orphanage shook with paradisiacal rapture. He could hardly loosen the grip of a three-year-old wight with a running nose and a sore head who would hang onto his trousers. "The heart is forever inexperienced," asserts Thoreau; "Feed my lambs," says Christ.

The whole day was a Lacedaemonian exercise. Everyone had his daily work; no one was ever idle. There was the toilet-broom boy; and others to clean and Sapolio the troughs and the bowls in the washroom; four sweepers for the playroom, the window-washing platoon, the pick-up boys for the yard, wardrobe boys, laundry helpers, the garbage collectors who emptied the cans of refuse into the furnace next to the chicken coops at the edge of the hill. What the boys had to do every day brought them the reward of heaven, and, on rare occasions, kept them from getting fifty demerits.

They were disciplined for warfare, which is a benefit to the poor in will. Nobody suffered from that malady, velleity, which disables the soul. Any kind of work that does not harm the health or brutify the spirit is essential for children. Epictetus remarks: "For since you must die in any case, you must be found doing something, whatever it be— farming or digging or trading . . . or suffering indigestion or diarrhea."

There were a few lucky ones of the male gender: unprincipled orphans like Bonehead Balaam who had saved his first and second picnic money and invested it in white leghorns. He sold a few eggs to people in the city but he preferred to drink a raw egg himself to settle his blood and increase his weight. Bonehead was such a miser that he wouldn't go "in whack," that is, "divvy up" his eggs and chickens with a boy who was going to be confirmed in a year. One couldn't beat him either, because an older boy was sure to forget himself and hit Bonehead on the head and break his hand.

In January the orphans skated on the frozen pond. Midway between the clinkered hill at the edge of the yard and the bottom of the gulch was a hummock. When a boy on a sled struck this bump he rose several feet, then passed through the dead, mangy bushes and went around the bend as far as the pond and the oil tanks. All the fights with the tough Irish Micks took place in the ravine.

Every winter the Irish Micks came from Kinsman Road and the slums of Superior Avenue to fight with the orphans. These January battles had been going on for years, and though an 8th-grader wasn't afraid of anybody, he was always on his guard with these brawlers who had knives and hid stones inside icy snowballs. Once when a fight with the Irish was about to start, and Mush Tate was waiting for souvenirs—a mumblety-peg knife, marbles, nails or a

77

penny—to fall out of somebody's pocket, he said to Hans, "I'll hold your coat for you so that you can lick that Irish bastard," and he did.

Achilles was no fiercer than an orphan fighter. Hans, who got a glass of milk every day because he was underweight, had merciless fists. He had whittled a broomstick to a fine edge, which he dug into the belly of a timid boy warming his pants on the radiator pipes of the playroom. When he saw a boy mumbling to himself on the window sill, he beat his knuckles until they bled. No one escaped Hans's punitive broomstick except Moses Mush Tate, who made him laugh. Mush Tate was the Socratic dialectician of the orphan home. His words fell out in prophetic order and with such good luck that only a whole orphan with half a wit would argue with him.

On Sunday evenings, when they got stewed prunes for supper, the orphans said Kaddish, the Hebrew prayer for the dead, for Christine the cook. Not even Mush Tate would touch that supper of Hecate. Everybody in the refectory was starved and bored. When the governors were not looking, an orphan might take a prune pit, put it on the handle of a spoon and then strike the bowl as hard as he could with the palm of his hand. The aim was generally accurate, and when an inmate who wore senseless eyeglasses was hit in the head with a prune pit and yelled "Ouch!" the governors, followed by the Superintendent, came running to the table to discover the malefactor.

Not only did one receive demerits for running out into the city, a capital offense, or throwing goulash or green-pea hash at a "newcumber," but he was summoned to wait in the marble hall after supper. If there were seven or eight culprits, they had to stand in this holy alcove and wait for Doc to finish his meal. They would study the names of the deceased donors which were chiseled in gold in the marble: "In memory of Abraham Cornhill . . . $500."

Doc was a stubby, corpulent rabbi with a white beard;

no orphan would have doubted that he was God—had he not picked his nose. He occupied an oak-paneled apartment opposite the memorial slabs, where he slept in a large, downy bed and had incredible meals; broiled fish, spring lamb chops and lettuce and cucumber salads dressed in olive oil were as unimaginable to the J.O.A. boys as ambrosia or nectar.

Doc had a long and seasoned experience with the Old Testament and the retribution of Jehovah. He had many ruses in disciplining the orphans. He would commence in a solemn, gentle strain, holding his hand on his bad heart; he was sorely grieved for the circumcised offenders before him. He took his place in front of the line of boys, usually beginning with a reference to the golden calf or the trials of Moses after he had descended from the holy mountain that spoke. Then, while he admonished an orphan at the extreme right end of the line, he would strike another at the other side. In spite of the fact that these stratagems were well known, Doc sooner or later caught someone off guard because of a poignant allusion to Leviticus.

When Doc asked Mush Tate what need he had to defy the Mosaic dietary laws by running out into the city and eating gentile jelly rolls and Washington pies, Mush Tate hung his head, and as soon as Doc saw he was lost in the throes of meditation, he gave him an uppercut.

It was during the first World War; there were new sore heads, "Becker's Bakery boils" and ringworms every day. On the third day of creation there was grass, but after the Lord had rested the orphans had pimples, spinal meningitis and rickets. But it was the time of the harvest for these gnomes because the physician had prescribed white bread for them. What a benediction were all diseases. Had not the Lord given them measles, mumps, chicken pox, scarlet fever and made them dwarfs in order that they might receive an albic crust?

The lavatory had become more popular than usual;

79

this was the agora of the orphanage. Mush Tate went to the water closet to meditate and to jot down neologisms he claimed he had received from Mt. Sinai. By five o'clock every seat was taken. Human beings eat to defecate; the orphans dunged as a pastime. When the meals were the most repulsive, both Doc and Simon Wolkes told them to rejoice in their swill because of the famine in Armenia and the floods in China. Their poverty was so equally distributed among all the orphans that no waif, unless he coveted the indigence of another, had any cause for envy.

These children with senile, swollen heads were already as wrinkled as Adam who stood in the River Gihon and wept. When they were unusually hungry, they invented word games, or just relieved themselves.

Pete Kayte was drumming on the wooden panels with his lopsided knuckles. Gabbie, with his trousers spidering down his naked legs and his suspenders dragging on the cement floor, had a harmonica in his mouth on which he was playing a J.O.A. classic:

We'll fight for the name of Harvard . . .

Mush Tate was musing over his prophetic J.O.A. lexicon. Beans Mugsy was howling:

My little girl, you know I love you.

A *Cleveland Plain Dealer* was lying on the lap of Benny Marble's woollen drawers. He was counting the number of Canadian, Australian and English casualties for the week. The boys computed the war fatalities as if they were baseball scores. They made wagers and the one who came closest to the number of soldiers who died on the battlefield during one week won an every-other-Wednesday biscuit or a Friday-supper *kuchen*.

When Simon Wolkes walked by the toilets in his black

kabbalistical suit, he gave Number 92 a brief, prayer-hall face and pulled the hair of Pete Kayte, who was then whittling into the wooden partition: P/K. Conf. 1917. Mugsy went on howling, paying no heed to the Assistant Superintendent, who, he said, would not be earning $6,000 a year, plus his apartment, free meals and laundry, had not Mugsy's mother and father died. Number 92 descended into his legs while the water sang in the urinal with the Jesus-pensiveness of the brook Kidron. The hallowed Adonai had forsaken Number 92. Why must Wolkes make his daily inspection of the toilets when 92 was sitting on the hole and the Lord had fled?

The real Pythian augur of the orphanage was Moses Mush Tate; he would say as he passed a shoal of mites in the playroom, "Lo, I am the living water; for does not Pharaoh's daughter say, 'He is Moses, for I have drawn him out of the water.'" Mush Tate had a great round head like a nimbus. Being of an oracular bent of mind, he did not trust anybody, particularly himself; he carried his pennies, marbles, shoelaces and horsehair braids in secret pockets he had sewn together inside his jacket and trousers, so that neither he nor anybody else could find and filch them. Though a liar, a thief and a rhetor, Mush Tate was wise and good because he had never been known to call another boy a perjurer, robber or just clever. But his character was not without unusual defects. During the war he described himself as a conscientious objector, and the big fellows were so impressed by his vocabulary that they did not molest him.

One day it was noised about that Mush was to deliver a discourse. The door-monitors stopped all roller-skating in the basement, and the 8th-graders bawled out, "All quiet now, bastards and newcumbers." Those who had been skating, or sitting on the toilets and defecating to pass the time, gathered around Mush.

Mush Tate had enough genius to understand that language is as unreasonable as life. He paid scant heed to grammarians, who imagine that literature is the result of reason. The Moses Mush Tate Bible was a two-penny composition book which he had stolen; he also had two hundred lead pencils, ten pencil sharpeners, one hundred erasers, twelve bottles of Waterman's ink and fourteen copy books which he had taken from the schoolhouse supply room. He said that they were the essential paraphernalia of a doctor of literature. Moreover, Mush Tate's playroom box, number 13, was a mystification to Mugsy, Pummy, Sid Corman and Bah; for where did he get the horseshoes, the twenty agates, the Washington pies and stale crullers? No one violated good principles who purloined Becker's stale cakes; Becker was a miser and a war profiteer anyway; but what good was it to send Mush Tate to chapel on the Lord's Sabbath and force him to starve on Yom Kippur when he had no more ethics than to steal the cakes which other orphans had carried out of Becker's bakeshop?

Moses Mush Tate never had an equal. The only reason he had not been expelled years ago was that he studied the Psalms and Proverbs, which pierced old Doc and made his bad heart flutter when he listened to this orphanage Lazarus through whose words flowed the blood of Elohim. The mediocre had no better reply to Mush Tate's Mosaic argument, which he had received on Mount Horeb, than the tawdry, brutish rejoinder of the witless: "Knock this off my shoulder"; but Mush Tate was enough of a seer to ignore that. Besides, there are many ways to sink the Theban towers.

It was his custom to commence his hortatory dialectic with: "God humbles the proud, and the lowly He raises. Think you're much? Know you're living?" Which is unanswerable, as no one really does know. A waif in the Kosmos, who had walked through the Valley of Hinnom and had drunk contempt in Orcus, he went on: "Though I walk in the valley of the shadow of death I shall fear no evil, for Thou art with me."

How many times had Mush Tate climbed over the fence and, going by himself along Pushcart Boulevard, wearing the stigmata of Ishmael, the flat, dusty-gray uniform of the *weisenhaus,* heard a passer-by say: "There goes a poor orphan." What is sealed to the unsuffering—hunger and rejection—had ripened for him; for gall, derision and the world were his birthright. A warrior of ten thousand chagrins and a soldier of sorrow no less than David the harper in Jerusalem and Christ at Golgotha, he knew by heart the hymn of the fallen when he sang: "Say it not in Gath, publish it not in Ashkelon, lest the daughters of the Philistines rejoice."

By now the orphans surrounding Mush Tate were lost in the throes of words no Midian could comprehend, and the body of Mush Tate had passed over into the soul of Gideon as his words marched on: "I will open my mouth in a parable . . . Doc's overalls, Christine's stale drawers, Benny Marble's bungers, Watermelonhead's ringworms, Mooty's dandruff, Doc's marble hall and his stiff-necked Israelites . . . He maketh me to lie down in green pastures, He leadeth me beside the still waters . . . Down the hill, down the gully, around the bend . . . Green-pea hash, goulash, Sunday night's stewed prunes . . . Man is born unto trouble . . . Mount Zion, Mount Carmel, Shaker Heights . . . Who shall ascend the hill of the Lord, and who shall stand in His holy place? He that hath clean hands and a pure heart . . . The Lord is my shepherd, I shall not want Christine's green-pea hash or her Polack Hungarian stew . . . Come on, talk, think you're in school, think you're much, know you're living; fifty demerits, a hundred demerits, you're a sorehead; you're in company, you're expelled, confirmation day . . . Yea, though I walk through the valley of the shadow of death I shall fear no evil for Doc is with me . . . Talk, Bonehead, think you're an orphan? . . . God is our refuge and strength; I drink up the scorn of the world . . . My God, my God, why hast Thou forsaken me? . . .

God humbles the Micks and the lowly Orphs He raises . . .
My soul is weary of my life . . . Psalms, Proverbs, Exodus,
Leviticus, Numbers, the five books of Moses, the asses of
Kish, Saul's dead march . . . First picnic, second picnic,
going out walking, Euclid Beach, Euclid Avenue . . . *Pirke
Aboth*, the sayings of our fathers; Abraham's bosom, Isaac's
bedpan, Jacob's mumps, Isaac's measles, Moses' scarlet
fever; Rosh Hashanah, so's your Day of Atonement, so's
your New Year . . . How's your circumcision? An eye for
an eye, a tooth for a tooth . . . May Jehovah destroy all
mine enemies, lest the board of trustees rejoice; I am thy
rod and thy staff; my cup runneth over . . . Smite me on
the other cheek, smite me on the other ass . . . Kaddish;
*Yithgadal, yithkadash, sheme raba . . . Baruch atah Adonai
. . . Had gadya*, and you got me . . . What is man but dust?
. . . My bowels, my bowels . . . Aw bull, say something;
think you're a newcumber, a Pharisee? . . . So's your uncle
in Milwaukee, so's your illegitimate gentile cousin in
Akron."

When Mush Tate had finished, his face red with the
energy of the prophetic afflatus, he strode through the
door, and no monitor stopped him. He had gone out of
matter into ritual. After which he disappeared from the
home for a week. The orphans were sure he was dead and
that he was secretly sepulchred on Mount Nebo. Doc swore
that before he resigned because of his bad heart he would
expel Moses Mush Tate.

Mush Tate had caught an M-K-T freight, for he
wanted to be free—though nobody can, because each one at
the same time that he aches for liberty also pines as the
ancient Israelites did for the cucumbers, the leeks and the
melons of Egypt. He was picked up by the railroad yard
dicks outside Toledo and brought back to the orphan
home.

As he stood in that burial place, the sacred alcove on
whose walls were the memorial tablets in marble, he studied

the amounts of money each deceased trustee or his relation had given to maintain five hundred castaways and wrote the following in his Biblical composition book: "Fred Lazarus, donated $1,000." He hung his head because he knew Doc would expel him and he would not receive the confirmation blue serge pants, the Roman toga of virilia, and a Bible with his name engraved in gold letters on it: *Moses Tate*. No one would shine his shoes, and he would not have fifty cents to bequeath to Frank Lewis, with whom he had been in whack. He would never sob the confirmation liturgy: "Father, see Thy suppliant children." He would go back to nobody, and the world would be a stranger and a foe to him. Should he cry out as Jesus did. "Oh, I have overcome the world"? Every day away from the Home would be Golgotha because he would be absolutely kinless. Once he left the J.O.A. he would be an orphan.

Doc expelled Mush Tate, and everybody thronged about him; two 5th-graders showed him all the respect due a confirmation boy; they shined his shoes and gathered together all his real estate from box 13: the marbles, the agates, Becker's stale cakes, the plaited horsehair chain which Mugsy and Pummy closely scrutinized, the ball bearings he had taken out of Mooty's box, who had stolen them from Mushmelonhead, but who had the heart to be virtuous now and claim his own possessions.

They walked Mush Tate to the front gate, and he turned about just before passing out of their lives and said, "Mark my word, my address will be 1036 Mark Twain Place, Hamilton, Ohio," and he bequeathed his Mosaic ledger from Mt. Sinai to Bonehead Balaam, who was as illiterate as the twelve disciples. He knew that the word had corrupted the whole earth, and that the Pleiades and Lucifer, the Morning Star, tremble only in the breasts of the fallen.

Soon after Mush Tate was expelled, Doc resigned because of his bad heart and Simon Wolkes succeeded him as the rabbinic lawgiver of the Jewish Orphan Asylum. Salt and pepper shakers were expected any day. Diogenes was able to be a philosopher on the scantiest fare of apples, millet, barley, vetches, lentils and acorns, but filth deforms the soul—Christine's watery mush, green-pea hash and the dead stewed prunes produce Shorty Joshua, Pummy, Shrimp, Prunes, Mooty, Mugsy, Give-eye Newman, Sachemhead and Watermelonhead. They expected loaves, as white as the shewbread on the holy table in the temple, to be loaded on porcelain platters. The big boys would wear city knickers and go to the public school, and the older girls were to be clad in white middies and wear blue skirts; they would have ribbons for their hair—as dear to the orphan-asylum Eros as the wimples of the damsels of Zion.

Imagine an orphan, who was not really a human being, wearing a necktie, having a cotton handkerchief instead of a bandanna rag and being able to look at girls without shame. Gabbie, the leader of the harmonica club, gave a symphony in the basement and played three favorite J.O.A. classics: "Und der kuchen schmeckt so gut," "O wie schön es, O wie schön es," and "We'll fight for the name of Harvard."

Everyone in the washroom, latrines and dormitories kept the monitors up after the lights were turned out, gabbling about the innovations Wolkes was expected to introduce. Shortly after he became superintendent, Simon Wolkes summoned the 8th-graders to the schoolhouse. The boys were so rapturous that they kicked each other in the pants and spat on each other's shirts. They sat at the desks with folded hands and waited for Simon Wolkes, who strode up and down the classroom in his hundred-dollar Talmudic suit, to tell about the new orphan-home commons. In a long, solemn sermon, he admonished them not to be slaves of their stomachs; he delivered a Levitical caveat, warning them never to use public toilet seats lest they come by a venereal disease. Then he told them that they would be gray-haired and senile before confirmation day if they masturbated. After Wolkes' potent exhortation the 8th-graders were crestfallen; many now thought they were no better than fish who rub themselves against something rough, as Dio Chrysostom says, when they have the need to eject their sperm, and they were sure their legs were too hollow and decrepit to stumble back to the basement.

The hopes in the breasts of the orphans were cindered. The fare was still the same dirty Spartan mess. What else could Mugsy consider but food? Shrimp, thinking of Lizzie's boy, asked Mooty what an orphan could get out of puking all the time and walking by himself. Bah, utterly disgusted, went to the court on the top floor, climbed the basketball post and with a knife dug a memorial into the wooden board from which the net hung: "Bah Birnbaum, 307 days before Conf."

Though Number 92 called on the Lord for help, he could not stop retching. After he had vomited on the school desk, Simon Wolkes, showing an underlip upon which the scrolls of the Torah had soured, told him to control himself. And how he did want to control himself—so that he could walk by the side of Wolkes and touch his bony, Jehovah fingers which smelled of Cashmere Bouquet soap.

On various occasions the boy endeavored to gather together the face of his mother; he had not seen her for so long, and though he willed to perceive her he could not. At unexpected moments, she appeared to him, on a sudden, and when afterwards he did his utmost to grasp her image he was unable to identify her, and he wept, and his heart sat down by the River Dan. He knew her eyes, nose, chin and mouth, but each time he tried to put them together, instead of seeing a whole face, he saw nothing. Even when he caught her short, upright gait, which he could clearly imagine, he looked into the palm of his hand for that image of her, but it was empty. What parts us totally from others? Is it that they do not exist? Did he have a mother? Suppose he had placed the six-year-old child alongside the same boy who was now Number 92, would he even recognize him? How many people are sepulchred in us?

Number 92 praised the God of Abraham, Christine's tomato soup, Hans the bully, the Standard Oil tanks, Sunday evening prunes and graham crackers, and accursed *Ivanhoe* and *Silas Marner* because his hair had begun to curl. He brushed and folded his gray, lank pants and wiped the buttons of his shirt with saliva because of the *weisenhaus* Shulamites who now wore ribbons and plaited their tender hair. When young boys are filled with the virile seeds of the serpent Samael, they faint with desire as they hear the April elms and the opening of flowers. Holofernes was overcome by the sandals of Judith; 92 swooned when he saw a black, elastic garter around the leg of one of these skinny, chaste doves, and he rejoiced in the seminal song of Solomon: "A garden is my sister, my bride, a spring shut up, a fountain sealed." But who would notice a puking orphan?

There was at least one hosanna in the hearts of the orphans. Hans was confirmed and for a whole week everybody sang the Sabbath hymns as though they were the little glad hills. Hans had been the defender of the old martial traditions of the Home. He would kick a boy in the groin because he wore eyeglasses. When he saw a crookback warming his frozen pants on the steam pipes his high cheekbones became feverish. His underlip shot out at the sight of a lopsided cranium. His tongue, always lying in wait for the prey, crept out at the corner of his mouth when he beheld the squint-eyed or the sorehead bandaged in smelly Unguentine.

Hans carried a bunch of marbles, ball bearings or a rock in one hand, which he tightly shut as he beat an orphan. A bleeding 5th-grader who said, "I'll report you to Wolkes," had to lie in the dead scabby bushes by the diphtheria stream or run out into the city to escape Hans.

Were he weary of his bleating prey, he would go bare-
footed upon the cinders, cross over from one icy window-
sill on the fourth story to another or walk in the tin trough
hanging from the gabled eaves of the main building. The
spoil of the snail is the plant, the hyacinth and the summer
leaves of the melon, but man pants for the soul of his
brother.

Three months after Hans was confirmed, Simon
Wolkes told the orphans to howl for Heshbon and weep
for Tyre. Out of the coffined throat of Wolkes fell the
funeral words: "Our beloved son of Zion, Morris Hymson,
was crushed to death by a freight elevator while perform-
ing his duties at the Richman Brothers' warehouse."

Each orphan had to sit in his place on the wooden
benches until Kaddish was said in the prayer hall. A
former inmate donated an oil painting of Sir Galahad to
the orphanage; it was pensively framed in gold leaf, and
Mr. Martin, head of the manual training class, made an
engraving for it on a metal plate: "Morris Hymson, Confirmation 1916." It was hung in the venerable oak room of
the board of trustees.

Hans was buried in the orphanage cemetery near
Cherry Farm. Not even Moses Mush Tate became a greater
myth than Hans. The inmates spoke with awe of Hans's
Homeric fists, his war with the Irish Micks and his battles
with the J.O.A. Skamander. Man is as homesick for the
grandeur of Caligula as he is for the prophet Jeremiah. Hans
was no less ineradicable in the soul of the orphans than the
gully, the measles-and-mumps infirmary and the M-K-T
freight cars alongside the Standard Oil tanks. All that is sepulchred in the bosom of man is sacred, and nobody will give
up a single remembrance of a chagrin, wound, shame or
infamy.

Our past is our only knowledge, and, good or ferocious,
it is, for sublime or baleful purposes, the sole viaticum of
the spirit. We can digest our childhood but never our

present deeds, because no one knows what he is doing while he is doing it. The present is an absolute sphinx to men. Had Peter really known that he was walking on water, he could not have done it, for every act, small or great, is a veiled trance.

Now every day Lizzie's boy walked in the wind when the rain scribbled round drops on Bonehead Balaam's chicken coop. Soon he too would receive his blue serge long pants and five dollars—he would be a former inmate. He could return and look into the face of Simon Wolkes without having to drink up the derision and the waters of Marah from his Levitical mouth.

Suppose Simon Wolkes should die and he would never be able to prove that he had walked to Capernaum, and that he had been at Golgotha. Could it be that after he had come to manhood he would still be no more than puking Ishmael, Number 92? He wept and he shook the mountains and the hills and the rivers because he would never be able to say that his miserable orphan dust was anything more than Number 92.

The day of leaving the Home had come. He stood on the stage in the prayer hall and sang the dirge of separation together with the other orphans who were in the confirmation class of 1917.

A boy had died and a man had sprouted. Whatever the child had been, the man must overcome. Would he long for his homeless boyhood? Are there children whose years are watered by the four rivers of Eden? Give us love and justice and the heart to sorrow for others. O heaven, earth and seas! He who is not pursued by the Erinyes has no love or justice or sorrow for the house of flesh. It is an infernal tragedy to be too fortunate. Pitiless is he who has not been harried by the furies.

He left the Jewish Orphan Asylum, but he was never to obliterate its hymn, because all experience is holy unto the heart which feels:

Father, see Thy suppliant children
Trembling stand before Thy throne
To confirm the vows of Horeb
And to serve the Lord alone.

IV

For all our actions derive from concupiscence and unregenerate nature.

A sneeze absorbs all the functions of the soul as much as the sexual act.

Pascal

After Ishmael, Number 92, was confirmed and had left the orphanage, he returned to Kansas City, his mother and Henry Smith, and went by the name of Edward Dahlberg. I had been nameless since birth and had only that knowledge of myself which I had derived from the streets, towns, stables and rivers I had known. I have avoided the use of "I" because I was obscure to myself, and no Pythian oracle either then or now has helped me. Until my seventeenth year, when I left the orphan home, I was suffering locality rather than a person.

I had been gone for six years, and everything had changed. The barbershop at 16 East 8th was now a skinny cranny, and the two electric fans, which I had thought as a boy represented so much money and rank in society, were a pair of noisy, scurvy grasshoppers. How beautiful I had once thought the brass cuspidors were—unimpaired vases of an early Mycenaean age. But now when I saw a railroad switchman spit tobacco juice into one of them, as he was getting a haircut, I winced. Christ cured the blind with a little spittle and clay, but this is the love of others.

I could no longer bear to watch my mother fawn upon an old codger in smelly, bepissed overalls, and I cringed when she announced: "Star Lady Barbershop, you're next, sir." What would I have given not to eructate, piss, gender, grunt and hiccough: yet, according to Aristophanes, Zeus urinated. We love to lose our strength on women—and die for doing it. The philosopher studies the Logos in order to forget that by the time man has attained his three score and ten years, he has passed a hogshead of wind; or, as Rabelais writes: "I moisten my gullet, I drink, and all for the fear of dying." Ursula, the pig woman, says: "I do water the ground in knots as I go like a great garden pot."

The stigmata of my mother's trade had by now become intolerable to me, and my heart, otherwise a stone at this time, was a vial of tears because my mother earned her livelihood as a lady barber. When anybody asked me what my mother did, I said she was a hairdresser or operated a beauty parlor; why such a trade was better I never knew.

There is no fault so difficult to eradicate as affectation. "*Toda afectación es mala*," says Cervantes. Assassins are pretentious, thieves are boastful and professors imagine they have knowledge. It is not because we do not know who commenced the Kosmos, or cannot examine the Milky Way or Arcturus in a limbeck, that we are ignorant; it is that we were born to be stupid and are such bookish jackanapes as to forget it as often as we can. Why the Platonic *Dialogues* and the long arguments in the agora? Why philosophy? Why mathematics and letters? I know the questions, but not the answers. Why, too, should the barber trade be more despised than that of a politician or a banker? The one is a windbag and a clumsy liar, and the other a pawnbroker, now the patrician of the American polity.

I had acquired some refinements and believed that I was more intelligent than my mother. She had sense, which I lacked, sexual understanding and a charitable pity for others, which is education. I could not claim a knowledge of good human entertainment; I was an incredible gawk with women, and I thought that because a fly on the wall upset my stomach, and because I was mawkish about sunsets, I was sensitive. Spite his taste, who is better than a porter, drayman, gamp or lout? There is no doctrine worth a straw so long as man has a pair of ballocks and a fundament. "As for reason," writes Rabelais, "we use none of it here." A man could be truthful save that everything touches his skin.

The truth is that I was not sensitive about anybody else except myself. Did I think that perversity was sensibility, or that even the latter meant that I had the scantiest compassion for those who suffer? The Lord hardened Pharaoh's neck, but I was not a Pharaoh in ancient Egypt, only the son of a lady barber who had provided me with the shaving mug which I had to translate into the helmet of Mambrino. My mother had given me that gallant desperation without which we cannot change objects around us into ideal thoughts. Whatever energy I had, and was later to employ with some comprehension, I had derived from her. Had I not received some moiety of her strength, I should have long since perished, or made the hapless mistake of the average who are sure that they are alive solely because they eat, excrete and sleep. We are as dead as Lazarus, and we wear our mediocre conceptions as Lazarus did his cerements.

Often I had heard my mother repeat that no matter how she labored with her ten fingers to advance her fortunes, she could make almost nothing beyond our bread and lodging. How weary I was of hearing this. And yet how can one have a just commonwealth so long as trimmers own rivers, thousands of acres of wheat, fruits and livestock, which they cannot possibly consume?

My mother told the truth, and, though she reiterated it countless times, it was still the truth which I was yet to understand. Moreover, people always do the same thing, and the only relief they have from this monotony is that they imagine each act to be different. It is doubtful that the uneducated repeat their pelting stories and the few maxims they have derived from experience more than do the learned. A peasant is likely to have a much better memory than a pedant; the reading of many a book is as fatiguing as the writing of them, and neither can be said to make us less tiresome to others.

The only Holy Grail for mankind is the imagination. A stupid man can comprehend this but an average person cannot. Even the ruses my mother prepared for herself—with what self-knowledge I did not know—plainly showed that she was not mediocre. She was too easily deceived to be common. Whenever she heard the fruit and vegetable chant of a huckster in the street, she invariably asked him, "How much are you charging today—is it cheap?"

He always replied, "Lady, what do you take me for? Of course, everything I peddle is a bargain."

After she had gone to his wagon and handled a few bad peaches and several mealy apples, she would ask him, "Are you sure, mister, these are very good?"

To which he replied, "Would I sell you anything that was not the best?"

She never failed to buy them. This was a parcel of the sport that makes our days underneath the sun dear to us.

In the years I had been away Kansas City had grayed in my soul. A hot, wanton town, that pallbearer's Sabbath had ruined a large portion of a coarse and good-humored populace. The city was now filled with Christian Scientists, spiritualists and impecunious bachelors who went to the tabernacles and religious gatherings to meet spinsters who thought maidenhead and godhead were indivisible.

The city was no longer my parent; I could not saunter along Locust, Maple and Cherry Streets. Kansas City had become a great, soulless town, and the laughter had expired underneath the 8th Street viaduct.

Each man's past is his Nemesis, and as Lucian has it, our remembrances are "the burning lake of Phlegethon, Cerberus and ghosts." Where was hapless Gizella, that fat, dropsical Proserpine? She had become a streetwalker in Chicago; Noah Taylor was selling newspapers in Portland, Oregon. Catholic Mary had quit to become the mistress of the saloonkeeper next door, who was reported to have set her up in diamonds and cut glass. The cashier of the M-K-T had embezzled ten thousand dollars and skipped town with Blanche Beasely, whose marvelous buttocks were said to have been worth it. Tisha's mother now owned a house with a pecuniary lawn in a very refined and quiet street near the end of the Troost Avenue trolley line. The humble Italian fruit dealer at the corner of 8th and Walnut was no longer there. His two sons, gentle boys who had never molested me, had robbed a mail train, but no one thought the less of them except those who were expecting registered letters or money.

What a beauty I had imagined Venus Hickman, who was always decked out in vestal white silks, satins and laces. When I returned I met Venus again. She did not have a small, turned-up Christian nose as I had believed. She was dark, bony, and had a long Hebraic nose, quite classical, but very disappointing to me. She had become an ardent devotee of Mary Baker Eddy and played the violin in a high-class motion picture theater on bawdy 12th Street.

The alley in back of the Star Lady Barbershop had

dwindled, the viaduct was of dwarfed dimensions. The barbershop was a little hole; everything had diminished as I grew up, except Venus' nose.

I had no idea what I wanted to do or to be. The plain truth is that I had no conceptions worth the remembrance. Nothing seemed to me so enchanting as those monied gardens in Swope Park and on Linden Boulevard. Although I now had a passion for books, I had read only the dross of the orphanage library. Besides, of what profit to the spirit would the imperishable books have been to me? They increase the sensibility, provide us with a more exquisite understanding of a landscape, the sea or a room, but do not make us more tender. Can the knowledge of all the Canticles of Solomon make us more moral? We are the sons of Adam, and when we long for a chine of beef, will Anaxagoras do? Seneca would make wise reading did not man scratch himself. Aristippus the Cynic said that the body is the *summum bonum* of man.

Let me now say that I have not the least respect for my moral nature. I do what I am, and though I would do otherwise, I cannot. I do not say this easily, but with infernal pain in my heart. Perhaps, after many years in libraries, I can prattle better than I did. Has not Addison or Steele asserted that no one was any better for beholding a Venus done by Praxiteles? Some are the worse for having read Swift, Defoe or Chaucer. Several thousand volumes are the making of a marvelous mask, for aesthetics is a style of living, enunciation—and affectation.

My one aim at this time was to become a Sardanapalus without being a drudge. When people talk about the wealth, lands, herds, lakes and granaries they own, they are usually stating how many concubines, ladies and wives they can buy. How could I possess Aphrodite? For by then what vexed me most were my privities. In spite of the prolix sermons on the shameful parts delivered by Rabbi Simon Wolkes, little else occupied me.

97

Every piece of female apparel maddened me: a crisping pin, wimple, the tire around a woman's flocky hair, her gussets and the orient sound of her stays gave me furious transports. To the ancient Romans, a woman's comb was a symbol of the muliebria.

At the age of eighteen I was shaken by every chit. I was so tormented by seminal nights that I was beside myself. Dioscorides alleges that a person mocked by lascivious dreams could be healed by taking nymphaea. At the orphanage we were told that Onan, who dropped his seed everywhere, died because he no longer had the strength to stand on his feet. After weeks of such involuntary seminal paroxysms, I spoke to my mother about it, and she took me to see Dr. Joy, a new physician who had been recommended to her by the saloonkeeper. For weeks, following his dietary injunctions, I ate no animal flesh.

Had I criminal inclinations, I would have ravished any Helen or even Webster's "old morphewed lady." Whoring is as natural as rain, snow and defecating. The practices of Venus Illegitima, the goddess of various turpitudes, is the way of all flesh, and those who pluck down the bawdy house and banish the prostitute have made it a peril for a woman to walk in the streets in the evening. Let him who can keep his pudendum on a leash for seventy rueful years cast the first stone; I swear by Abraham's codpiece which lies with Sarah in Hebron that either he has no genitals or is a barefaced liar. Meanwhile, blessed be Saint Scrotum, hallow the name of Father Prepuce and Friar Priapus, for they have been martyred by the beadle and honest folk. Absolute continence gives us chilblains, the quartan ague and the vapors. Chastity is 79 degrees north latitude, and many an imprudent explorer has lost all his parts in that frozen terrain.

Could I have been ascetic, I should have relinquished voluptuous entertainments or the thought of them. Origen castrated himself to be pure, but to the horror of the

Church Fathers of his age. Who cannot be sorrowful over the sexual pangs of Antisthenes, who exclaimed: "I would rather go mad than feel pleasure"?

Never having been innocent, I had not deteriorated. "He who seeks Me will find Me in children of seven years old" is the Gospel according to St. Thomas. But we are fallen children, and who has such naive libidinous conceptions as a child? For him copulation, though he has no knowledge of the use of bodies, is an angelic sensation. He thinks pleasure is a perfect Platonic circle. The Epicurean hopes that all his ecstasies will be as wondrous as he imagined they were when he was seven years of age.

— At this time I had two infernal perplexities: my erotic appetite and what sort of work I could do to earn money to gratify it. I had been thoroughly uneducated at school for twelve years and was completely useless. I had no skill at anything, either to dig potatoes, caulk a boat, shuck corn, look for haws—or talk. When I met a female of my own years, I could not open my mouth; separation from girls at the orphanage had turned me into a hapless dunderhead. Santa Teresa said that it was a cross for her to converse with anybody. I was as drumbling with a slut as with a virgin.

When I was eight, fat and overgrown Gizella did her best to allure me. I could not imagine that there could be so much delirious, Titian flesh in one person. She described to me all the edenic raptures of cohabitation, but I was afraid to handle her. She was too young to scorn me, but years later she showed me her whole derision. Even if you reject a woman who does not want you, she will never cease detesting you for it. I had another fatuous amorous experience with the eight-year-old daughter of a lady barber who worked for my mother. She offered herself to me, but I was just as helpless with her. Rozanov declared that when he was impotent five virgins threw themselves at his feet. No wonder he wrote a book called *Solitario*.

Having nothing to do, I walked up and down Independence Avenue and peered into doorways, hovels, cheap dry-goods stores, bakeries and shanties; I imagined that poverty and prostitution were intimate companions. I loitered about the expensive Baltimore Hotel; women who travel, if they have not mildewed maidenheads, are often available. Ransacking every thoroughfare, alley and mangy street, I could not find a woman who would lie with me. I became a street-walker. By now I thought it were better to be androgynous. It has often been comforting to hear Ovid tell that the fish *channe* conceives without a mate.

Let nobody think I am peddling my impudicities for the few pennies a truthful author gets in this world. Stendhal understood the affliction we name passion, and without a tittle of hypocrisy, he wrote: "I shall be taken for a madman among the people of the North."

No matter. There were harlots in Gaza and Gath, and in underground Independence Avenue, but none for me. I wore the clothes of suffering from which everyone flees. I have always had the wounded face of Lazarus. A woman has the most clever scent: she can smell another female on a man, which multiplies her desires; but if the same man approaches her long after the odors of the aloes, the myrrh and frankincense in Solomon's bedchamber have vanished she will reject him at once.

How fortunate was Jean Jacques Rousseau, who received his bedroom education from Madame de Warrens when he was fifteen years old. And how frequently have I been envious when I thought of that lascivious cleric who tightened the laces of her corset.

Max Stedna, who had made his fortune selling mules to the government during the war, still came into the shop because it was a parcel of his memories. Morris, his son, who ran around with chorus girls that he met at the stage door of the Orpheum, asked me what I did for recreation. What a plain and homely question it was, and I was not simple enough to give him a straight reply. He would have introduced me to a fast woman in the lobby of the Baltimore Hotel had I not been so embarrassed.

Americans are the most embarrassed people in the world, and are too ashamed and surreptitious to acknowledge that man is miserable when he is deprived of a woman. How English we are in our brutish sexual hypocrisy. With what pain and discomfiture did William Hazlitt, in *Liber Amoris*, write of his infatuation for the daughter of a conniving landlady, and how quick were the scribbling Philistines of his time to pound him with a pestle in the public mortar of the commonweal. His only sin was that he said in a fine English prose style what the dissembling, lickerish Puritan feigned was bad manners. O God, sink all social manners!

Before leaving Cleveland, after my release from the orphanage, I had found temporary employment as a messenger boy for Western Union, and had rented a cot from another "boy" who delivered telegrams and was sixty-six years old. Two girls, cousins, who had fled from a small Ohio town, lodged there also. One of these girls had the most well-fed legs and tempting bosom; she had gotten her posteriors from Aphrodite Kallypygos—meaning a marvelous rump. She sat on my cot one evening, paying me what I thought were pinchbeck compliments, and tousled my curly hair. Although I was quaking I did nothing. Imagining that I was an hermaphrodite or had no masculine seed, she gave over, but said that if I wanted her I should knock on her door. A thin partition separated the two buxom cousins from me; several hours afterwards I rapped lightly on the door, and then shook the knob, but there was no reply. A few days later when she was making her bed I looked at her with the wildest yearnings, but she then despised me no less than Potiphar's wife had abhorred Joseph.

I have always dreaded dissolving that chasm between

the woman sitting at my side and me. Though hyssop and gall have been my portion, I fear more than most chagrins the rebuff from a female. After I have been rejected I am undone, and I walk in the snows and upon the steppes, the bitter waters of Marah on my lips, and as I pull up the collar of my overcoat, I despise God, the grass, and am a nihilist.

I got a job at the stockyards in Kansas City, herding bulls and heifers from one pen to another; it was necessary to get up at 4:15 to be at work by 6. My poor mother awakened me, made my breakfast and prepared meat sandwiches for my lunch, since the quitting hour was not until 6 in the evening. After that I drove a laundry wagon, but I spent more time stroking the red-brown flanks of Fred, the horse, than I did collecting dirty towels, drawers, sheets and shirts. It was an unusual elation for me to harness and hitch Fred to the wagon, and we often trotted out to Cliff Drive or took a small excursion to the Paseo. Unfortunately we were parted after a month, as I was discharged. Whenever I think of that gentle animal, who never harmed anybody and who had a moral nature superior to Seneca's, I grieve for his carcass.

What should I do? I wanted to be a thinker—but I had no thoughts. Suppose I went to the University of Missouri as I considered doing, what would I learn? As Epictetus remarks, I might find out how to resolve the syllogisms of Aristippus, but what good would that do me? Would the knowledge of a theorem teach me how to walk, speak, caress a woman or understand a river? One can learn from Lewis and Clark that the Missouri nourishes cottonwood, alder, cypress, lynn, coffee nut and the oak, and yet be sluggish. What makes us tremble, and what dilates our affections? I was to discover this much later, but as I was always going into the grave or coming out of it, this was dying knowledge continually to be re-examined and to be relived.

I thought that I knew more than my mother. She

earned her livelihood and mine, and she had accepted the cruel limits of everyday drudgery. I was rebellious but did not know what I was opposing.

Still doing nothing that was either good or bad, which is ignominious, I became a street-walker again. Always accosting a woman in a whisper, muttering, "Isn't it a pleasant evening," or "What a dry summer it has been," I was either ignored or taken for a noddy. Dressed in a loud green suit that appeared very stylish to me, I must have looked like a Lithuanian factory worker. Sometimes I was so nervous when I approached a woman that she took me for a plain-clothes man and fled. On other occasions, when I mumbled, I aroused hauteur and coldness, even in a harlot.

One night after going through the archives of all the whoring streets I believed I knew, I found that I had not, as a result of my scholarly diligence, been rewarded with one pedantic footnote on lechery. Worn out, I sat on a wooden railing in front of a gas station. A woman with swelling hips passed by, and I vaguely guessed that she had made some reply to my wan and defeated smile. I rose and stumbled over to her side. Had she taken pity on my desperation?

What she expected to derive from such a bottlehead as I, I could not conjecture. She put up with me, and did not seem to mind my stupid declamation about the weather. Since I did not indulge in the American titter, she might have thought I was serious and reflective. I have never learnt to treat any woman as though she were a tart. How often have I lost unusual raptures because I was polite and taken for a weakling; I can be so excessively civil that I am able to persuade a light woman that she is really a prude.

When we were in this woman's room she asked me to go to a nearby saloon and fetch a pail of beer. I was certain then that she was a whore, and was afraid that she would give me a venereal disease. I almost ran away.

Prostitutes are as essential to a society as potatoes,

bread and meat, though they may not be rhapsodical food. There are various kinds of love; the most common and dreary is that which men get from strumpets. The patron saint of the house of ill fame is Venus Vulgivaga. Cato, a Stoic, said that when young men had swollen veins, it was far better for them to go to the public stews than to grind their neighbors' wives. For coition to be entirely satisfactory, there is that love which is under the amorous tutelage of Venus Urania.

My experience with this woman was very brief, and of no value to her. It is told that twilight in Quito lasts no longer than three minutes—which was longer than my intimacy with her.

I hurried into my trousers and shirt as if I were getting into my morals. What else are clothes but social cant? As I was making ready to flee from this woman, I considered it only respectable on my part to offer her money. Giving her two dollars—which was all that I had—I thanked her. She tore a piece from a paper sack and wrote her name and address on it, and I made a great show of placing it carefully in my wallet. How relieved I was to be in the air, fine, tonical scruples blowing through my hair. Sure that I was now rid of such infamous appetites, I tore up the paper on which she had written the address of the wooden house she occupied. How good and right our conduct is when our testicles are empty.

A week later I covered every block and house in that part of Kansas City, looking for her, and wept because I had been so foolhardy. The body is a burden of Tyre, and it is also the only wisdom we have. He who refuses to fondle the breasts of Theodota will live long enough not to have the occasion again.

Plato is a seer when he declares that "pleasure is one of the veriest impostors in the world," but few can read the *Philebus* with composure unless they have a woman with whom to be an ascetic! Aside from Eve, there is no Anticyrean hellebore to purge lechery. All we have to conceal our depravity is a little rose water, good manners and a pair of breeches. Contemplating a pentagram would be an excellent receipt for such fevers, did not the sight of plump hunkers overthrow the whole of Euclid.

Panurge says, "Madam, know that I am so amorous of you that I can neither piss nor dung for love."

The Kosmos is the seminal cornucopia, and the Kabbalists speak of the massive genitals of Jahweh; St. Paul says that the whole earth groans and is in constant travail. The life of the universe depends upon the pudendum. As soon as the Word was made flesh, man was unable to be quiet, or work, or think, until he had dropped his seed.

V   *Pleasure of life! what is 't? Only*
       the good hours of an ague.
                                    Webster

My mother and Captain Henry Smith were still together
when I came back to Kansas City. He was almost as
much my habit as he was my mother's. Since I no longer
leaned against his sweaty, fleshy shoulders, he did not dislike
me or find me the nuisance I had been as a boy who needed a
father. He had grown stingier and now lay around the 8th
Street flat all day; he had had no employment on the river
for several years. There had been talk of converting his
freighter, the *Chester*, into a pleasure boat, but Captain
Henry Smith thought such a change would be parasitical.
A rounder himself, he had absorbed all the hypocrisy regarding human delights that were not associated with utility
and money.

Now he only stirred to go to the shop to carry back
Lizzie's basket of food and canned fruits. He had room and
board free and no matter how late Lizzie came home she
would wash his socks and underwear, or if it were a hot
July night, she would prepare a pitcher of lemonade for

him. He never said thanks because he was embarrassed; how distant is the heart from the tongue when one is obliged to be grateful.

When Lizzie became provoked and said to him, "You old grouch, am I your dog that you can't even wag your mouth when I scrub and clean for you?" he would fatly amble off to the parlor. He would occasionally lock himself in his room, or just break wind, which sometimes made her laugh. They had long since dropped all those niceties and romantic manners which make us forget that the only difference between us and animals is that we use words. There was seldom any reference to matrimony, though Lizzie wanted to give up that rotten barber trade and have a home. Why should she be more unfortunate than Tisha's mother or Gladys, a chippy from Tulsa, who had married a cowboy star of the films?

Captain Smith had considerable ability as a mechanic and he talked of opening a garage, but did nothing about it. He had invented a trolley signal which a passenger could press with his foot when he desired to let the motorman know that he wanted to get off.

Henry Smith's streetcar bell might have brought him a fortune had he troubled to patent it. But he was torpid and hardly had the courage to get up from his chair and shuffle from one room to another.

He had, however, property in Louisville and houses in St. Louis, and Lizzie thought he was well-fixed. At about this time he built a clapboard bungalow in a grassy village called Northmoor, which the interurban car passed as it went along its route from Kansas City to St. Joseph and Joplin. When he had finished it, he registered the deed on the house in his own name. Lizzie said nothing but was very stung, and from that time on she had no use for him. She did not hesitate to tell him that he was a cheap skate—that during his entire courtship he had treated her to a few ice-cream sodas at

Jenkins' cigar store and had only given her a gilded clock one Christmas.

Lizzie hoarded everything. She even saved orange peelings for her marmalades, though often they lay on the window sills until winter or the following spring. She was clad in the wildest rags: stale tattered aprons, torn stockings that she could not keep up, a yellow, rindy corset and shoes that were smeared with food and jellies. Had her face not divulged her desperation, her slovenliness would have done so. Yet she always had a good breath and a pink tongue. She took cold baths the year round, and when she rubbed her body and paps with a towel, she felt she had exceptional good health. She used to say that as long as her heart and lungs were sound she did not have to worry. When she looked into the mirror and saw how her mouth and throat were beginning to fail, she would step back a few paces to examine her strong torso and bosom that were far younger than her eyes, hair or neck.

Both Captain Henry Smith and Lizzie were small of stature and short-gaited. She always held her head high to increase her size—and to add to her lorn hopes; formerly Henry's slow steps were cocksure, but now he moved along as though he thought he would die or felt that he could no longer bait a woman.

They would amble along together, he carrying the basket of food in one hand and holding her arm with the other—because it was good form. He was very listless—which is real atheism, for what we do not see with exuberance does not exist. However, whenever a woman passed by, he ransacked her body with all the fever of a libertine who can still admire rather than perform. If Lizzie complained, he joshed her: "What do you think I have eyes for?"

When man has finished his destiny he waxes obese and feeds to excess because his genitals are sleepy. He resembles the pocky, devaginated shrew rather than the heroic warrior who mounted the bed of Circe with a sword. After the long water-sorrows, gullygut Odysseus ate more of the swine, goats and sheep in the stalls of Ithaca than all the suitors of Penelope consumed during his absence.

Henry Smith developed a bad cough and told Lizzie it would be better for him to take the bed in another room so that she would not catch it. Then after he had recovered he kept to the separate bed, though continuing to hawk and rasp his throat and, when he thought of it, going to the kitchen sink to gargle. Had he not done any of these things he could have been clever. Men are fatuous liars because they are imperfect beasts, but women are seldom deceived as they are the most artful brutes in the world. When a man is preparing to leave his wife or mistress he seldom succeeds in hiding his intentions. On the battlefield he may be a marvelous strategist, but with a woman he is a nincompoop, and all the secrets he thinks are hidden in that driest of crypts, the arid and deceitful heart, are known to her long before he has any knowledge of his own designs.

Finally, Captain Smith packed his suitcase, rubbed Lizzie's arm and, with a puerile titter, said he had to go to St. Louis to secure a mortage on one of his houses. Lizzie said nothing but went to the window sill to water the geraniums and to pile together the dried orange peels she was saving for marmalade.

How practical women are in such passionate moments. At such a time a man considers what skill he has had in dissembling and is even troubled because he is injuring his paramour; he is very sorry that he is doing it, though he would do nothing else. But a woman scours the kettle, washes the tablecloth or rinses her stockings. She even sews a button on the shirt of the man who is about to desert her.

There is no herb in Paradise that can gratify our hunger any more than henbane or nightshade. Male or female, we give our paps to the wolves because we are starved, just as the Mexican women nursed the deer and the dog. Does not Lucian, like our modern, wretched hearts, say: "Are not poisoned fountains necessary, and stinking fires, and filthy dreams, and maggots in the bread of life?"

Shortly after Captain Henry Smith had left, Lizzie received a letter from his sister who lived in St. Louis telling her that he had taken lodgings with a common hussy whom he intended to marry. Lizzie went to a round-shouldered, impecunious lawyer who sat in his office in summer underwear and spent most of his time reading Ingersoll and Henry George; this man positively detested fourflushers who deceived widows, impregnated farm girls or jilted females. Lizzie told him her whole life story: how Harry Cohen beat her out of five hundred dollars, how the saloonkeeper had sold her worthless oil stocks in a wildcat company and how she had supported the captain for seven years when the steamboat business on the river had failed. She could not omit telling him, as she told everybody, that she was a hardworking widow with a son to earn bread for, and that nobody could say anything against her noble heart.

The lawyer put a lien on the clapboard house at Northmoor and notified Captain Henry Smith by letter that he had been instructed by Lizzie Dalberg to bring an action in court against him for payment of seven years' lodging, board and laundry. Jacob had not hired himself out to wily Laban for seven years to secure a Leah, nor had Lizzie cooked and washed and provided Henry with room and spending money for the same length of time to be robbed of respectable matrimony. What she wished above all was a place in society.

Lizzie wanted so much to improve her lot and to sell the shop. Her trade had made her an untouchable; a lady barber was a Mary Magdalene, though her sins were not venal. The worthies of the synagogue despised her, and the Brahmin hardware dealer and the owners of small dry-goods stores looked down on her. So greatly had her occupation affected me that when I later became infatuated with a salesgirl it took me several months to tell this daughter of a junk dealer that I was the son of a lady barber.

Several weeks later Captain Henry Smith reappeared in Kansas City on a Sunday afternoon. He asked Lizzie to play an old-fashioned tune on the upright mahogany piano, but she did not move from the settee. She wiped her pince-nez glasses and smoothed her soiled, wrinkled apron. She remained taciturn while he took the mandolin out of the case, jigged on the dust-swollen tatters of rugs in the parlor and sang in his best vaudeville manner:

> Oh gee, be sweet to me, kid,
> I'm awfully fond of you.
> I'm blue when you're cross to me.
> Come treat me square, kid,
> I love you for fair.

In earlier days she would have smiled at this jolly, foolish ditty, but now she watched him dancing in his fat-slobbered pants and stooped to make a bow of her shoelaces which were always untied. She was about to pull up the stays of her corset but checked herself, thinking that improper.

There is no rage like the madness of the heart, and it is most dangerous in a woman. When she prattles and gossips she is transparent, and boring if she is unloved, but when she is silent there is no animal in its lair so menacing.

Lizzie was in no mood for the captain's ridiculous and shrewd nonsense. Had he ever had a single fine or noble trait? We provide people with honest, jolly or good faces, but when the eye is distempered or sick with disenchantment, the countenance once contemplated with so much ecstasy is empty, vain and motionless flesh. The blood Jesus sheds comes from our own tender hearts.

Henry Smith laid the mandolin aside and said, "Come on, Lizzie girl, I'll blow you to dinner at the Electric Oyster

House. And tomorrow evening we'll go to the Willis Woods Theater; you need a little recreation—you've got the blues."

He stepped toward her, pulling her up from the settee, but when he attempted to kiss her he could not find her mouth, which had disappeared. Her body was cold and rigid, and her short, stubby fingers were clenched.

She pushed him aside: "I'm tired, Henry, and it's no use. I've been your sucker, washerwoman and cook long enough. You want that St. Louis chippy, and I want the house in Northmoor. I think I'm entitled to something."

His face fell; who had told her? Several days later he came to the conclusion that it was his sister Clara who had betrayed him. Two women always unite their strength against the common foe, a man. Then, as my mother later told me, he broke down and cried like a baby, begging her to take him back. He still did not mention marriage, which was the only trump card he had to renovate a romance that had never been celebrated by epithalamiums, or even by a nosegay of roses.

After Henry Smith had gone, my mother thought again that she was old and she counted every line in her face. Would she ever bloom again? The electric light bulbs wore out her eyes, and raising her arms to cut hair made her so heavy with weariness that she said every bone in her body was aching by the time she locked up the shop at night. Had the sport of the sun gone out of her? Nature was against her. Why dust should wrinkle more in one than in a thousand churls is an enigma for apes.

She was listless when an old-timer said: "Come on, Lizzie, let's shake for a cigar." What gaiety there once had been in throwing the Indian dice on the front showcase. No more than forty-five—what had dried up in her? We are disappointed ten thousand times and believe that we do not hear the turtle rains or the maples leafing. Would she so soon give a surd ear to that love song of Solomon which stirred in her when she listened to the street huckster cry, "Watermelon, cantaloupe," or a Mexican vendor bawling, "Hot tamales, hot tamales!"

There is no physic for the crabbed bones; the dotard cannot be purged with rhubarb or civet. Go mad rather than grow old; wear the livery of the fool, 'tis a saner custom than to be clothed in the wry, flensed skin of sapless age. When the fig is cindered, not virtue or goodness or charity will truss up the chaps and the hams.

Sometimes, while walking, Lizzie imagined she was touching the elbow of Captain Smith, but when she realized he was not there, she took the streetcar back to her flat. Business was dull, and the three hens working at the chairs were no show for the barbershop. Many of the wooden ramshackles near 16 East 8th Street had been torn down and the two-story commission houses had long been boarded up. The shanties on Oak, Cherry and Locust, those tree-streets that vined the blood of the midwestern American, were gone. How dear and sacred is the *memento mori* of our poverty.

I was born to sorrow, but as a boy I did not know that my desolation was to be not much different from my mother's. Between the Kosmos and my mother was an immense void. Ben Jonson says, ". . . we must live, and honour the gods sometimes; now Bacchus, now Camus, now Priapus. . ." What God had my mother save frozen solitude?

I was making ready to go into the wilderness of Beersheba, but what angel would there be to furnish me with a cruse of water? That angel was to be my mother, who had herself longed for the fountains in the wastes that never would water her spirit.

VI *The Merrimack, or Sturgeon River,
is formed by the confluence of the
Pemigewasset, which rises near the
notch of the White Mountains, and
the Winnipiseogee, which drains the
lake of the same name, signifying
"The Smile of the Great Spirit."*

Thoreau

Kansas City had been my Jehovah, but now, at the age of
eighteen, I felt I must leave. I no longer had a hearing
soul for the maple and oak trees, or the Paseo, which had become a seedy, colored section. Going down to the West
Bottoms, I listened to the locomotives on the tracks and to
the coupling of freight cars, and the four rivers of Eden
passed through my soul. The manure on the boots of
cattlemen from Montana had been dropped by the heifers of
Uz! People who have withered spirits do not of a sudden
become succulent stalks by going elsewhere. Pascal has said
that ". . . man's unhappiness arises from one thing only,
namely that he cannot abide quietly in one room."

However, always going somewhere else is a lust also; it
is a song of the maggot, which tickles us and deprives all

skin of patience—which I was never to have. Bunyan counsels us, " 'Tis not best to covet things that are now; but to wait for things to come." I had not one drop of quiet in my whole body and could not even wait for death to annihilate me. By traveling I believed that I would be the free wind that blows in all lands. Was there nothing to ease me except pestilence, the desert and the wilderness! Every time we think, we die—and a forest springs up in the obscure heart.

Most of my errors have come from that rudest of shibboleths: I want to be free. Yet we only do what we are. Prometheus suffered every day for the same reason; he wished to have the liberty of Zeus, who himself could not alter fate. Although Prometheus invented philosophy, he was the prey of the vulture that devoured his liver each night. Was I to eat myself? It would have been a meal for paupers.

So I purchased a ticket to Omaha and told my mother that I was going on the road as a drummer for Libby's canned milk. I lied to make sure that I would be an orphan. She was unable to be my mentor, for neither she nor I knew how to use our lives. How could she open the Star Lady Barbershop at 7 o'clock in the morning, shave whiskered chins and cut hair until 9 or 10 at night, and still have the strength to guide my wild heart?

My mother was as wise as trouble, error and waste. All her knowledge came too close to her death. But what she did was not so often mistaken as unlucky. Her sadness—which was to be mine—was solitude. Nobody cares to keep company with grief, indigence and mishap.

My mother wept when I told her of my decision to quit Kansas City. I was fleeing from her to find my life. Every leave-taking was a lamentation. Since my childhood my greatest apprehension was always that I might not see her face again. Could I even remember what apron she wore, or how she sat in the rocker on the back porch? Wherever I was, I endeavored to perceive her nose, mouth and eyes, maimed by the driest of gods, hopelessness.

In Omaha I took a room at the Paxton Hotel, which was a garden of Midas for loungers who slept in the cane chairs on the sidewalk in front of the hotel. I tried to get a job as a traveling salesman—I wanted a large territory and a fine expense account—but without any success. I had no trade; I was no vintner, miller, harness maker, fuller or tailor. Already plagued by ennui, I had no desire to perform futile and bestial work. What could I do that would not sink my faculties? Could I shed Adam's guilt by simply toiling, though the products I made were loathsome and immoral? Was man born to be tethered to a machine or to sit at a desk and reckon up another's avarice and sloth? He who makes others produce stupid baubles for the doting multitude "lies in wait to catch the poor."

Before long the heels of my parched shoes were run down at the sides, and my suit was stale in my nostrils; worse, I was a week behind in my rent. And I thought I smelled because I was separated from everybody.

Then one morning I came down the carpeted stairs, and the bellhop grasped my valise in his hand and took it outside as I instructed him to do. Meanwhile, I ambled easily to the desk and examined a Union Pacific timetable, casually bought two packages of Spearmint chewing gum, tipped the clerk a dollar and then walked out through the side door, where I handed the bellhop a half dollar. A block away from the Paxton I caught a streetcar which happened to be going to the railroad depot. I shipped my suitcase, collect, to Los Angeles.

Then I went to the Nebraska State Employment Bureau where I found an agent inspecting applicants to shovel gravel and handle railroad ties in Green River, Wyoming. I stood in a long queue, but when I was asked to show the palms of my hands, the agent pushed me aside. However, I noticed that each laborer who had been accepted for the section gang now had a green pasteboard card with a number scribbled in pencil stuck in his hatband. At a moneylender's, where mandolins, guitars, cornets and jewelry were sold, I pawned my Hamilton railroad timepiece, a gift from my mother, for $12. After that I went to a printer's office and bought a square of green cardboard; then I squandered a moiety of the day in that stygian American whorehouse, the movies. That night I slept in a 25-cent bed in one of those commercial communes for peeled oafs and nomads.

In the railroad yards at dawn, I skulked among the bushes, waiting for engine 213 on track 8 to move. When the train came by, I hurled myself forward, my fingers clawing the rungs of an iron ladder attached to the side of the caboose. As quickly as I could I made my way into a dirty, raw coach up ahead, steerage for the working class. There sat the workmen with the green passes in their hatbands; putting the one I had made in my own hat, I settled down to doze on one of the rough wooden benches. By eleven the workers took sandwiches out of paper sacks and tin dinner pails. I had had no food for nearly twenty-four hours, and my belly yearned for a mite of beef, ham or bread. The men ate, blew their noses, chattered and drank their coffee without taking any notice of me. There was a tank in the coach, next to the toilet, out of which trickled tepid, metallic water; that was all I had.

At Green River, Wyoming, a soulless blank town, I heard the hobnailed shoes shuffling out of the train and saw the inspector outside counting the men as they descended the steps. I got out on the other side of the train, trudged along the wooden ties for a space of fifteen minutes and then returned to the center of the town. Putting my hand in my pocket for my wallet, I discovered it had been stolen. I wiped the grime from my face and fortunately found a dime knotted in my handkerchief, with which I bought a package of Loose Wiles graham crackers. After filling my rueful stomach with crackers I drank some water that flowed cold out of a lead pipe which moistened a little grass in front of the depot.

Toward the fag end of the afternoon I caught an Acme freight going west. On both sides of the locomotive and inside the boxcars rode white and Negro vagrants; there were about twenty-five of them in all. I hid from them as well as from the brakeman, for by now I was a wild ass of affliction, my hand against every man's, and every man's against mine. Toward evening I overheard one vagabond say that a platoon of detectives was waiting for us in the railroad yards at Ogden, Utah.

A houseless beggar, I preferred to starve rather than be locked in an iron cage like a feral beast. Besides, the soul only tolerates the suffering it requires. I did not go out in the world to have every bad experience there is, but my will had spoken, and though I did not know what I was doing, I must needs obey that oracle within me or live dead. A few miles outside Ogden I jumped from one of the boxcars; the freight was rattling against the tracks at about forty-five miles an hour. I lay bleeding in the soot and amidst the sharp clinkers of Acheron.

The ancient Talmudists divided hell into seven parts, each parcel of slough and darkness piled one on another: Beatrice, Abilene, Green River, Ogden, Salt Lake City, Reno and Eureka were Sheol, Abaddon, Beer Shaḥat, Tit ha-Yawen, Shaʿare Maweth, Shaʿare Zalmaweth and Gehenna, the seven divisions of the Jewish Hades.

Instead of a new world, I stumbled into Ogden, and there was not a street paved with mercy or alms for the poor. I sat on curbstones or lay in doorways as though I were a dead Tupi doubled up in an earthen pot. Who would hear the cry of my ribs, bruised and hungry? "My strength is dried up like a potsherd."

How long was it since I had worn a clean shirt? Could I have but changed my smelly socks and flesh! I had journeyed almost as far as Cabeza de Vaca, who went naked from the Atlantic to the Rio de las Palmas, but he had to become a serpent, sloughing his skin twice a year. I had passed through a peopleless region and knew not that I had walked through two thousand leagues of myself.

Later, I slept in a stiff wind beneath a tree at Roseburg, Oregon. And many weeks after that I was lost in the Mojave Desert. Arriving at an abandoned hovel, I saw an iron keg filled with water. I leaned upon the barrel, thrusting my head into it—and drank kerosene!

How or when I came to Needles, California, I do not know. What had I gained from my misfortunes? I crept into coal cars, and snow, hail and rain were my roof. When I had to flee from a brakeman with a club or from a plain-clothes man, I would slink into a town of asphalt taken from the Dead Sea. Trudging over countless guts of cement that ran like slag in Gehenna, I stuffed my scabrous shoes with newspapers. My suit was a sickness; the moth sighed in my shirt and trousers. I was threadbare, hungered when I ate and imprisoned when I was free. I swallowed sleet, wind and confusion. Was I wandering on a peopleless comet without herbs, grass or ocean? How much punishment can the body take without corrupting the spirit? Could I feed upon my sores and not stink? My hair fell out in large clumps, and when I viewed the miserable remnants of my boyhood, vultures appeared. I moaned for my youth, for I was only nineteen at the time; baldness had come upon Gaza and my bones sang in the cinders and waste places of Jerusalem.

I begged when I was able; at the mission houses I was offered as a guerdon for two hours of dreary, canting piety, coffee and a cruller. At times I was a scullion, peeling potatoes and scalding dishes for my wretched meat and sleep. Epicurus said, "I feed sweetly upon bread and water, those sweet and easy provisions of the body . . ." But seldom did I have either. My Delphic oracle was my ceaseless hunger. As long as I was starved I would not be the refuse of the cormorant; for the will that languishes skulks among the melons and the leeks.

I had looked for the seven cities of Cibola; but each place was the same as the other. The streets were discharges of mucus; and trade, gain, deceit and money had left their scum and foul breath in the gutters. Wherever I was I cried out, "See, I am clothed in the miserable stuff of the spider and the caterpillar. Help me."

Had the American forgotten the privations of the settlers, hoary with suffering? There were mullet and bass in the bay, but the Pilgrims did not know how to catch them. One, going to gather shellfish on the Cape Cod beach, was found dead, stuck in the mud, having fallen down because he was feeble from starving. Did the American no longer remember how inhospitable and rocky were Mattapament, Pamaunke and Topahonock? Chickahamania and Powhatan were viperous rivers. What, too, could he get at Patuxet, Masuet and Satucket, Indian hummocks, save groundnuts and clams?

The Arctic Circle is not the coldest place on the earth; for there are no grounds so bleak or stony as indifferent flesh. In Needles a man walked by and my fingers were bleeding between his teeth. Another who had eaten his lips slinked into one of those festering wounds in a wall where the American lunches; there was one whose jowl was filled with morose hymns and suety sermons. They carried my youth in their bosoms.

Everywhere the people were clad in the cloth of death; the buildings were dead, for avarice, meanness, mammon and hatred had drunk up every drop of Abel's blood. The owl and the bittern were in the mouths of the churchgoers. The mouse skulked among the rafters, and the termite nested in the sullen, barren twin beds; the roach had taken possession of the plate, the porcelain, the iron pots and the skewers. These were a young people already in their dotage, who stored within their breasts the blood of their neighbors.

Natural affections die more quickly in civilized man than in beasts; there is no climate so polar as the fat, comfortable heart. Human charity is so short-winded that it cannot fetch a second breath before it is weary of the scantiest lees of its purse and table.

Poverty is fierce, savage water and terrain; Lake Titicaca is in the arid, wintry country of Callao where there is no wood, and where the aboriginal Indians use the dung of the llama for fuel. But who warms his hopelessness by burning his own manure? I am not unmindful of the admonition of St. Augustine: "Go not abroad, return unto thyself; in the inner man dwelleth truth." But I was not ready then for the sage rebuke of the saint. Had I looked within myself I would have seen nothing.

In what latitude did I wander? I was neither in the ice nor in the fire. God helps those who are themselves their sole food, for we eat our natures when we do not know our surroundings. Those who remember little are already senile though young. It was said by Humboldt that nothing remains of the lost Guanches at Teneriffe but the sepulchres, and that each skeleton and its ashes weigh six pounds. What would I not have given for six pounds of recollection?

Had I been able to recognize sorrel and the purple saxifrage, my days as a vagabond would not have been so peeled. I could have suffered for understanding; but I had ranged a great part of a continent, and it was as insubstantial as my dreams and the First Void. How was I to raise this shamble of rags from the grave? Can *no-feeling* be taken from the ground? Was I already as old as the age of water —upon which neither God nor man leave one word, thought or impression?

The worst misery is not an empty belly, but a vacant

mind: the fell pain of not seeing. Allen Tate, our poet, has said:

> The thin grass picked by the wind,
> Heaved by the mole; the hollow pine that
> Screams in the latest storm—these,
> These emblems of twilight have we seen at length . . .

Was I looking for the fiery clouds of Magellan? Was it the Polar Seas or the Southern Cross in Antarctica? Was I seeking the burning zones where the Mauritius palm tree grows? What could I do? Ask the larvae of ants and the polypi, ask the eider ducks flying eastward? Would that I could have crossed the shoals to the headlands where the narwhal sports. Oh, where was I going? And why could I not see? Does excessive punishment corrupt the gaunt eyes?

How many epochs are there in a man? How many millennia do the Cordilleras contain? What remains of that boy who flits like a sapless phantom through my memory? I am more familiar with Theophrastus, Bartram or with Thoreau than I am with him. Where is that vine in my blood, more ruined than Heliopolis or a relic at Borsippa? Could I meet him face to face, I pray that there are yet enough tears in me to cover him, for he was naked.

In Cuzco there was a street called The Lady of Mercy, where the poor could exchange their rags with one another. Let me beg for my victuals or stand in the street of the pauper and barter everything that I have save my heart and my mind, for the meat and the bed drink up the whole life of man.

I will be a hunger-gnawing fate in the ravines of Callao and I shall drink the raw, orphaned waters of Lake Titicaca. Angelic bed and pillow are sterile wastes and the bitter winds at Potosi. I strive for my will; this is my sole understanding. Only by my will can I exhume my own tombs. Woe to him who is easy grass and tepid water. We are worms long before the maggots compose our epitaphs. Comfort is my false seraph; the perpetual snows of the Andes are my abode and hearth; wind my garment, and paleolithic gravel my living bread.

VII

I love him who desireth not too many virtues. One virtue is more a virtue than two.

Nietzsche

L os Angeles is a sewer of Sodom, though once it had been a grove at Lebanon. "A great city is a great solitude," says Aristotle.

When I arrived there in 1919 I was clad in moth-eaten penury and I had no place to lay my head. At night I crouched on wooden porches on Figueroa and Flower Streets. If I saw a gaping ground-floor window of a Japanese or Mexican rooming house, I would creep through it and crawl into a vacant bed—and awaken and flee before dawn so that I would not be discovered and cast into jail. I was rotting every hour. One midnight, coming into a bedroom, I heard sounds from heavy, swinish matter heaped on a mattress. In a pair of sour, beer-sodden trousers were four crimped one-dollar bills which I took. For several days I filled my belly with 15-cent beef-stews and purchased a bed for the night for 50 cents. After the money was spent I drank the morning for breakfast, my midday meal was a light zephyr of hope and at dusk I licked the smell of a week-old broth on my coat sleeve.

One day I tottered into a lunchroom, ordered two hamburger sandwiches and a cup of coffee which I gulped down, and, taking the check, stepped up to the cash register behind which the proprietor sat and asked him whether he needed a dishwasher or somebody to peel spuds. When he replied that there might be a job for a scullion in a week, I thanked him for his unusual courtesy and, stepping out through the door, tried my best not to scuddle.

During the noon rush hour I patronized sundry drug-stores, devouring avocado salads and two glasses of milk, after which I approached the pharmacist and asked him for an ounce of herb grace. While he was occupied searching a catalogue for this medicine, I left straightway.

I had moulted my honesty in a far shorter period than the serpent needs to slough his coat. One requires a friend, or even the driest stubble for fuel in order to keep one's principles warm. By now I had become a soulless array of clouts, and lived wild, and stank.

Some afternoons I visited that plaguy plot of cement surrounding a few scurrile patches of grass called Pershing Square. Almost every American park is a lewd tryptich composed of a cannon, a sign reading KEEP OFF THE GRASS and a homosexual. Cruddled pederasts and sulphured her-maphrodites slouched on the benches, waiting to ambush an urchin who had just come to town by freight train from Columbus or Detroit.

Another refuge for the waif was the cinema, where men and boys are pewed in a pit of darkness and are mad-dened by dithering photographs of whoring Venuses. There were also the mission houses operated by the pimps of God. They gave vagrants catarrhal doses of hymns and prayers for a plate of soup boiled in Acheron.

Nineteen years old, I was more ashamed of my ravaged pate than I was of my rancid drawers. Already an old child,

I studied my hairline every day. One evening I attended a spiritualistic seance and instead of handing the medium a note asking her to speak to the dead in my behalf I told her to beg Esau to give me his hair.

The medium repiled, "Do not be despondent, my infant; take heed, and eat only wild locusts and honey, and you shall be as hirsute as St. John the Baptist." For a whole hour I was jubilant, and that night I saw the hairy saint in the wilderness; when I awakened I found a sheaf of my locks on the pillow.

After that I went to a Christian Science reading room and sought the help of a practitioner. Laying on of hands, he promised, would heal the impotent, the palsied and the bald. He admonished me, "Keep your intestinal tract clean and do not go into women. Be not puffed up, for in much hair is much vanity."

On a Sunday I was standing in front of the YMCA at 7th and Hope Streets. Services were being held on the mezzanine floor. I went upstairs to grub up godhead for one cruller. By noon there was a covey of YMCA pariahs reading in the lobby. Looking over the shoulder of one member, I read: "And he who hath to be a creator in good and evil—verily, he hath first to be a destroyer and break values in pieces." When I heard this adage, what manna and quail were in my wild heart.

A castaway vegetarian, this stranger in the Y asked me whether I had read *Thus Spake Zarathustra*, and I smarted under my ignorance. How reluctant I have ever been to admit that I am not familiar with a savant, and I have told falsehoods, claiming that I knew the author, because I could never endure the infamy of stupidity. Though I accepted long ago the Socratic admission: "I know nothing," did I ever have my heart in it?

Zarathustra restored in me the visions of the night which had departed from me, and I said to myself: Do I not regard the dream as a god?

Nearby in the lobby of the Y sat a rough, carroty urchin who was throwing hazelnuts into his mouth while he perused George Gissing's *By the Ionian Sea*. And in the corner of the room was a thin, piercing man who had a volume of Epictetus's *Moral Discourses* on his knees. Endeavoring to scan one of the pages, I stumbled against his spruce trouser cuffs and scarred his polished shoes. He gave me a hard kick and laughed at me. Laughter is the Kabbala of the bowels, and since we must quit this world weeping, it is better to come into it laughing, as Zoroaster is said to have done.

This man, I later learned, liked to call himself Lao Tsu Ben, and he was to be my mentor. From him I learned of Gissing's *The Private Papers of Henry Ryecroft*, Samuel Butler's *Erewhon*, *The Upanishads*, Daudet's *Sappho*, Gautier's *The Golden Fleece*, *The Meditations of Marcus Aurelius* and Wilde's *De Profundis*—books which I bought in the secondhand shops by selling my overcoat. He was also, in part, a disciple of Mary Baker Eddy, and was positive that Plato had not been mistaken about the existence of Atlantis. In his twenty-third year, when I made his acquaintance, I thought all intellectual speculation was packed in his spare body; he gave off, besides, an agreeable odor of Storax. He was like the tyrant Montezuma, who would not allow anyone to come into his presence until his menials had fumigated the space surrounding him with copal.

As for me, I made a delirious impression upon Lao Tsu Ben. On one occasion he followed me when I stepped out of the YMCA door, keeping a yard or two to the rear. I had rushed out of the lobby, choked with Emerson's "Over-soul" and the *Rig-Veda*. Going up Hope Street, I recited aloud: "*Bhagavad-Gita, Rig-Veda*, the *Upanishads*, I'm the Over-soul, yea, a lord of language, an autocrat of passion."

Having memorized pages of Emerson, Wilde and Ibsen,

I stood at the corner of 7th Street and declaimed whatever happened to come into my head:

O Rhodora, if the sages ask thee why
This charm is wasted on earth and sky,
Tell them, dear, that if eyes were made for seeing,
Then beauty is its own excuse for being.

Tsu Ben was so convulsed that he fell into the gutter, and when I turned around to see what the noise was, he got up and punched me in the ribs, blaming me for his fall. Tsu Ben had no doubts about me; I was the most original fool he had ever encountered. A crazy waif of the Muses, I was one of his most remarkable pastimes.

He took the greatest care in shaving his handsome, peaked face and dusting powder on his pimpled cheeks; were I in the room while he was making his toilet, I always somehow managed to step on his shoes which he had just shined or to jostle him so that he cut his chin. Had he not found me so droll, he would have gotten rid of me forthwith. Though he roared at any ineptitude or waggish act of mine, he had a skulking compassion for sorrow, and I already wore the maimed face at the place of the skull. Without understanding what I was doing, I had become a rapturous believer in Saint Teresa's saying, "Suffer, O Lord, or die."

By now, finding that ordinary, brutal work was unbearable, I asked my mother for help, and she sent me $15 a week. I seldom ate more than one meal a day, saving my pennies for filet of sole and tartar sauce in the YMCA basement cafeteria, and keeping what I had left for the books of Tolstoi, Gorki, Chekov, de Maupassant, the Abbé Prévost, Andreyev and Thomas Hardy.

I felt sure now that I was born to write—but I did not know what. I was already hankering for a pseudonym when I read that Gorki had asked the following question in a Russian newspaper: "Who conceals himself behind the name of Leonid Andreyev?" To which that author replied "Leonid Andreyev."

When Lao Tsu Ben was not reading Shakespeare, denouncing Mr. Bowdler, taking upper and lower colonic irrigations or considering the transmigration of the soul, he was studying the columns of the newspapers, giving Talmudic attention to *Personal, Lost and Found* and *Business Opportunities.* He had no time for such rabble parts of the paper as *Help Wanted—Male.*

During this period of unemployment he came upon a man who told him ecstatically that a Christian Science healer had restored the sight of his son. The Christian Scientist and Ben decided to organize a company and buy machinery for excavating gold from the bottom of Lake Tahoe. Tsu Ben had no difficulty in persuading some mediocre businessmen to invest money in this venture. Unfortunately, it cost more to dredge than the gold was worth, and the corporation went bankrupt. Bakers, contractors, a mumper, a pair of ironmongers, a vice-president of a bank and a trimmer in real estate had put thousands of dollars into this scheme; they were all looking for Lao Tsu Ben. However, he had sundry addresses: one in Desert Hot Springs, another in a mean, wizened room on Flower Street, as well as a familial arrangement with a man, very flaccid in bed, whose wife Tsu Ben solaced. He also kept a pelting ramshackle on the seashore at Venice. Always hiding, either to avoid a concubine or a bumbailiff, he acquired a clandestine nature. Living in the Midi of America, he suffered from the pangs of terrible boredom, and he had no way of relieving it except by starting a new intrigue with a slut or a broad-hipped matron, or commencing another business.

Lao Tsu Ben next became an impresario, resolving to bring Mozart, Beethoven, Bach, Saint-Saëns' *Samson and Delilah* and "Just Awearying For You" to sterile Los Angeles. He engaged Edward MacDowell and several renowned pianists and violinists; the recitals were held in the Mauve Room at the Ambassador Hotel, but in spite of the fine performances of the virtuosi, the majority of the residents still went to see Mae Murray in "On with the Dance" or other gaudy films.

Tsu Ben found a convert in Redondo Beach and there gave himself over to new cogitations and adventures, for he was positively determined not to be a grub harrowed by a populace of churls. His attitude was no different from that of Alexander Hamilton, who had said: "The people, sir, are a great beast."

While Lao Tsu Ben was away—he had become interested in a copper mine not far from San Diego—I formed a rhapsodic friendship with a boy named Asa Hyams, who introduced me to Evelyn Underhill's book on mysticism and William James's *Varieties of Religious Experience*. I met him in the lobby of the Y when he was at the piano playing "Underneath the Stars," an American semi-classic. Asa Hyams was a Greekish, seminal lad with licentious lips who pored over the volumes of Berkeley and the works of Ralph Barton Perry. Like many another YMCA ceno-bite, he took enemas each day and was addicted to raw carrots, walnuts and waitresses. Asa had run away from rich parents in the Singapore Straits Settlements. When he was out of pocket, he waited on tables at stylish resort hotels in Monterey or at San Juan Capistrano for three to four months so that he could be free to read for half a year.

Asa once asked me whether Anatole France's *Thaïs* had troubled my privities, but I retorted that when I read literature I was entirely continent. However, the real truth is that my priapic, Socratic syllogism has always been: I have secret parts, I am ashamed of them, therefore I am mortal.

Tsu Ben thought me an exceptional gawk with women. He had eight or nine houris in as many lubricious beach towns within fifteen to twenty miles of Los Angeles. When he had a sexual connection with a chit in Venice—the syphilitic bitch of all those cheap California spas—he told her he lived in Oakland.

I cautioned Tsu Ben not to cohabit with venereal women, as he had many beady pimples on his face; at this he was overcome with glee and lay down on the cot to compose himself. He advised me to read Lombroso's *The Man of Genius;* the treatise of this man from Turin made me even more of a buffoon. After I discovered that Goethe, Heine, Beethoven and Nietzsche had all had syphilis, I thought I could not be a genius unless I found a woman who would be lenient enough to share this disease with me.

I began to look about for a whore who might help me become a man of letters. There was King Solomon's Penny Dance Palace, which was known to the YMCA heteroclites as the temple of the Three Rhea Sisters. Sporting a chartreuse-colored handkerchief that sprouted from the breast pocket of my pustular green jacket, purchased secondhand on Spring Street, wearing somebody else's pawned spats and a velours hat that also came from a moneylender, I thought I was such a dandy of the Muses that I would have distempered testicles in a fortnight.

Both Tsu Ben and I were certain of my afflatus. It was the last time that I was to be certain of anything; for doubt was to be my Rock of Peter; I took this Petrine stone and beat every shibboleth and thought in my breast. Whatever can be proven is dross.

Continuing to live as an ascetic, I pined for erudition, a half hour with a prostitute and a magnificent infectious disease. But nothing came of my aspirations; I was so helpless that I could not even get the pox.

Tsu Ben thought that I should have a woman in any case and he offered me one of his mistresses who had become burdensome to him. But I was unable to take her; as she lay in my arms, I was myself a corpse because I could not eradicate the thought that I was duping my friend—even though that was what he wanted me to do. I could not warm over one of the cadavers he had buried, and he was interring one love or another each month.

Tsu Ben came of a feral stock of speculators; his father, a great, raw-nosed man, had come to California for gold in '49. He belonged to a little rebel band of alchemists who attempted to turn every event or mishap into a precious metal. Standing on a curbstone one day, he saw a streetcar accident; the trolley had left the tracks, and many hurt persons were being carried away on stretchers. Tsu Ben's father sneaked around to the other side of the tram, crawled through an open window and a few minutes afterward was himself taken out by two men. After his confinement in the hospital for delirious spasms and nervous shock, he collected six hundred dollars from the insurance company.

Before Lao Tsu Ben was twenty-two years old he was the vice-president of the largest ladies' wearing apparel store in San Francisco. Although adept in all the arts of trade, he loathed commerce, and so resigned. At one time he was several months behind in his rent at the YMCA; whenever the secretary had the effrontery to ask Tsu Ben for money, he showed him his Masonic membership card. Tsu Ben spoke of the Masonic order in a whisper, only disclosing that as soon as one had been received into this hierophantic sodality he was given his winding sheet. I was impressed with the secret rites of this lodge and I wanted to meet the overlords of business in order to get a fancy position as an elite wastrel. Tsu Ben was so abashed by my lack of idealism that I had to renounce this opportunity as well as the special Masonic cerecloth.

However, Tsu Ben was in a sorry predicament and in spite of his bloated principles one night he had to fasten a long rope around his trunk and let it down little by little into the alley from his eighth-floor room at the YMCA.

Then he moved to a clapboard flat with an unemployed milliner who needed an abortion.

During this period I shared my fifteen dollars a week with Tsu Ben. I had persuaded my poor mother, still lady barbering in the shop beneath the 8th Street viaduct, that I would soon cut a great figure in the commonwealth of literature. Though I was the most searching reader of Gorki's *Tales,* Tolstoi's *The Death of Ivan Ilyich,* Ibsen's *Emperor and Galilean* and George Moore's *The Confessions of a Young Man,* I could not understand why the scenarios I wrote as a free-lance scribbler for the movies were invariably rejected.

Whenever I got a registered letter from my mother, I ran to Tsu Ben's rooming house to announce, "Today, O my friend, we eat chopped chicken liver and pumpernickel bread." At times I could not find him; he was clandestine, either by nature or as the result of failures and the fear of court writ.

Our usual rendezvous was a kosher restaurant on Hill Street which we had converted into an almshouse. Our companions there were Asa Hyams, now a part-time pianist in a moving-picture theater at Altadena, Sebastian Bach Honig, a seventeen-year-old violinist who had left St. Louis to play "Hearts and Flowers" on a Hollywood stage-set, and, of course, Tsu Ben's current bed-morsel.

For twenty cents we could get a meal of chopped chicken liver, along with three platters of pumpernickel and extra portions of butter. We were furtive feeders, keeping our heads low over our dishes so that we would not attract too much attention from the proprietor, who might turn us out.

Tsu Ben, now reduced in health by few and irregular meals and excessive fornication—for was it not said by the Argives that Aphrodite was the opener of graves?—continued to study the newspapers. One week there was a small notice about the owner of a chic ladies' wearing apparel shop in Laguna Beach who was accused of seducing a boy at the YMCA. This was not an exceptional occurrence. The Laguna Beach man had been lying in jail for over a month when Tsu Ben visited him. The prisoner thought he was too vile to notify his relatives of his plight and was certain that no counselor-at-law would defend him.

Crates the Cynic copulated with his wife on the porch in full view of the Greeks in order to show men how to overcome their shame. Another philosopher of Attica erected two statues in Athens, one to Insolence and the second to the Water Closet, so that his acolytes would be brave enough to insult liars and dissemblers, and in order that there would be no affected nonsense about sitting on the closestool. Are eating, blowing one's nose, hawking and spitting less fastidious than fornication? All flesh is hypocritical; there is hardly a depravity we condemn that is not a parcel of our dreams.

Lao Tsu Ben retained a lawyer and paid fifteen hundred dollars to the detective who had arrested the shop owner. Tsu Ben's ward had provided all the money. The detective now admitted that he had made a mistake. Tsu Ben also bribed several city officials and then took the prisoner, who was now out on bail, across the state line to Nevada. The man could not give Tsu Ben enough groveling thanks for his achievements. He signed over his bank account to him as well as his shop and promised him a partnership in the business should he win his freedom.

Now that Tsu Ben was the proprietor of a fashionable store, and since all his customers were women, he became more wary of them. He mused upon the worth of carnal entertainments, considering whether it would not be more sagacious to muzzle his secret parts. Schopenhauer held that joy is the absence of pain, but Tsu Ben opined that if man could have no more than a neutral experience, he was no better than dead. Rueful as the thought was, Tsu Ben could recollect no amorous experience without wincing.

After Tsu Ben seduced a woman, he would rummage through his mind for a subterfuge whereby he could escape from her. He had graved well over a hundred maidenheads; abhorring injustice, he believed that only a scoundrel would allow a virgin to grow cold and musty. But well did he comprehend the caveat in the Book of Proverbs: "A woman hunteth for the precious life of man." He refused to re-examine the remains of a deceased love, and was always put out with me because, if he passed her on to me, she was soon back on his hands; I could not exhume her either.

Lao Tsu Ben was a gourmet in feminine flesh. He would not couple with a woman whose husband had a corrupt breath. Having wise nostrils, he could divine smells before they were apparent. If a woman had a good scent when the air was blowing off the sea, he knew beforehand whether she would have a tarnished odor when the wind came from the land. Nor did he relish a bedmate who hiccoughed, eruc-tated or sneezed—unless she was moved to do so while he was lying with her.

However, he was not averse to hackneyed meat or to a deformed body, any more than the Spaniards who were with Balboa were opposed to eating the repulsive alligator, as its flesh gives off the vapors of musk. He was prescient enough to reject an angelic Venus who might resemble the South American mancanilla, which looks like a beautiful apple but is extremely venomous. He preferred a woman who had a husband, finding it more convenient for the latter to provision her than for him to keep her. Also, he believed that ground grubbed up by another would prove more arable for him.

Tsu Ben was most prudent before having sexual com-merce with a female. He not only considered the weather of her nature but also mapped her contours as if she were a bay, so that he might surmise what rocks, shoals, sandbars or islands there were in that cove where he might be shipwrecked. What gales stirred her? Was she *mare dulce*, sweet river water or the brackish sea?

At first he would wanton with his paramour on a hard, rough bedstead or on an uncarpeted floor—so that she would always remember that she had received him in the worst of circumstances. When he was beginning to be jaded, they moved to a feather bed or paused to take a comfit or cheese.

But now that his health was declining, Tsu Ben developed a passion to be a hermit and to live on a rock. No experience seemed so ecstatic to him as to be quiet and not to be vexed by his prepuce. He resolved to relinquish his seraglio. Moreover, the one he slept with in Venice he had suspected for some while because she spent long hours eating chocolates at the front window. He did not regard a casement facing the street as good for the general deportment of mistresses, since adulterers are always on the pavement looking up to see whether the curtains are closed or not. Besides, a window is the lascivious aperture of a house. A view of the ocean is also disastrous and will keep a beloved one in upheaval; she will have her high tides when a man is absent. He did not think it sensible to provide a mistress with a flat that was in the rear of a building; he felt that using the back steps would make her surreptitious. Nor did he like a woman to take the air by herself; a female wears her house as she does her clothes, and when she goes abroad alone she sheds two principles to which she is attached: home and raiment. Finally, he refused to marry, imagining that so long as he remained a bachelor he could never be considered a legitimate cuckold.

Meanwhile, Lao Tsu Ben had given his latest impermanent companion a stylish wardrobe out of the large stock of the Laguna Beach shop, and had withal bought her a baby grand piano and an abortion. When she announced that she wished to be his wife, he told her that sexual intercourse would be fatal to him. He had already disposed of several concubines, or forgot them. Let nobody think that Tsu Ben did not have a marvelous memory, though it must be acknowledged that on occasion he failed to recognize some to whom he had given an evening. Once he was having a ravishing night with a virgin who furnished him with extraordinary vagaries—until he recalled that he had possessed her the year before in La Jolla. But then a man travels from one bed to another in order to be with a woman who is the duplicate of the one he has forsaken. If he is accustomed to a hundred and ten pounds of flesh, and has been irrational enough to suppose that he could dote more on more skin, he will find himself starving on two hundred pounds.

Notwithstanding all of his priapic woes, Tsu Ben did not overlook me. He gave me money for books to dilate my wit and afflatus.

Regrettably, the fugitive in Nevada, feeling after some months that the accusations against him must by now be forgotten, returned and demanded his shop and money. Tsu Ben was virtuous when he least expected it, which is natural. Everything is unpredictable in this world, especially a moral act. He returned the business and departed, asking for nothing.

He now fell ill of poverty and, worse, of consumption. He had lost considerable weight and precious tufts of his silken hair. Of late he had not fornicated at all and could not understand why he had not been compensated for his recent abstemious habits and had his health restored to him.

Since the Kosmos no less than Society was his implacable foe, he did his best under the circumstances; he applied tincture of iodine to his scalp and washed it in salt water, besides drinking raw eggs and three malted milks a day. He was so emaciated that I feared my friend was disappearing in his suit. When I grasped his bony elbow affectionately, I cringed. Eager to serve him, I scuffed his shoes while polishing them, broke one shoelace and tore out the tongue, too.

As usual this put him into such convulsions that his lungs and ribs pained him.

A doctor advised Tsu Ben to go to the Mojave Desert for a few years. My heart was stuffed with grief, and I wept over him more than Joseph did when he fell on the neck of his brother Benjamin. We were children of penury, and who is so zealous a friend as a boy? Later we are too curried to love; when our blood is stale we call it mature. Who flows wisdom constantly? Not even a river.

We Ishmaels of the YMCA had no doctrines. All castaways, we disclosed our raw, bleeding indigence to one another, and only other pariahs, wounded to the quick of their identities, had anything to give us. The citizens were too full to vomit their dregs for our beggars' table. Those unable to give friendship are poulpes who eat their own tentacles.

In the Mojave Desert Tsu Ben bought, without paying any money down, a wizened grocery store containing a few shelves of dismal canned goods. He promised to collect for the previous owners the unpaid debts incurred by the desert rats who camped in huts or made hovels in the sand hills. In addition he gave them a note for two thousand dollars to be paid in eighteen months. The store was in a barren settlement called Joshua Tree. There he sold canned peas, figs, pears and peaches to tubercular steam fitters, paper hangers with heart trouble, rheumatic plumbers, whom he referred to as ordure-artists, and to lickerish, ailing divorcees. During the day, when the heat was one hundred and twenty degrees in the shade, Tsu Ben slept. Walking at night, as he coughed and expectorated blood, he observed the jack rabbits galloping over the dry lake bottom or browsing among the verbenas and lupines, and wondered how he could become independent. He would rather have been the sole maker of his own evil than be under obligation to another for a single benefit.

Not yet in his twenty-fourth year, he was obsessed by

old age and poverty. Still in his heyday, he wished that he were younger, but not as foolish as he had been. We are charitable at noon, pensive in the rain, fools when the Fishes are quivering on the horizon and perverse all day long. But drink mulled wine while the acacia blooms, for tomorrow you will die. With such thoughts in his mind, Tsu Ben found himself one evening in the midst of a stud poker game.

He was playing with the members of a Hollywood company that was on location not more than a mile from Joshua Tree. By daybreak he had won six Sears Roebuck cottages that were being used as a set in the film. He erected the cottages adjacent to the grocery store and now had a hostel for overnight tourists. The money he received for rent he spent to build a café; he bought a truck on the installment plan and shipped in avocados, grapefruit, oranges, flitches of bacon and ice cream from Barstow. He planted alfalfa and trees, which were gnawed by the cows of two burly ruffians who were his neighbors. After warning them several times to keep their heifers away from his herbage and trees, he shot all eight of them. After that he put up a garage and invested money in a gold mine in Death Valley.

Lao Tsu Ben had always abhorred the rabble, but now he became more surreptitious than ever and locked himself in the house that he had built, as he considered the sight of every mean or wormy face a chagrin. When I came to visit him, he declined to be seen except at random moments. A tyrant, he had been too good a Buddha for me not to learn the subtle crafts of despotism. I was deeply stung. Was he hiding from me to be contemplative? We have all the quiet we need in our lives to brood. He who demands more is asking for the tranquillity of the grave. I could never tell a man, particularly my beloved friend, that I was too oc-cupied to see him. When one tells another that he is busy, he implies that the other's time is his refuse.

Tsu Ben had a small fortune by now—how much, I did

not know. Would he be able to endure success? Man survives disease, paralysis, a thousand humiliations, almost any travail but success. May the harpies excrete upon everybody who has more money than he requires for his conceptions and livelihood.

Our quarrels became numerous; I had by this time misread about fifty more good books than he and I was now a young blade of letters! Lao Tsu Ben detested the neologisms in the new literature which had already reached us. It took me thirty years to come to his sane judgments about authors. Young and coarse, I argued and gabbled, unable to resist either temptation. Arguments dry up our oracles.

He eclipsed me in many ways, but in his returning to that toad called trade I detected the carrion of the herd in his spirit. Moreover, though I owed him everything, I could not pardon him for no longer having any need of me. Yet he had plenty of good sense, of which I could claim only a little. This is an autobiography of my faults; were it an avowal of my virtues, I would have nothing to confess.

All my life I have been a vagabond in the winds; I have even been the underling of those who came to ask alms of me. Now I was solitary again. Before we parted, I strongly reproved Tsu Ben for having become gross. Each morning every man should burn incense and pray God that he be not too vulgar that day. Tsu Ben had bragged of his connections with the bailiff at Barstow. All my life I have loathed the gendarmes of the penal state. Tsu Ben, my mentor, had fashioned out of his intellect a blade of imperial Toledo steel, and I now cast it at his bowels, and he fell down before his pupil. The man who had been my Emerson and Epictetus bowed his neck, wherein is lodged the most crass and obdurate egoism.

Tsu Ben feared nothing but the intellect. He had taught me to distrust the rout; for nothing stinks so bad as the spirit when it is a crowd. Had not our sage, Nietzsche, still a pariah in the worm-eaten academies of philosophy, warned us: "Everyone wants the same; everyone is equal: he who hath other sentiments goeth voluntarily into the madhouse."

But when I was seated in a truck, making ready to leave for the university at Berkeley, which he had persuaded me to do, Tsu Ben tenderly wrapped a blanket about me. He was a monarch who humbled himself, and I have not met one man since who could be as meek as the dove though as wise as the serpent. Lao Tsu Ben was of the elect; but I could not relent. How stiff-necked I have always been after a quarrel; such pride has been the Golgotha nails in my body.

Lao Tsu Ben became a wealthy man, but utterly removed from me, while I remained a beggar, with windmills in my brain, going to and fro in the lazar house of literature for a few pennies a page. Lao Tsu Ben was the one friend of my soul, and no matter who has since said to me, "I am your friend," I sit in my waste places without anyone except the owl and the bittern.

VIII

I had a sister much older than myself, from whose modesty and goodness, which were great, I learned nothing.

Saint Teresa

Berkeley was strewn with large, round hydrangeas and winelike broom, and surrounded, save where the bay was, with soft flanks of sensual hills. Only the swamps and brine gave me some quiet, and the harsh and acrid odors of fresh paint were hygienic; had not Abraham waited for the angels beneath the terebinths, which were turpentine trees?

I had matriculated at the University of California in the middle of my twenty-first year, enrolling as a special student. Most of my courses were in philosophy and anthropology.

I soon found that the work and the talk in the classes at Berkeley were tiresome and bootless. I had chosen one course in botany, and the lectures were given by such a drab that the notes I had jotted down on paper I gave to the goats, who devoured them. Any love of natural history was spoiled for me for at least a generation: I would never have believed then that I would some day go to the works of Buffon, Humboldt and Darwin with such joy.

What need had I of the sour pedants of humid syntax, or of courses in pedagogy, canonized illiteracy? I saw that anybody who had read twelve good books knew more than a doctor of philosophy. Had I not studied on my own the works of some of the Russian savants of letters and read the great English and French authors, I should still have been thoroughly uneducated at the time I received my Bachelor of Arts. Was I not ignorant enough without walking the earth with several degrees? A grocery boy with good sense is more learned than many an American professor in the general arts whose stock in trade is ambiguity and circum-locution. His wine is a footnote to a platitude. There is a Spanish proverb: *Llamar al pan pan y al vino vino.*

Again I was sorely vexed with libidinous dreams. What could I do about that fever that comes with virilia? The Greek doctors of *materia medica* paid as much heed to seminal visions as to the cure of elephantiasis, leprosy or poltfoot. The plant called Nymphaea, used in a medicinal beverage, was drunk by persons who cohabited in their sleep with Aspasia or Helen of Troy.

We know less about amours than the bramble frog; the absence of elms, alders, willows and the vitex, or even marshes, bogs, rivers and brooks in our cities has produced every imaginable deformity: impostumes, senility, short groins, groveling bums, sniveling ballocks and a simpering anus. What we do not inherit we catch from fools, and stupidity is more contagious than the pox. We should know in what months it is best to be continent; the matrons, dur-ing the Greek Thesmophoriazûsae, strewed their beds with the vitex, not unlike the willow, observing at that time the strictest chastity.

The Goncourt brothers wrote that they set aside one hour a day five days a week to discharge those vexsome vessels, so that they could have the quiet and sanity they required for their work. I had had no amours, but had known a few prostitutes—from whom I fled after one or two encounters. That was better than sensual madness. Christ said, "The poor ye always have with you," and Tolstoi remarked that the whore you always have and *should* have.

Bodies seek each other until their demise—and nearly always in vain. How was I to find that darling bud of truth? Many are wed to women whose breasts are plain, coarse bread and whose hair is sexless. As they walk they drop the odor of kitchen soap rather than nard. I would never be satisfied with the gap-toothed wife of Bath.

Often I chanted: Oh, let her loins quench my famine and her belly be a comfort against the winds; may her skirts be my tent of Kedar and her petticoat a wonder in Lebanon, for I am in the dust, O my God; let a maid come out of Jerusalem and kiss me before I die.

Was I to have a marriage song or a hymn of woe and failure? What gentle arms would bind my wounds, quell my anguish and warm my barren hills? Meanwhile, I shaved my head and led the exemplary life of the ascetic. Had I not been sorely troubled by the flesh of woman, I should have been content to walk and to give myself over to amorphous vagaries which I then imagined were mountainous conceptions. Thucydides taught me much later that there are no ideas which are not clearly defined or written. I also thought about suicide, because I considered that sort of nebulous cogitation as a part of the style of the literary man. Of course, I had not the slightest intention of taking my life. One of the reasons that I did not kill myself, as others had done after reading Goethe's *Sorrows of Werther*, was that I found the novel a bore.

Among the intelligentsia at Berkeley was a graduate student who passed himself off as a great doctor of amours. He claimed that he had gathered more maidenheads than the number of foreskins David collected from the Philistines.

He was a stumpy Uriah who annoyed me because he fed among the lilies while I ranged the campus coveting any giddy skirt that came within my view. One day this philosopher of lechery showed me his erotic morsel, Angelica, and I was quite beside myself. My one thought was how could I take this lovely away from him. No Machiavelli in love, but full of spleen, bile, ill nature, clogged veins, and unable to tether that ungovernable organ that is a pest to the whole human race, I was either at one moment mad for the delicacies of Venus, or resolved to be abstemious the next.

I rose at five o'clock in the morning to catch the pure, hard air from the hills; I used no eggs, milk or meat, nor touched any of the fruits in season—including the fig, symbol of the wondrous matrix since ancient times. Taking only a Spartan diet of nuts and the coarsest bread and water, still I could not rid myself of that terrible sting which the sight of Angelica had given me. When I considered her dear, tender nipples, which I saw so gently browsing beneath her white blouse, and remembered a moiety of her thigh which she had revealed when she reached for the steps, I was close to tears. Whenever I met this Hittite who had her I abhorred him, and adored her the more.

Some days I haunted the library waiting for this maiden. I could not think of her otherwise, for every woman who is loved is a virgin, and her chestnut tresses and slender exhalations were holy to me. Feigning as best I could, since I had no skill as a hypocrite, I tried to learn from the graduate student what classes she attended, whether she was in a sorority or on what street she lived. He was a hard and cunning rogue, and having realized that he had committed one mistake, he had no intention of making another. After this I became his implacable foe, and he mine, though we had never spoken in rancor to each other; but as Zachariah has said, "I abhorred him in my soul, and he loathed me in his."

Then suddenly I began to cut a figure at the university. What with a shaved head and walking about by myself—

which is usually the most boring of company—and having contributed to the college magazine an astounding piece of belles lettres with the impressive title, "The Sick, the Pessimist and the Philosopher," I was sure that I should now have those apples of Haran. Though I imagined I saw one very enticing creature in my French class ogling me, my deportment remained rigid and aloof. Why should a burgeoning Heinrich Heine run after women? Since not one came to kneel at my learned feet, I had no other course but to resume my literary work.

I had already composed one foolish novel grounded upon *Don Quixote:* another was written under the influence of Beethoven's symphonies and a third I did in the style of Dostoevski's *Poor People.* It was to take me many years to realize that one has to be very lucky to write one intelligent sentence. Since whatever falls out, ill or good, is the result of an accident, I have always had the most hopeless feelings whenever I commenced a book.

Then at a freshman dance I saw Angelica alone. The softest wind blew from the tops of Amana through my fainting soul but I was at the same time glutted with seminal egoism. I would be the craftiest Hannibal and take her from that varlet. My experience in dancing I had gotten at King Solomon's Penny Palace in Los Angeles and after one clumsy foxtrot I thought it better judgment to turn to polite letters. As I was chattering about Gautier's *Mademoiselle de Maupin*, with Paul Bourget's *Le Disciple* in my mind—for his adage was: give a maid three books to read and you can seduce her—the president of the university approached me. He was General David Prescott Barrows, who had been at the head of the American Expeditionary Force at Archangel. I had read with great wonder Karl Liebknecht's *Militarism* and some of the precious letters of Rosa Luxemburg, and so I managed a stupendous choler against this man. He offered me his hand and I refused to take it. He grew quite crimson, which I am now ashamed to remember, for I do not know unto this day whether he was a good or a bad man, though I imagine every general to be a bandit. Worse fortune than that, Angelica had vanished. Dolt that I was, I had failed to ask her where she lived. The truth is that I feared she would give me a rebuff.

Angelica had disappeared, and my design of making her lover the archbishop of cuckolds had failed. Whenever I imagined that eighteen-year-old damsel in his ignorant arms I writhed. He drove a big automobile—which I regarded as compensation for a small erotical tool—and had hands for changing a rubber tire but not the tender fingers of an amorist.

Shortly afterward I met Portia Kewling. She had a fine, clever nose and a most delightful mouth, but one composed for wit and a quick rejoinder rather than for the kisses of a harper in Jerusalem. Four years older than I, she introduced me to Hegel and to Empedokles and Parmenides, and under her guidance I read with far greater understanding the *Timaeus* and the *Phaedra* of Plato.

By then I had taken a room on Buena Vista Way in the house of a German woman. She had a fifteen-year-old daughter who took a great fancy to my eccentric haircut. Always a foe of the stupid education in our schools, I introduced her—with the most virtuous motives—to *La Maison Tellier* and to *Manon Lescaut*. Some afternoons, when the sun was warm, she used to comb her hair on the upstairs porch within my view, sitting so that I could enjoy her supple and orbed knees. Assuming the role of a preceptor, I disregarded her.

I spoke to Portia of my moral conduct toward this ripe little chit, and with a great deal of pride—only to be laughed at. Portia, showing her fine, intellectual teeth, ridiculed me as we strolled through Strawberry Canyon, saying, "Don't you know you are an immoral Mephisto, and that you will seek the philosopher's stone only to turn all dross into the most precious of all ore—sin?" I reminded her that the girl was fifteen; to which Portia replied that Juliet was only fourteen. Moreover, I was soon repaid for my grandiose moments of goodness: a sophomore began coming on a motorcycle to the house on Buena Vista Way, and very shortly the girl regarded me with scorpion-like hauteur.

One day I stopped at Newbegin's Bookstore on Post Street in San Francisco and purchased a copy of Turgeniev's *Smoke* from a twenty-two-year-old virgin. I was smitten. Consuela had the features of a *mater dolorosa*—and the calves of a peasant. Now I could sing my epithalamium: "I will tread all my woe in the wine press of her flesh." I began seeing her frequently and after two months I was utterly distracted; whatever territory I acquired one week I lost the next. I was allowed limited freedom; her body was divided into precincts, and some were forbidden me. Had I been too virtuous at the outset, I wondered? Any familiarity gained is a step forward, and if one is timorous on the first night, he is sure to be thoroughly routed on the second.

Each week I revised my military strategy; my hands were not utterly famished as she allowed my fingers to pasture on certain swelling flanks, and even her posteriors were not a bastion that could not be taken. However, I mused, if the nipples, those most exquisite morsels, could be captured, then all would be won.

By the third month I was out of my head, as I had been forced to make a cowardly retreat, having been denied certain meadows and grassy lands that had been my free grazing ground. I was put on a soldier's savage ration of a few kisses a visit. I had to cease seeing Consuela, though my agony for her continued to rage.

One night Portia and I were in the back yard of her house, lying on the ground close to an acacia tree. In spite of Portia's unusual mind, she was too prudent—and her mother was more so. The mother had read Sir Richard Burton's pornographic life with terrible dismay and regarded me as no less of an obscenity, although we were always most civil to one another. Yet the mother was no fool and she did not find me completely bad, if only because I respected her intelligence. Only in very stupid moments with women have I failed to show the most unusual esteem for a female's mind. The error in woman is not that she is not extremely clever, but that she often forgets that all her understanding comes from a clear knowledge of her body, which is her imperial intellect.

Portia's mother was a Puritan lecher and she had the bawdy laugh of a Mistress Overdone. Though Portia gave me wise counsel, always reminding me that wit was my genius, I in turn beseeched her not to marry an oilman, or an obstetrician who would be poking about in every matrix he could, or an ironmonger who would give her a pair of Philistine sons or a dry, wary Martha. That night Portia asked me not to take her, and I did not because I was put off by her own penny passions and pocketbook control.

Portia began to avoid me—probably because I had not taken her when she forbade me to; Consuela was most willing to continue our relationship, provided that I refrained from raveling her undergarments. I had seen her only once since we fell out and had told her that Prepuce was as much a saint as Abraham, Isaac or Jerome. She blushed, and I knelt down and kissed the hem of her skirt—which she asserted was less an apology than a lascivious act.

I knew a giantess with the shanks of a stork whom I could have pursued. However, after taking counsel with myself, I decided that it would be far more difficult to win such a deformed trull than Lais of Corinth. An ugly woman has a grudge against nature, including human nature, and she will not countenance the least defect in a man.

On rare occasions I went to a vast hall to hear lectures on botany. There were a thousand and one drones in the classroom—the students and the professor. One Saturday morning, as I was standing in front of the hall, wondering whether I should attend class, I turned to the left and saw a fond smile pooled in brown eyes. It was Angelica. She had been in the botany class all term! All of beauty is in gentle manners, and I will forget the almonds of desire and the plums that purple in the tender months if I ever forget thy gentle pulses.

"Angelica, Angelica, Angelica!" I cried out. When I glanced at her and imagined the hands of that automobile Hittite on her dear, white raiment, I shut myself against her. As the mangled hordes quit the hall I whispered to her, or believed I did, asking whether I could see her. Then I fled before hearing her refusal.

I absented myself from that class, took to my one-room cloister on Buena Vista Way and read. How good it was to be done with the happiness of the flesh, which is nothing more than itching and scraping. Are we not singing worms when we are dead, and do not corpses comprehend true felicity when the flesh is separated from the bones and the skeleton chants as it squirms?

Filled with the false wine of Pater and the wild celibacy of Nietzsche, my plenitude was: "Be mad, O my seed." "But guard it," spoke my sepulchre. In that moment I had a marvelous certitude that I translated into a psalm: I will gaze upon the mandrake apples, and my soul will be content; may I reverence the womb but never go into it. My specious tonsure gave me enormous confidence, and for a time I was not plagued by Satan Pudendum.

But by the following Saturday my monkish room had disappeared, and though in a peripatetic fashion I was reconsidering the *Critias* and the *Apology* of Plato, I discovered that I was on the steps leading to the hall near Sather Gate where another lecture on plants was to be given. What strategy should I now take up? Though she had awakened the seven trembling Pleiades in me, I feared that courtship might imply weakness. What I dreaded most was that infernal moment when I would attempt to breach the chasm between us by placing my hand upon her. I would rather have gone barefoot to Gethsemane than be rejected. Should I not risk a galled denial, I could still have the amorous pangs of a lover. But while I was adopting the canting manners of a polite courtier, the Hittite would still be bruising her teats. Though I had never possessed her, I should be the cuckold. It is not he who comes first or last, but he who desires most who is the real lover, and I reasoned that I had already been a ridiculous wittol for a half a year.

I looked about the lecture hall for Angelica, and I sank; she was not there. Ah, the worm! Like Hamlet's Ophelia, she was babbling about country matters with that churl in some rotten, depraved crevice in Oakland, which was the town of assignation for the rakehells of the campus.

The following week, however, Angelica was there in class and as we walked from the hall I resolved to take her. "Hardness of heart reigned till Christ's time," says Tertullian. But the Messiah had bled in vain for me. I was very unsure of her; besides, whenever I was certain of anything it fell out ill.

I really wanted to go off and be rid of the whole grubby situation, for by now I had not the least sensual desire, but some perverse angel pressed me, and we walked into the Berkeley hills. She repelled me with all the vehemence of her body. My hands were surd and numb, and though she was in my embrace, the globe had soured in my flesh. It was an amative battle. Whether it was on that evening that I possessed her I cannot tell. We think because we are obscure to ourselves, and we shed the night in our hearts and call it light. No matter; whatever transpired, Angelica was no longer the Hittite's.

What occurred later was an orgy; I cured my Sundays in a hotel room in Oakland with Angelica, and later groaned because of my excesses. Then I hid from her, lurking in the darkling thickets of books. Angelica never complained nor came to the monastic cell on Buena Vista Way. It was only when we went for walks together, sauntering along inhaling the joy of broom or acacia buds, and I did not touch her, that my felicity was boundless.

I was now racked because I made a bacchanal of our days in Oakland. Was it to be Golgotha or the bed? But then I could not oppose my demons without entering the swine. I dared not make a covenant with myself, for every resolution I had ever made I violated. What was I to do not to harm Angelica?

When Angelica twined me about her chestnut tresses, I wanted to fall at her feet and chastely press my lips upon her nude body. Spite of my many days with her, I cannot recollect a single pleasure. Why then do we torment ourselves for delights we cannot later recall? The rueful truth is that now I only remember her naked, and worse, though her flesh were the softest prayer of the kneeling heart, I was still as one hungered after our hymeneal celebrations. Was she too slender, her leg too spare? Brantôme has declared that the learned doctors are of the opinion that a big woman is more apt and more delightsome than a small one.

On one Sunday when I was taking my pleasure of Angelica and had come to that moment of music out of our timbrel and sackbut, I cried out, "Consuela!" Angelica had brought manna and quail to my desert, and God, earth and river know I had not thought to commit such a fell offense against her. Do we also sin without intention? He who has had bad dreams knows that he would be good were not his sleep a vile worm in his vision. What with hunger for Angelica, thoughts of Consuela, and then moaning for peace, I sought a remedy for my plight.

After a few unquiet weeks I believed I had found a simple for the dilemma—but another woe for Angelica. I imagined what I was preparing to do was reasonable and good. Oh what moral fangs there are in our rational decisions! Pray unto God, O human gnat, for a wise mistake.

I decided to quit Berkeley, planning to continue my studies at Columbia University. After several months I left

California. What epistles did Angelica later pour out of her sweet flesh, and how many times she called me Christ. She had her revenge against me, but without one drop of malice, for New York was to become a place of the skull for me. Not satisfied, I waited for her to ask me to marry her!

How shall I atone for the beloved Angelica, the bereaved one, the interred one, save as every Edgar Allen Poe who must bury his seraph? How shall I pour out my lament to her to whom I should have brought the torches of Hymen? My grief is in that raw, open grave where all my ghosts walk day and night, and to and fro, wailing before the cock crows: "Nymph, in thy orisons, be all my sins remembered."

IX   *And so . . . my mother . . . .*
Hamlet

Before going to New York, I returned to Kansas City, the burial ground of all my memories, and where my mother was still the proprietor of the Star Lady Barbershop. She was fifty years old now, with scrawny, nervous hair colored with a cheap henna dye. Ever since Popkin, her second husband, had taken all her savings, she had lost her bloom, though she was still vigorous. Her strength shone through her clouts.

My mother's appearance humiliated me. When I regarded the loose, dangling throat and the skin of her face that was beginning to yellow, or looked at a straggling shoelace, I thought no other son was so unfortunate as I. How I once envied Marion Moneysmith, whose mother had been a pretty woman with such a tidy figure. The young are savage and do not realize that after a short while they too will be dry, crumpled leaves. But wrinkles and rough guts in the skin are symptoms of compassion—that were not seen in the same man when his complexion was radiant but his features blank.

My mother continued to prate over her respectability,

mentioning how noble she was, though there was always some man hanging around her. Still a very passionate woman, she once told me, as we sat on the front porch at the 8th Street flat on an August evening, that Captain Henry Smith had been all played out by the time she met him. How many regal and delicious women, who ache to eat of the tree of knowledge because the fruit is a delight, have tolerated impotent men.

When I considered my mother's privy sheets and illicit pillowcases I abhorred them, though I myself was weaker than grass. If I saw a milkwhite rump, my body became a seminal song. My flesh cried: let me smell her sandals or clap my nose upon her navel, for I hunger, itch, piss, eat and die. In spite of my own incontinent blood, I refused to see that a grim angel had warped my mother's luck, and that she was deprived of one constant man who would cherish her paps.

That she was a drudge in a barbershop and spent the pennies she earned on a son more useless than a gnat did not occur to me. Nor did I realize that she was far more honest than Society, which had rejected her. Was she not an angelic pariah? Little wonder that I myself would roam through the earth, and that wherever I was a wild forest would spring up around me. However, by the time I had come to have a moiety of my mother's good sense, I was more afraid of virtue than of vice.

For a while Lizzie saw an old-time railroader named Circlear who had previously been a steady customer. He was a fancy tipper in the old days and after having a massage, haircut and tonic, Circlear would get up from the chair in his sporting braces and, bantering me, he would say, "If you'll cover your Jew nose with your hand, I'll give you a dollar." The girls believed this was a tremendous piece of wit, but I never thought about anything except the dollar, though I was sometimes chased by neighborhood boys and called a Sheeney.

Although my mother had stopped investing in imaginary oil wells, or in Coca-Cola when shares were offered for sale to the public, she was now speculating in something far wilder—the man business.

Circlear was no longer a sport nor connected with the Burlington Railroad. Formerly, he revealed, he had been a vice-president of that railway company and had had a private Pullman car for his office. He confided to my mother that during the War his Chinese cook, since deceased, had buried a million dollars for him and that when the time was ripe he would take the fortune from its hiding place and share it with her.

The imperial offices of the Burlington Railroad were on Walnut Street, no more than a few blocks from the 8th Street viaduct, but my mother was too timorous to enquire whether his tale were true. She cringed when she thought of asking a high Burlington official whether he knew Circlear; she was sure that a prince of such a realm would exclaim: "Madam, will you leave these premises at once, or must I call the police!" She had an infernal fear of rich people; the invisible grace of money that is represented in the visible grace of the law was never questioned by her.

Circlear washed clothes for Lizzie at the flat, swept up the hair from the floor before the shop was closed, counted the dirty barber towels, mopped the linoleum, cleaned out the spittoons and carried home her basket filled with grapes, St. John's bread, Winesaps, jars of orange marmalade and marinated herring. But after a time he drifted away.

Then Lizzie complained of a flaccid, dropping belly. She had gone under the knife three times; her new surgeon, in whom she had the utmost confidence, was a Doctor Joy, who had a medical diploma from the College of Hippocrates, which was somewhere in a Mississippi bog. Whenever she had the blues, she thought of having an operation. However, if she saw a marriage opportunity she became quite spirited again.

On the first evening that a new beau came to call, she would primp, daub her seamy neck and face with several kinds of creams and dust her breast with talcum powder; then she put on the gold-embroidered linen dress that Popkin had brought back from Jerusalem and pinned her watch to her bosom. Tokay grapes hung over the rim of the cut-glass bowl, and the settee was polished and placed near the sofa, so that they could talk to each other and be close but still refined. She had no intention of hurrying into the flabby arms of a short, stale miser.

There was not much variety to the sort of beaus who came into Lizzie's parlor; they were stubby, with round, parsimonious necks, and wore blue serge suits and vests with a pocket for a watch that was as large as a silver dollar. If the evening courtship were not going well, or her guest took out his Hamilton railroad timepiece from his vest pocket earlier than he should have, Lizzie hopped to her feet at once. She would help him into his coat with a flurry of haste and show him to the door with more passion than she had anticipated.

Usually when she had a visitor she would walk very slowly toward the upright piano, almost swaying as she tiptoed, and after wiping the yellow keys with a chamois cloth—which she had already done before he had arrived— she would run over her scales for several minutes. She then played a few notes from *Cavalleria Rusticana* before turning to her favorite semi-classic: "I was jealous and hurt when your lips kissed a rose, or your eyes from my own chanced to stray."

She had a thin treble, quite soft and courteous, and sometimes she removed her pince-nez glasses after she had turned one of the pages of the sheet music to give her recital a professional touch. She was extremely proud that she could read the score and did not have to play by ear like some of the common 12th Street trash.

Following her performance, she would set a saucer and

napkin near her guest on the oval-shaped mahogany table so that he could put the grape skins on the dish and politely wipe his chin with the napkin. She nibbled a few grapes—so that she could part her lips just enough to show what kind of a family she had come from; delicately spitting out the seeds, she heaped them into a cultured, neat pile on her saucer. The embroidered napkins smelled of moth balls, since she never used them except for such occasions.

Lizzie was the most finished listener for the first night or two. She wanted to find out whether she had a four-flusher on her hands; she felt sure she could recognize an old two-timer or a shrewd windbag the moment she smelled him. If her bladder troubled her, she did not make shift or put herself out, and often she grew tired of the game before she could believe in it. Otherwise, she did her best to give herself the right sort of advice, and I often heard her speak aloud to herself without knowing it, saying that one had to take a chance with a two-faced schemer just as one did with any other risky business proposition. Had she not learned that much from those low chippies? Give a man his way, but just so far, until he lost his footing. Well, a piece of he-nonsense was a big gamble, but she would come out all right.

She showed the visitor every civility, bowing now and then to words whose sense only came later to her mind, but her thoughts were of Captain Henry Smith. What a dandy, rosy future they would have had together; he was a stingy one, but jolly, and what company over a solid rib steak or a plate of stewed oysters, with a bottle of Bock beer.

In her mind she could still see the Captain with his hair peeled off like the gilt of a picture frame. He had often been grumpy and he belched, broke wind and sometimes smelled sour, but how she used to enjoy washing out his drawers and smelly socks! He was a pot-like man, a big, sweaty laugher, small where he should have been long—but you can't have everything in this world. The steamboat trade was finished;

the Missouri River was dead, but it was so much better to have a man fill the rooms. Pshaw, you can have all the clean white linen there is, but if there isn't some man-dirt on the sheets what good is it? Then he had run off with that rotten little piece from St. Louis; his sister, Clara, had written her that she was a good fifty-seven—an old hen, you could be sure of that.

Kansas City remained still half rural; the elms and maples lining the streets gave health to the heart and the lungs. Yet there were those long periods of dryness in her, followed by that gentlest rain in the spirit, hope. Yes, it was still a wooden rather than an iron town, and the rocky hills, and the clothes hanging on the lines and flagging in the breeze eased her.

But when my mother asked herself what could she do with her life, God was as deaf as the adder. The Lord chastises those whom he loves, but why had He placed a heavy rod upon her neck? For what reason must she drink the bitter waters?

The tears that spring from the flood of Noah and which cover our nights ran down Lizzie's loose cheeks. What was left of her mouth? My God, where do the swelling hips go? And the skin dries on the wrist and hand, and the leg shrinks. Her bosom once could make a man forget that he was in the dumps; and her calves—the skirt-chasers would turn their necks around to look. But that was past, and so much of her had disappeared. Good Lord, we die all day long and every hour; each minute we age somewhere in our bones. She examined her hands and half shut her eyes so as not to see too plainly the coarse, tortoise-shelled veins. How much she had accomplished with her fingers! But how hard they had grown; you can't handle steel scissors and a hair clipper all day long and have a smooth, lady's hands. How honest can you be when you have nothing in this world except a pair of hands—and with a son to take care of, too? Poor Emma Moneysmith used to say it was fine to have principles—if you were rich enough to afford them. Not even Cromwell, that good old soul, who was an alderman, could swear that all the dollars in his safe were legal. Oh, sing the song of money, the psalm of deceit! Who isn't a cheat? And who has a sock on his foot, a shirt button or a corset that is not ill-gotten and whore-rotten?

Should she not be rewarded in some way? Had she not held her head high? What had she gotten for twenty-seven years of drudging, cutting hair and shaving the tough, gray whiskers of switchmen, railroaders, deadbeats and bluffers, and of massaging old rounders? And oh how she ached when night came. . . . O God, do not forsake me; I have nothing between me and the gutter except my pair of scissors, my razor and hone and hair clipper. Let me live long enough to hear the grass coming up in Northmoor, and to bend over my plump, red tomatoes. Give me, for I am alone, another fifty summers and Aprils, and fifty more hopes; it's so little to ask. Do not go away, O God, lest I die. Die? What is that? Can that be? Is it possible to disappear? Look, I am a womb, a belly where I had my son, Edward, two hands and a pair of stout feet. Do you, O Lord, really kill people? The Holy Living God is no thief that comes in the night and breaks into your soul and carries it away. This cannot be. I know it; for as I breathe, I will never die; would not my body, my lungs, heart and bowels tell me! . . .

Lizzie, on a sudden, awakened from her reverie. Her small, wrinkled brown eyes were slyly peering over her glasses at the man in the parlor; the skins of the grapes were slobbered over his meaty, nether lip. His loose buttocks spread morosely over the chintz cover on the settee. How could she take a worm-eaten crank like that into her polite bed? He told her of the ketchup factory he owned in the West Bottoms, and the thousands of shares he had in the brand-new $50,000,000 Union Station out at 15th and Main Streets. Nearsighted, she was positive his vest was frayed;

she could not keep her eyes off the grape pulp that slopped about his mouth, though she endeavored to show the strictest attention to what he was saying. Wasn't he wearing a secondhand blue serge suit? But then every bachelor was a born miser. Yet one had to have some confidence in the public; there was, she had to admit, a kind of pleasant odor of high-tone money about him.

He now assured her that he would lend her a thousand dollars at six per cent interest, or if she wished she could give him a second mortgage on the cottage Captain Henry Smith had built in Northmoor. Lizzie had spoken of her desire to invest a small sum in property or land in that country village. Before another suitor had come up the steps, she had earnestly made a vow to herself that she would be patient, wait and let him slip a little into the net—and when she had caught him, she would make a real bargain for herself. Let him propose first, and then she could make him a plain speech: "Sir, I know you have a noble heart, and I regard your offer of marriage as true blue; but don't you think it would only be respectable for you to set aside so many thousands of dollars in my name? God forbid that anything should happen to you . . . well, let's not look at the dark side of things." Her original elocution was far more eloquent than this, but after all why should she take such pains and be so careful with a short slob? He must certainly be past his seventieth year. Look at his old stomach, and rumbling all evening, so that she could hardly hear what she had been saying to herself. What was there in it for her, except a marriage license, if he refused to cough up some of his fortune?

As usual she was too nervous to wait, and her blood was so heady that no matter what a miserable prospect a man appeared to be, she had to go on with her intrigue, just to discover how it would turn out, though she had not the least intention of marrying this sort of man. She was mighty particular about her brass bed in the alcove. If he thought he could get under the blankets without first putting everything down on paper in black and white, he was too stupid for her.

Accustomed to grasping the meaning of what others said some time after it was uttered, she leaped up abruptly when she caught the words *lend* and *second mortgage*, which had reached the bottom of her nature and by now were coming back in a great tidal wave. She rose at once to her feet to show that cheap skate out of her courteous parlor.

Then when she remembered that he had called without even bringing her a box of Lowney's chocolates or a bouquet of roses, or so much as said, "Here is a sack of fruit," she went into the kitchen and watered the geraniums and afterwards made a broken prayer, half in Hebrew and the rest in midwestern American: "*Baruch atah Adonai Elohenu* . . ." Deploring her situation, she sobbed, "I'm the most unlucky woman on the earth; my eyes are so strained from cutting hair I can hardly see straight, and my bladder has dropped, Doctor Joy told me. . . ."

After the curmudgeon had left she closed the mahogany piano, picked up the one good rug, which was the meal of the moth, and put it away in the clothes closet. Then she took off her parlor dress, removed her one pair of patent leather shoes and put on a smeary kitchen apron. She shuffled aimlessly from the sitting room to the alcove, while the pince-nez, fastened to one ear by a thin gold wire, kept falling onto her breast.

She dusted the postcards in the parlor, then stumbled back to the kitchen to light the gas range and heat the pot of soup she had made the day before. Suddenly she became frantic because she could not find her glasses. Sitting in a straight, oak chair next to the table, and staring at the mouldy crumbs, flies and chunks of sodden bread she was in the habit of tearing out of the loaf, she moaned, "I'm blind; I cannot see, O God." Her hands fumbled over her heart, and she felt the pince-nez against her apron; with a sigh of gratitude, she went on with her orison—perhaps God would not forsake her after all.

The next morning she got up and took her cold bath, which she believed would keep the seams out of her complexion and would invigorate her lungs and heart. She shook out her blanket on the latticed back porch which was strewn with sun, and when the air was upon her bare neck and cheeks she revived. A very deep sleeper, she had awakened earlier than usual this morning; she had to open up the shop herself; that acid hypocrite Harney was in bed, either with the drummer who sold Rogers' silverware or because of her troublesome appendix, and wouldn't be at her chair that day.

For a short while Lizzie sat on the rear steps that were four stories up, putting cold cream on her face, neck and arms; it was the latest vanishing cream for wrinkles. She wished she could sell the Star Lady Barbershop and be rid of those chippies; they were always tramping from one bed to another or chasing a rancher or a sucker from Oklahoma City. No wonder she stole their checks—they were no good anyway. And why not? Business was business.

When she walked along 8th Street to open the shop, her feet were so slow and she had a miserable, heavy feeling; what she needed was an operation. Then she remembered her son who still lay sleeping in one of the bedrooms at the flat, and she cried, "O son of my bowels, and of all my troubles, you whom I carried in my arms from Dallas to Memphis, to Louisville, to New Orleans, to Denver, to Kansas City. What a skinny one you are, and still so green around a woman. You ought to fill out a little. Why don't you run about with a hussy or two, like Stedna's son? O Edward, my son, son of all my hopes!"

My life was a heavy affliction to me at this time; the chasm between my mother and me had widened. I blamed her for everything; whom else could I find fault with except my sole protector? Why had she not provided me with a family? Could the bastard issue of a lady barber with dyed, frizzled hair amount to anything? Why had not my mother given up that common trade? Was I to stumble in the winds, too? No matter how we begin our lives it is a misfortune. One has to overcome the best as well as the worst of circumstances. But thinking this did not help me; my grievous childhood stuck in my gizzard, and I recalled how Captain Henry Smith had persuaded my mother to send me to an orphanage.

Now the sight of a suitor in loose, acid pants and slept-in suspenders made me prudish. How could my mother stomach such men? How immoral was her sensual hymn of flesh and sweat to me. It is everybody's folly to judge others; did we not do so there would be no morals at all. Lizzie always tried to keep me from seeing what went on between herself and her admirers. They were of use, though swill to her imagination. Nor could I bear any longer that cranny at 16 East 8th Street; when I saw the cuspidors bespattered with tobacco juice and watched one of the barber girls step away from her chair to cast her phlegm into one of them, I ran out of the shop.

I had acquired airs and prejudices that I believed were natural. How much difference is there between the educated and the commoner sort except in the way they spit and rasp their throats? It takes no more than a single adage from Lord Chesterfield to make a debonair fop: "Do not look into your handkerchief after you blow your nose."

Who is my father? was my continual liturgy. Was I got upon the knop of a little hillock, like Gargantua? It did not matter. Not where or how, but who? Has not the pismire a sire? (Eber was born unto Shem, and Cush begat Nimrod, but who begot me? In an old midrash it is told that birds are fashioned out of marshy ground saturated with water. Was my origin similar, or did I come out of the loins of the maggot? We live in an unfilial age, and though the son curse the father, he ranges the whole earth looking for the Cave of Machpelah, where lie Abraham, Isaac and Jacob.

Had I no progenitor? Christ can revivify mouldy Lazarus, but who can raise the living from the grave? I wanted to feel, but had no emotions, and I sighed for thoughts and had no conceptions. My sleep spoke to me, but it was slack and shoaly, and it came up only as far as my ankles, and I could not drink it. I was a dark root of nothing, and my own emptiness groaned. An hour would come when morning, like a cerecloth, would be wrapped around me, and I would say, "I never had a mother; she neither was nor is." I heard the pangs of this phantom, but she was invisible. She was next to her son, and she was not. There were myriads of galled and palsied phantoms who gnawed themselves, and yet were starved, for they ate their ribs that did not exist and supped upon a vacant chin or neck. They wailed all night and at daybreak, when the cock crowed, they fled. What ailed them most was the cold; for unless they could warm themselves in some other wraith's pulses or find a covert in a coat pocket or crawl through a hole in an imaginary gloved hand, they could not be seen. Sometimes they hung upon a neck that had been kissed and embraced, and were perched there like some great pensive bird or cherub, and though terrible winds blew upon them from the Void, they would not leave this nesting place.

We are nothing, we know, though God has feigned we are something. We have been deceived, O First Cause and Mocker—you who told us we were created. What is there betwixt our coming and our dying but the fumes rising up out of Nowhere? The fool licks the fat and scum of this non-existence until he is gouty and swollen.

How long is misery? I cried; how much space is there between Nazareth and Capernaum, those apocryphal, pneumatic towns that lie in the gullet of the paraclete?

I said, "Let there be darkness, for I cannot see in the light; and my sepulchre laughed at Him who pretended that on the fourth day He had made the moon, the stars, fish, birds, mice and the dream, and who thought He had created Adam on the sixth day." But I spurned Him and said, "When Thou gavest man dreams, he knew that Thou hadst lied to him, even to Thyself, for Thou hast created nothing." And I bellowed, "Take away Thy follies and images and Thy six days of Void, for all that I require is the DREAM. Why didst Thou plague Adam with a conscience, for what need has man of it when his visions of the night judge him?" Wrinkled and old, I lifted up my voice and wept, "Thou knowest well there are no days, and that time is only the noise of the wings of the seraphim. Away with Thy sun; are not ashes wiser than the flame, and does not the moon know more than the sun? Thou nihilist, does a phantasm require anything which is nothing, except the dream, for if a man perceives as he sleeps, what has he but a trance when he awakens?"

Meanwhile Sirach sat in my ear, which was stuffed with the adage: "And forget not thy mother who bare thee in pangs." She sat in the parlor on the oak rocker, hiding behind the *Kansas City Star*. She knew what was in my mind. Was I not her belly, hand and feet, and did she not comprehend her own flesh? On a sanitary inspection tour of the rooms, I glanced about the kitchen; what a babel of greasy dishes, bent, charred saucepans and pots. Flies hovered over the crumbs and smutty cups and dishes on the oilcloth. Another pile of plates, slimy with yesterday's food, stood in the sink. There was an aluminum casserole filled with a withered scum of soup and suet. I opened the door to the oven of the gas range and saw a copy of Fielding's *Tom Jones* inside. It was stained with butter, and pieces of bread and orange peelings lay on top of it. My mother had resolved to be educated.

A few days before, in one of our easy, jocular moments, when we were playing pinochle, she had asked me whether such dirty words as Fielding used were literature, and her eyes were rinsed with tears of mirth. While she was relating that the picaresque language of Fielding was no different from the everyday words of chippies, I caught her cheating. My cheeks burned with fever and I said that she had no principles. We had the fewest of agreeable moments with one another.

Carrying the soiled volume of *Tom Jones* into the parlor, I upbraided my mother; why had she put Fielding into the bake oven? But she made no answer. I stared at the copious brass bed in the alcove where my mother had lain with Harry Cohen, who had burnt his team of horses to collect money from the insurance company. I heard that he now had a pair of upstairs rooms in Independence Avenue where he lived with a decayed whore. Harry Cohen was a parcel of my boyhood, and I yearned to look upon his face. What is foul feeds the eyes also; besides, I was so alone and had nobody to speak to but my own tomb. And so I visited him, but when he turned to his bony prostitute who called him "Daddy," I went away undone.

Moving around listlessly in our sitting room, I looked at my childhood. All my kin were in this room: there was my aunt, the mahogany oval-shaped table; the cut-glass bowl in the center of the table was my sister; in the corner of the parlor was an avuncular oak table, and the settee, which was for company, was my cousin. What an orphan I would have been without this familied room. My fingers would have been waifs in the world, and my hands no part of my body, if my mother moved away from the 8th Street flat. I had been begotten in Boston, but this was my borning-room; here I had hoped and dwindled and now I died every hour.

I had forgotten that my mother was in the parlor with me. Then I looked at that woman, less than five feet of relentless will. Oh God, her stockings were sick and raveled again. Could I have come out of such wild rags? She was still sitting in the rocker, the upper part of her torso covered by the newspaper. My neck was hard. She rocked slow and sly, peering at me, I knew. How could I wrest from her the knowledge of my beginnings?

When I turned toward her, all my interred bones groaned: "I am a man, and there are ghosts of trees and a ravine howling within me, and at the root of a mountain sits a man. Who is he? You have always talked to me about your father, sisters and brothers, but I never saw one of them. What relations have I ever had or touched or smelled? In what city are my father's footprints? Does he walk, does he breathe, and is he suckled by the winds? See, I am a shade emptied of ancestors; I am twenty-three years old and grown into full sorrow."

The rocker was mute, and I stood there filled with a fatherless emptiness. Stepping backward, I slipped on a tattered, woolly rug and I shouted, "O heaven, these rags, all our hopes have been moth-eaten rags."

Then I caught sight of the rusty tin rack of stale post-cards on the wall. What paternal finger had grazed that faded brown wallpaper? For a moment I stood bowed in front of these holy relics: there were three scenic views of Swope Park, one of Fairmount Park, one of Cliff Drive, another of Swift's packing house. There was the Grand Opera House where Chauncey Alcott had sung so many times, and the Willis Woods Theater where I had seen Anna Held when I was eight. There were the photographs of the old-timers; Lizzie never threw anything away, not even a reminder of her most wretched experiences.

I studied a card that showed Lizzie when her hair was still brown and tender and her face had a meditative contour. Next, the U.S. Major, bald, with a stylish military mustache, and in uniform, stared at me—but he had been too pallid for my mother's bed. I passed him to glance at skinny Birdie, then Gladys from Tulsa, and Blanche Beasley, for whose stupendous buttocks a cashier for the M-K-T had stolen ten thousand dollars. What a victual was Ruby du Parr, but destined for the public stews, and there was the dear, fetching figure of Emma Moneysmith. Such a big-trousered man was Hagen. Popkin had a spruce, carroty mustache, with tidy fringes of hair around his ears and neck, but he looked so quick and tailored. And old Cromwell, wearing spectacles, who was now in his grave; he would never let anyone give him a chin-scrape except Lizzie.

My origins were still unriddled. The rocker was creaking; the newspaper lay on my mother's crumpled kitchen apron. When I contemplated her untied shoelaces, I moaned, "You sent me to an orphanage because Henry was fat and I leaned on him; before that I was in a Catholic home, and then in a parochial school where the boys beat me every day because I was a Jew."

The woman, so distant from my anguish and the bitterness of my days, now replied, "My son, when I went under the knife, what could I do? I sent you to the Jewish home in Cleveland because I could not manage you. You were in the streets all day, and sick and puking, and I had the scissors and comb in my hands. I could not give you regular meals or control you. What could I accomplish with a widow's ten fingers, and who was there to help me? Do you think I could find money in the gutter? I wanted you to be high-tone; you have the aristocratic face, my son, of my brother Ignatz, may he rest in peace."

"Don't mention a brother or sister to me; even a worm has a parent, but nobody begat me. I am nothing, and I came out of nowhere," and I was filled with gall, and layers of grief lay over it. I heard Job on his muckheap: "The ox knoweth his owner, and the ass his master's crib."

I crossed the front room, returning to the tin rack of postcards, for these sepulchral memories bound my mother and me together. On a sudden, I was gazing at a hand-tinted picture of a man with the curls of a dandy; he wore the dude's chestnut-colored vest with the usual fob, gold chain and watch. He was showing the teeth of the fox that spoils the vines. It was Saul! Whenever business was slow or her bladder gave her that desponding, dragging feeling, Lizzie would often exclaim, "May Saul burn in hell," and then breaking off into German, she would let out a blasphemy: "*Verdammter Saul!*"

I pulled the tintype out of the rack and leaning against the cemetery of postcards, I roared, "It is Saul! Who else could my father be? I know it is Saul. My blood is ruined; a thousand lusts boil in his skin and in his tumored brain. But where is he? You must know. He is my father. Tell me, I must know . . . or live and die unborn . . . for I will wail all the hours of my flesh if I am unfilled by a father!"

She sat immovable. No grave was more silent than she, and no matter what words and sounds I made, she did not move. I stared at her helplessly, for she was a terrible headstone without an epitaph, from which no secret could be wrung.

Fortune ruleth in everything: disposing of them according to her will rather than unto truth.

Sallust

In 1925, my mother sold the Star Lady Barbershop and moved out to the grassy Missouri village called Northmoor, a short distance from Kansas City. There she had acquired a two-family stucco duplex, one half of which she occupied. It was about fifteen yards from the clapboard cottage Captain Henry Smith had built. Also, in exchange for the barbershop, including the value of its good will, she had obtained a wooden bungalow in North Kansas City. With the help of her son, now teaching school in New York after his graduation from Columbia, she bought four hundred Rhode Island Reds and Plymouth Rocks and sold eggs and broilers, thus adding to the pittance she derived from renting her three small properties.

A very agile woman, mewed up in her four walls, chicken coops and back yard because she feared the galling bigotry and gossip of rural folk, Lizzie resolved once again to improve her circumstances. In order to find a suitable companion, she inserted an advertisement in a matrimonial gazette. She had rewritten this notice, before sending it to the periodical for publication, above twenty times. She requested that the following item be printed as soon as possible: A highly polished widow, a young forty-four, with five languages at her finger tips, as well as an accomplished pianist, desires to meet a cultured bachelor who is a good conversationalist, and a man of considerable means. Object: Marriage.

Shortly thereafter Lizzie received a letter in which a gentleman expressed himself in lengthy sentences that were both emotional and gallant. He described himself as a retired manufacturer, though still in the prime of life, and very light on his feet. Not given to boasting, he added, he had the highest taste for literature. Though neither tall nor short, he had a rosy complexion and was withal not fat nor a skeleton either, and could prove at first blush, and without peradventure of a doubt, that he was a seasoned talker. Although in the middle of life, he had hardly come to the beginning, and if he were not stylish in appearance, he could amend that by his faultless deportment. He said he was not looking for any kind of brutal or cheap amusement, since he had the most elegant and lofty regard for the opposite sex. He wrote that he would call on Saturday.

Lizzie was exceedingly impressed by his educated language, but was confused by the three snapshots of himself which he had enclosed with the letter. In one picture he had wavy, chestnut hair, parted most tidily down the center of his head, and a well-bred though conspicuous nose. The second picture was puzzling to her, for it did not resemble the first: here he had on glasses with thick, bifocal lenses, and his jaw was long and loose. His face was far more sparse, looking as though it had been flensed, and the nose appeared to have spread or grown up since the first picture was taken. With even more gravity and suspicion, she scrutinized the third photograph. In this one he was standing on a front lawn shaded by a large, rock-ribbed house, and either because he was in a shadow or the snapshot was poor, his hair looked more like a January frost than August foliage; he was emaciated, if not wholly dilapidated. More baffling, his mouth was so sunken that it occurred to her that he must have forgotten his false teeth that day. In all three pictures he had on big galoshes, a winter coat, a heavy flannel muffler, and carried an umbrella. Since the pictures were taken outdoors, the sun must have been shining, but what was he doing with rubbers on and an umbrella? She hoped he was not a crank or had weak lungs.

Saturday morning Lizzie wore a freshly laundered kitchen apron and silk stockings that did not match; the evening before she had retouched her hair. Awaiting her prospect with the utmost impatience, she rubbed off the Marsha's Tennessee Face Cream she had smeared on her cheeks and forehead, and sat in the oak rocker for two minutes trying to read a page of *Moll Flanders*. She then hurried out to the yard and stepped into one of the coops to see whether her hens had laid any eggs. She thought about the stature of the gentleman who had not yet arrived. Even if he were short, she prayed that he had not a sickly, sallow complexion borrowed from the tallow of a candle. Still, if a man were no taller than she, he would not be the energetic type; a man ought to have enough ambition to be higher than a woman. Lizzie was also troubled about the effect she might have upon a debonair bachelor. Naturally she had lied about her age; she was sixty, and though her skin was as clear as a babe's, she was worried about her throat, which could have been stitched together by the thread of a tailor. But a woman who is mellowing—and is thus far more serviceable to a mature man than a green bantling—has to cover her neck, which ages first. It was odd: her feet were quick, her torso succulent and buxom (and who could deny that she had young, virile nipples?), but the worst signs and symptoms of failure, disappointment and years, which were otherwise imperceptible, had showed themselves first in her throat. Hurrying to the dresser drawer, and throwing the pincushion, a pair of ragged woollen drawers, a torn pillowcase and a heap of moth balls on the floor, she found a small silk scarf that she wrapped around her neck—but quite loosely, as she felt as if she were suffocating if anything on her were tight.

Then lying on the bed and forgetting the pile of clouts on the floor, she endeavored once more to envisage the retired manufacturer. She did not care to have a miserable stump of a male dragging at her heels; were he skinny he would not be the enthusiastic sort. A poor feeder at the table made her downcast; she had never laid eyes on a man with a mean appetite who was not stingy.

At noon Tobias Emeritch knocked on the door. Lizzie greeted him and took him into the sitting room. After looking into her eyes and prancing about her, he began kissing both her hands. He smelled of cheap hair tonic. The odor was disagreeable, and although she had not yet had time to recover from his triumphal entry and to notice how old he was, she had already come to the conclusion that an old man smells worse than a young one.

Lizzie's ecstasy vanished. She was so overcome by the man's appearance that she fell into a painful reverie. Was this a nation of squat, pasty men with kitchen-garden noses? Circlear had had a low, slouchy stomach that ran into his lap when he was seated, and though this one had a far more frugal countenance, he was no different from her former admirer. When Tobias Emeritch lifted his insufficient mouth from her two hands and stood erect, she thought he was either sitting down or exhibiting only his bust. By now Lizzie herself was fidgety and her forehead flushed; without knowing how brusque her words were, she exclaimed, "For God's sake, sit down, or keep quiet, or stand still. What are you—a young bull in heat?" He sank down onto the couch, altogether worn out.

Having somewhat recovered, Lizzie began to take inventory of her suitor's visible merchandise. What was breathing or even rattling inside his secondhand suit she could rather surmise. His overcoat, which he had not yet removed, had a frayed black velvet collar. He wore a silk cravat with stripes that hurt her eyes, and he had not taken off his muffler or his galoshes. Still lounging, he was shaking the dust out of his umbrella. Lizzie jumped up from the rocking chair, grasped the umbrella as though she had a cat by the scruff of the neck and exhorted him, "Don't make yourself at home so quickly. Give me a chance to get used to a brand-new article like you. Besides, sir, I've just mopped and scrubbed the floor. Can't you see it is still wet?"

Whereupon Tobias Emeritch endeavored to put on his rubbers—which were still covering his shoes.

Lizzie now hopped to the window, drew the curtains aside, and seeing the sun was clear, she ventured to ask him, "Do you wear rubbers because you're cold? We've had a long dry spell, so what are you doing with an umbrella?"

She noticed the sleeves of his undershirt hanging out beyond his detachable starched cuffs, which made her positive that he was extremely wary and parsimonious. Lizzie herself wore long woollen underwear, winter and summer, but that was for her rheumatism, and quite different.

This creature seemed an unusual acquaintance already; if the first impression was hazy and perplexing, what would she make of him later on? The longer you know a person, the more nebulous he becomes; by the time you are friends, you may be strangers to one another.

As though he were speaking to nobody, he began, "You know, lady, it could pour, hail or there might be a sudden snowfall; I simply cannot afford to take chances."

It seemed to her that whatever remark she made he

did not hear it, and though now and then he cupped one ear as if he were hard of hearing, it was obvious that he had no intention of listening to her. Evidently, he also forgot whatever he had said and pursued his own thoughts, whether relevant or not, imagining them far more significant than somebody else's refuse.

"This is a duplex, is it not? Would you say your next-door tenant is in arrears? Without any prejudice to your lofty character, may I ask, do you indulge in foolish recreations, such as a worthless stage show? Are you in the habit of taking cognac or sitting in public restaurants by yourself? Do you go for a walk after six-thirty in the evening when you are sure to be accosted?"

Who but she could have discovered such a specimen? She was quite exasperated, for now he was digging the toe of one rubber through a hole in the rug. He started up again: "What did you do with my umbrella? It has a genuine silk lining, and I picked it up at the Salvation Army. Where is my flannel muffler?"

"Do you take me for a thief? You've got your umbrella in your right hand, and if you don't get out of that suffocating muffler, you'll catch cold. Maybe you're running a fever. Do you ever see a doctor?"

"See a doctor? I'm a discouraged man, but why should I be that despondent? If a physician tells me I'm sick, would it be prudent to give him money just for giving me bad news? A doctor who doesn't tell you that you're in perfect health is likely to worry you to death. Lady, I don't believe I caught your name, but never mind. Every time I meet a new person he gives me such a load of gas on my stomach that I am unable to sleep until I have evacuated him. You must realize that I do not have a sunny disposition; it's better, don't you think, to come right to the point, and not to deceive anybody. Did I not tell you that I was a big reader? I'm a disciple of Arthur Schopenhauer, the pessimistic philosopher. Whenever I have a little spare time I read him."

Lizzie had to admit that this man was no boor; in some vague way she regarded a book as a demigod and she could not help having elevated emotions about a man who had both knowledge and money—a very weird and abnormal combination in this world. Her son always told her that learning and money were never in the same pocket. But why did this guest have to be so melancholy?

Impressed by his mention of Schopenhauer, and now softening her manner, she suggested quite hesitantly, "Do you have to be dejected all the time? One should have a little hope."

"What will it get you but a little more hope? And one expectation weakens the next one, and in a little while you are so disappointed that you have no prospects at all. One's life is absolutely unendurable unless one's outlook on life is hopeless."

Lizzie was rocking and only half listening. She was utterly forlorn and wished she had something to do. So long as she was occupied her skin crowed, and since she had given up the barbershop, solitude hummed around the watery marges of her soul.

Perhaps she ought to excuse herself and get into her loud, geranium-colored dress; scarlet cottons revived her spirits, and made her look plumper. Moreover, red could make a fool out of a passionate man—but she was in no mood for such nonsense.

Tobias Emeritch, seeing that she was remote from him, felt that he had better do something to enliven their colloquy, and he commenced anew: "It must be damp. I've got such rheumatism."

Should she go out and examine her tomatoes?

"It must have cost you something," he went on, "to put up this stucco duplex." Tobias Emeritch was chewing the upper part of his lip and then feeding on the lower one, which he found more suitable to his cogitations. Now that the space between him and Lizzie had increased, he grew moody. Well, it was useless going on in that vein, and he asked, "How much is horse-radish this year? Do you know that during the War you could not buy German sauer-kraut? I wonder what a quart of sour cream brings, or if a barrel of smoked whitefish has gone up since last June? If you are in the market for coleslaw, I could do something for you, or should you be interested in pickles—dill or sweet, wrinkled ones, it makes no difference to me . . . I'm a retired manufacturer of pickles, myself."

How could she collect her own wayward mind? She remembered that another suitor had a ketchup factory in the West Bottoms, and that he had a similar kind of bent-in pot of a head and that his nose resembled a potato. Neither the former suitor nor Tobias Emeritch had enough energy to reach any higher than five feet one. She was sure Emer-itch would not be able to extend himself in any other way either.

Lizzie enquired, "Are you in the ketchup trade also? Are you positive, sir, that you don't have an uncle or a distant cousin who's a wholesaler in sauces, relishes or cucumbers?"

"Absolutely not. The reason that I did not mention cucumbers is that they remind me of my youth. After all, I was dilling cucumbers for nearly fifty years and, discon-tented like everybody else in this world, I wished that I had been pickling beets instead. Madam, I do have a brother who is also retired. He's past his ninetieth year, but still com-mercial-minded; one could say that he's in the life busi-ness, a very dreary and tedious occupation, though I admire brother Ebner. His only thought now is to reach his hundredth year. Imagine, as monotonous as life is, and thoroughly unbearable when you come to think of it, he declares that after his one hundredth year he will aim to reach a hundred and ten. Till this day, I cannot say whether people long more for something acid in a very dry season or in a wet one. With women, it's another matter; did you ever know an intelligent and healthy woman who did not hanker after a cucumber salad? You see, I am in the habit of brooding, though I am no great eater myself, for no matter what food you put into your stomach you're sure to get a disease for doing it. Peas give you gas, cabbage sours your whole system and one plate of spaghetti is enough to rush one of your relations to a dealer in tombstones. Frankly, I would not eat if I could avoid it. It would be more prudent to keep quiet also; almost every word that drops out of your mouth would have been wiser if it escaped through your upper or lower colon. Walking would be preferable if one had somewhere to go. It's terrible to take the air, knowing that nobody wishes to see you, and, after arriving at an inhospitable door, to realize that you would have been more cheerful, with a kinder attitude toward humanity, if you had remained at home and never seen anyone. If I could keep my mind on one thing long enough, I wouldn't do anything at all, for as soon as you do something you're sure to regret it."

She had never expected a miserable bargain like this. Should she pretend that she was a busy woman and that it was time for her to get the galvanized tin pail of chicken feed and scatter it in the poultry yard for her Rhode Island Reds and Plymouth Rocks? What did this acid nature want of her? Lizzie did not have the courage to tell him to go. She had never turned a tramp away without offering him a plate of split-pea soup, some leftover stew or a few homemade cookies. But this stranger paralyzed her and if he continued in this funereal manner, it would raise her high blood pressure or give her a fever. Why was she invariably unlucky?

Surely it was time to gather the eggs from the layers, count her cheeps and see whether the roosters with their erect, seminal combs were treading the hens. Lizzie grinned at that; her mouth parted enough to allow a little quantum of happiness to seep through it. What a compost for human bones is laughter. Oh my God, my God, laughter is a sweet country well. The rain cometh, and May and June come louder; the August corn silks the morning air, and the crickets noising in the evening yard put leaves again on your bare branches. Could we die laughing and sport in tombs, death would only be another season.

Should she put another advertisement in the matrimonial periodical? Maybe she could bait a rancher; a man around cows and horses has more sense with a woman. Certain that she had aged since Tobias Emeritch had arrived, she was having those hot flushes and nervous spells.

She raised her glance from the floor and was about to propose that she make food for him, but before she could open her mouth, he continued with his own ideas as if she were not present.

"My brother Ebner lies in bed all day without even a nightgown on and he can swear that he has not had a hole in one sock or broken a button or lost a sixteenth of an ounce in the fabric of his shirt in twenty years. My sister has Bright's disease. She is in the other bedchamber with its four large, beautiful bay windows, which she never opens as she is afraid that an unexpected draught will settle on her lungs. It is always what you don't anticipate in this life that you have to look out for."

Communing with herself and thinking of getting rid of him—yet afraid to lose him—she did not know what course of action to adopt. No matter where she was, he was elsewhere, and he had prattled so much about pickles, sauerkraut, coleslaw and cucumbers that she wished he would go, so that she could take an enema and lie down. She endeavored to interrupt him but was unable to; he went on as though he were hysterical and had not talked to anybody but himself for years. How could such a piece of skin and bones contain so much conversation?

"You must realize," proceeded Tobias Emeritch

apologetically, "that I feel it would be insincere on my part if I did not tell you everything about myself right away, so that later you won't be able to say that I deceived you. Suppose you got the idea that I was exceedingly cheerful, or that I had many appointments and was really too busy to come and see you—that would be dishonest. If you thought I took persons into my confidence easily, you could then call me a hypocrite. You see, after I gave up the pickle factory, I had a side line buying and selling second mortgages and was interested in foreclosures. Besides that I had an equity in an undertaking establishment. At that time people were dying like flies; it's peculiar the way everybody does the same thing, and generally together. Have you noticed how one week you receive from eight to ten letters, and from persons in different towns and cities though no one has sent you even a card for a whole month? Then, all of a sudden, you lose three relations; people so lack individuality and are so lonely that they won't die unless someone else does it with them. Human beings are only reasonable up to a certain point, and after that you can't do anything with them, dead or alive."

Extremely agitated, Lizzie had her hand over her breast; was her heart weaker or her pulse more rapid? Pensively scratching her nose, she tried to calm herself. How many times she regretted having given up barbering. What confidence she had had in those days; it had made her so high-spirited. Then there had been an agreeable leaven to the whole lump of her days because she was with the public. Frequently she would take close to an hour over a customer, honing her razor to the finest edge so that the shave would ease him. Poor old Cromwell, he had vanished; how could that be? She used to dab powder on his skin with the utmost delicacy and sprinkle tonic on his moral, gray head. He had larded the barbershop with his goodness when he came in, and how she waited on him, sometimes wiping his shoes with her sleeve or the tail of her white apron and, when she had no porter, taking the whisk broom and brushing the lint and the hairs from his coat, or hurrying to the counter for a towel to wipe a bit of lather she had missed when she scraped his neck. Had Mary, who anointed the hair of Jesus with frankincense, been more devoted than Lizzie when she massaged Cromwell's cheeks to relieve him of all the weariness of this life?

/ Now Tobias Emeritch brought thoughts of death to her. Was death made for everybody? Would not God protect her? Of late, insurance agents had been coming to her door, telling her to make her son her beneficiary. Whenever somebody came to the front porch she was usually ecstatic; it might mean an event or a windfall. Could she only take her hopes and put a leash on them! Oh, where do pleasant tidings come from, from what distant star? After she returned to her senses and comprehended what the agent was saying, and that he was no better than an embalmer, all her dormant force sprang to her words: "Mister, you should be ashamed of trying to convince people they're going to die just to earn a livelihood. Why don't you learn an honest trade? You could be a paper hanger, a plasterer or a union bricklayer."

After that she gently shut the door; she could not push it hard against his face. A man in the dead-business was acting against nature, but she couldn't endure the tumult of an argument.

Tobias Emeritch had gotten up and was frantically hunting for his galoshes and demanding his umbrella. Doubtless he felt that she was neglecting him, and was making ready to go. She had to remind him again that he was wearing his rubbers and that she had placed his umbrella in the tub.

Trying to placate him, she said, "Why don't I prepare a fine borscht with a boiled potato in it? And I could slice a few extra beets just to make it more solid. Then I'll fix up chopped eggs and onions, and for the main course a veal cutlet that will stick to your ribs. For a dessert you can have a glass of tea, Russian style, with a piece of lemon in it and three lumps of sugar, and my homemade cookies. Do me a favor; please talk about something else beside pickles, horse-radish and coleslaw. If it won't offend you, may I say that the business you were in must have soured you. Why don't you visit people on Sundays—a family or some friends?"

"Madam, if I must have others under my feet, or someone around me, I prefer an enemy. A friend will forsake you after a single misfortune, but an enemy will never leave you no matter how great a disaster has fallen on your head. Furthermore, a friend is always pretending to love or admire you for traits that belong to another man rather than yourself. Whereas a foe hates you for what you are and has the canniest insight into the weaknesses of your character that nobody else ever noticed. Did I hear you mention a meal? Why don't I lie down and take a nap while you eat?"

Outraged, Lizzie asked herself whether this was a courtship. So far as she could remember he had not discussed *her* at all. He had not told her what a handsome figure she had, and she was hasty to reproach him: "Did you come here to sleep, or to see me?"

But he was too exhausted to answer her. Should she continue to handle him with kid gloves or should she bring him his Salvation Army umbrella? Obviously, he was no bluffer; he probably had the knack of making money or of turning the worst into the best—while she always managed to turn every advantage into a loss. Even if she could scheme, she pondered, and work on a crab like that, when it came to trimming him she would stop short.

After nodding for several minutes, Tobias Emeritch was sufficiently renovated to start again: "I wish, Madam, I could be more entertaining and that I did not have to repeat myself all the time. The truth is I am no longer fit to be with others. As I always say, the poor are companions of the poor, the rich of the rich—but the wise associate with no-body."

These remarks fell deeper into her wilderness than she cared to think about; but still she hesitated to make it clear that she had no need of him.

"Sir, I'm not detaining you; however, I have the utmost faith in life. Be assured, I have always something to do. In the morning I'm up before six to feed my Rhode Island Reds and Plymouth Rocks. I pour fresh water into the wooden troughs and after that I take a broom and sweep up the poultry yard. If the chicken wire is broken, that has to be repaired; I have to be the handy man here. Then I clean out the coops and wipe the roosts, and put clean straw in the wooden boxes for the hens, and see to it that the roosters' combs are in good healthy condition. During the season for tomatoes, I pick them when they ripen, and they are as red and plump as a farm girl. What a joy it is to look at my patch of corn. My eyes used to be sore and strained, and now I hardly ever use boric acid.

"You can see I'm no lady of leisure. For breakfast I take a bite of toast and a little cup of oatmeal with sugar and cream, but I don't touch coffee, for I've heard it's hard on the arteries, though my digestion couldn't be improved upon. Afterwards I lay down on the bed and use my violet ray machine. You should see the violet electric currents in each glass tube. Let me give you a treatment with this miraculous machine; it would take some of the sores and aches out of your disposition and relieve you of all your despondency. Think it over—it's for your benefit, not mine. There are dishes to wash, and a woman has to be on her feet all day, inspecting the icebox, greasing the stove and filling the kerosene tank. And every day I go to my steamer trunk and unlock it just to give my deeds and legal documents the once-over, to be sure that they're safe. By one o'clock I reheat a stew, or drop a lamb chop in the iron skillet, or make a bean soup. In the afternoon, when there is no rent to collect or I don't have to see an attorney about my properties, I sit in the wooden swing on the front porch and relax my bowels by doing nothing for an hour except look at the green fields. Every week is so full—I could go on and on—but tell me, isn't that a day?"

Tobias Emeritch was chewing his silk cravat and he no longer felt sleepy because what Lizzie was revealing was profoundly reassuring and satisfactory. He said with the gusto of a man who has discovered that others are in no less of a predicament than he, "Madam, that's not a day, it's a whole life, and if you don't object to my saying so, a terrible one. You are always doing the same thing—rummaging through your heavy, tedious hours as best you can—and the only way you can endure the time you destroy is by pretending that one day is different from another. What's so unusual about Tuesday that it couldn't just as reasonably pass for Monday? And as for Saturday and Sunday, aren't they the same as the weekdays, except that they are worse? Be quite frank with me—what is so vacant, tiresome and lonely as Sunday? You take all the slops out of the business days and throw them away, and call it the Sabbath which is the emptiest day of the week."

Lizzie's discouragement had deepened and she scarcely knew how to respond to this crank and pessimist but she had to give some kind of answer. He was looking for a pretext to leave, and this made her stumble, "Didn't God invent the calendar?"

He was ready to go, but he didn't believe that a woman should have the last word. He simply couldn't afford the defeat. Following such a disastrous episode he would not be able to rest easily for a month.

Thank heaven, this time he was quick enough to say what was on his mind, and without delay: "If God divided the week into seven days and the month into thirty—besides inventing a year—he simply made another mistake. Anyway, what's so perfect about God? Didn't He create man also, and He made just as much of a botch of that as He did of Sunday."

Lizzie did not wish him to declare that he was leaving before she had brought him his umbrella. Quite courteously, she stepped toward him as if to help him get into his coat, which he had never removed.

Twilight fell upon Lizzie after Tobias Emeritch left. What was there to do? Her head was compressed. She could boil water in the kettle and lie down with a hot towel on her forehead. Doubtless she needed an enema. Her tenant, next door, was probably primping and getting ready to take the inter-urban train in to Kansas City. Her husband, poor fellow, was a night watchman. Well, that was none of her affair. They were behind in their rent, owed her for nearly two months—and were anti-Semites, too. How many times she saw that chit hanging out the wash in high heels, all painted up and powdered, and babbling with the cheap trash who occupied the Henry Smith cottage. Lizzie would be sweeping the back porch and neither of her two tenants would look in her direction or even greet her. How easing would a "Good morning, Lizzie!" have been. But when a tenant wanted a favor, how quickly would this same chippy come over with her mincing high-heeled steps, pretending that she was getting mud on her feet although it had not rained for a week. She would exclaim, "Oh, Lizzie, honey, do be patient—Emery was laid off a month ago." Then she would stroke Lizzie's crumpled, greasy sleeve or affectionately pat her on the arm where her torn woollen underwear showed, and Lizzie, melting, would wipe her sticky cheeks and tell her not to worry. Several times a couple who had taken Henry Smith's bungalow or the other half of the duplex would skip town, owing her several months' rent, and cross the Kansas state line to avoid being sued. She knew what these low Northmoor folks said behind her back about a Jew. Still, she could not be hard; it was too much of a strain on her to evict a tenant.

One day Lizzie was tweezing her eyebrows and imagined she saw a wrinkle around her mouth she had never noticed before. Taking the hand mirror, she held it up closer to her face, but she realized that the looking glass was cracked. Where had that brand-new, rueful line come from? Had she not massaged enough customers' faces to understand the beauty-parlor business, and was she not a complexion specialist who knew how to take care of every pore?

Maybe—and she shook her head mournfully—her son would return from New York where he was teaching. Was he not a buffer between her and every cruel mischance? Her own flesh and blood would shield her from old age.

My mother, peeled and ravaged by some trance, had heard, across the distance that separated us, the ghost that was wailing in my throat as I moaned, "Every mother, even while she lives, is the pit and grave of the son." And I wept, calling out to NOTHING, "Who will save my mother? What can I do? Shall I go soft and grovel before God who has mangled His saints and prophets?

"How shall I slumber, and where shall I sleep so long as I tremble for the vine, my mother? O mother, thou art my right hand, but my left is lame, and I cannot lift it up." I cried, "My father, my father! My left hand; half of my seed is spoilt. I am half born and half dead, always one part of two, though never two in one, the father and the mother."

And now I said, "I must guard my mother each moment against that corrupt phantom who is always looking over our shoulders. My mother must not be taken by surprise; I will watch over her with the spear and javelin of the mind. I hear the wings of that woeful archangel whose cry in our waters is like the screaming of a gray gull seeking its prey. We will conspire together against that skulking demiurgic glutton who, although he has devoured all the peoples of the

187

earth since the beginning, yet requires even one more body, my mother's. Though this fat, garbage cherub is swift and comes on a sudden, I will repeat each instant in that mocking dream that is death and not life the liturgy from Luke: 'Thou fool, this night thy soul shall be required of thee.' "

XI

Thales, being asked what was the most universally enjoyed of all things, answered, "Hope; for they have it who have nothing else."

Epictetus

For the first two days Lizzie was overjoyed at the riddance of Tobias Emeritch. When she was not obsessed with the mournful cypress or thrown down by her blasted hopes, she was not forlorn. She did not always stand in her doleful buskins when she viewed her life. On the third day it was still a benison to listen to the evening noises of the crickets and to the mumbling weeds that lay against the lattices. However, she accepted the fourth day of his absence with less composure and argued with him in her mind as she mopped the rear porch and threw stale bread to the chickens. She had dropped into the habit of reviling people long before they had proved that they were good for nothing.

Lizzie now described to herself how Tobias Emeritch had concluded his visit: he had given her a low leg which shook like the aspen leaf and covered her two hands with so many wet kisses that her fingers felt like sops. Why did he have to place his hand over his moth-eaten vest and swear that he would return to her after he had recuperated from their adventure? Also, the mouldy snudge had promised to bring her a box of chocolates. That exasperated her; did he take her for a simpleton? Lizzie could stomach almost anything—a poor appetite, diarrhea and even mislaying her glasses and keys—but when somebody said he would give her even a package of chewing gum and then did not keep his word, she raged about it for weeks. What could she do with a miserly bachelor who arrived to court her with nothing else but himself?

On the eleventh day she found a letter in her tin mailbox outside the gate. Before tearing open the envelope, she read: Timothy Andrew Smithingate, Counselor-at-Law. She quaked; who was suing her? Lizzie had a mordant apprehensiveness of the law, though she had no reason for it. Shaking all over, she sat down on the wooden steps of the front porch. Maybe she should not examine this epistle. Was this a court action? Was one of her tenants leaving without paying the rent? Why couldn't she drop everything into her saucepan, cover it with gravy, let it simmer and then gulp it down so that she could forget about it? Frequently she swallowed a regret or an insult so that she would not taste it afterwards.

Unable to control herself, she began to peruse the letter:

Dear Madam:
My benevolent client, Mr. Tobias Emeritch, a most circumspect gentleman of venerable means, has requested me to send you his appropriate appreciation for receiving him on the 16th day of September. He wishes also to call to your attention that this was in every sense of the word an informal, and an extra-legal visit. After some somber reflection, he deemed it advisable to make it absolutely clear that he is a retired man, and if you compass my meaning, that he is retired in every respect.

As it is imperative to eradicate any misconceptions you have regarding the social amenities between a gentleman and a lady, he wishes to convey, and without flatulent ambiguities, that he does not have the comprehensive appetites of the ordinary person. Albeit he finds matrimony despicable from almost any point of view, he does not care to give you the impression that he would offer a vehement repulse to such a step, which at this moment he has no intention of taking.

Nonetheless, he would not be averse to calling on you, could he be assured by you that he had no heart in it whatever.

It would avoid any embarrassment for either of you, could you express yourself in a letter, addressed to me, guaranteeing that you will never bring any action whatsoever against him for heart balm or alienation of affections or even, if I do not sound morose or abnormal, for adultery. It is of the utmost importance that Mr. Tobias Emeritch can feel that he is, as it were, sitting easy on his properties, securities, mortgages and sundry investments. After I have heard from you, I shall advise him accordingly.

Very truly yours,

Timothy Andrew Smithingate

While Lizzie studied this document, Tobias Emeritch himself was crouching behind the hedge; his mechanical buggy was parked a little way down the gravel road. Noticing that there was no postage stamp on the envelope, she suddenly looked up—and saw Tobias standing before her. His cheeks were hanging and plaintive, and when she said nothing to him, he cleared the mist out of his throat and, leaning on his umbrella, told her that if she did not invite him to come into her house he would catch cold.

Leading the way up the steps, she opened the door for him. Once inside the house, he wandered about aimlessly until he blurted forth: "If I'm not too bold in mentioning it, would you be so kind as to inform me which is the direction to the public convenience?" But Lizzie had her mind on the missive from the attorney. He became quite excited: "Excuse me, but I'm in a big rush; where's the blue room?" She walked toward the water closet and turned on the electricity, even though there was daylight, to show him how a noble-hearted person should act.

While waiting, she searched each word that the lawyer had written her and memorized his name: Timothy Andrew Smithingate. She wondered whether Tobias would lay out money for an attorney when there was not even a stamp on the envelope.

When he returned to the parlor he still had his hat on, his muffler wound around him and the umbrella in his right hand; his galoshes were on his feet and the overcoat upon his back.

She expostulated with him: "My God, it makes me sweat to look at you! The least you can do is to remove your overcoat—unless you're trying to suffocate me."

All of a sudden Lizzie's head cleared, and holding the letter aloft, her eyes dancing behind the tortoise-shell glasses, she queried him, "Who is Timothy Andrew Smithingate?"

He wet his lips, for although it was damp, he was dry, and hesitantly answered, "Timothy was a well-to-do building contractor who also had a cement factory. He died in 1908 or '12; I'm not positive—it is impossible to keep a record of all the corpses you know."

Lizzie's mouth filled with glee, and she jibed, "Don't you even know your own lawyer's name?"

Her triumph deepened the wrinkles in Tobias Emeritch's face. Momentarily his jaw hung like a bodkin, his nose grew and he whimpered, "Why should a man of my age recollect anything? Soon as something comes to my mind it grieves me to death. Besides, if a counselor-at-law isn't clever enough to remember his own name, what's in it for me to remind him of it."

Seeing that there was nothing to be gained by pressing him further, she suggested that she give him a violet ray treatment. Tobias Emeritch was fidgety; why is it that a man always baits himself and has not enough patience to wait for the woman to do it? Tears of laughter rinsed Lizzie's eyes, and after she had removed her glasses and wiped them, she asked him, "How is it that a man of your mature years has never been married?"

Tobias answered, "I was saving my strength."

"Well," retorted Lizzie, "judging by your appearance, you didn't accumulate much."

That remark fell out of her mouth unexpectedly; she had vowed to be gentle. She hoped she could get somewhere with this parsimonious curmudgeon if she handled him carefully.

Tobias was hoarding his own conceptions; it had occurred to him that perhaps it would be much cheaper to take a wife than to hire a housekeeper. His stale cheeks almost looked hectic. The letter had been a mistake, and now that she possessed that letter, which was doubtless grounds for legal action, the wisest step he could take was to marry her. Of course, it was also exceedingly foolish and improvident. What a harrowing situation for him! He would be up all night, scheming, arguing, passing water and complaining to her, although she was not present, and demanding that she return the letter. He found a tear on his trenched cheeks. What consolation was there in the fact that he had not aged, for he had never been young? It was tiresome to hear Ebner tell him every day that he would outlive him or to listen to his sister Martha complaining that the windows were rattling and that air was coming through them. Could one acquire a legal helpmeet and come out ahead? A consumptive had a better chance of recovering than a married man.

Wondering how long it would take to rouse him, Lizzie asked him again, "Why don't you do something with your life besides saving it?"

That nettled Tobias. She was always telling him to do something. Well, one had to answer a woman or she would master him: "Do you think that the possibilities of life are unlimited? After you've awakened in the morning, you eat, if you're gluttonous, and then, pardon me, no offense intended, you relieve yourself. If Ebner is asleep, because he wants to live longer, and Martha is too tired to ask you to close the windows tighter, you open the door and then shut it. If you have the temperament of Ponce de León or Columbus, you circumnavigate your room ten to twelve times. After that you go out for a walk; there is always, of course, a gross acquaintance who stops you and tells you that the sun is out, and that his doctor has advised him that his prostate gland is in tiptop shape.

"You wrack your brain for a couple of hours and wonder how you can demolish the remaining part of a horrible day. One should postpone every decision in order not to make a mistake; still, everybody is in such a hurry that he cannot wait to get to his grave. But say that it is already nightfall, then I often read the tragedies of August Strindberg, who really abhorred life; think of it, you only get one genius like that in a century."

Thoroughly impatient, Lizzie got a pen and a bottle of Waterman's ink: "Can you make up your mind, mister? This is no romance, and it's not strictly business either; but what's right is right. It may be that you're too cautious and you will discover that nobody in the world will look out for you but me, and if wed, am I not entitled to something? We're a lost couple, worse apart than together. Be noble, please, and set aside a few stocks and shares, a few thousand dollars. Keep most of what you have for yourself. Otherwise, what have you to offer me but your name? What's in Tobias for a woman, or in Mrs. Emeritch? Frankly, I find more honor in being Lizzie Dalberg; it's an educated name, and not common. I was born into my name and I didn't start from nowhere. Make a little contract with me, since you're so hasty to run to an attorney's office after one visit."

At this point, Lizzie felt suddenly reluctant to enter into such a bleak and desperate arrangement. She wished that she had not sold her upright Bach piano, so that she could run over her scales and sing in her high thin treble:

> Beautiful garden of roses,
> Kissed by the golden dew . . .

Had she reached that juncture in her own life at which it was essential to relinquish all her tenderest expectations? Why had it come to pass in this way? She recognized that this lonely old miser with his decrepit hopes was as miserable as she, and that neither of them had anything left. But, O my God, and my heaven, there is my son . . . if he could only come to my rescue.

Tobias Emeritch was oblivious of Lizzie. She might have thought her guest was asleep or dead, had she not seen his heaving hat and ruminative overcoat. At moments he arched his eyebrows, and then he shrugged his coat lapels, as if he thought that no matter what he did it would be amiss. Who knew better than he that a man could do more harm to himself than anybody could do to him?

Besides, why should he heed what she was saying? What had he to do with woman's gaggling? The best conversation is a monologue in which no one else can meddle. He renewed his musings: My watchword is prudence. When a female folds you in her arms, she is winding a sheet around you, and knotting it too. Luckily there's no woman who can feast on my jaw, or gnaw my sunken temples, or dig her rotten, amorous molar into my joints. I am grateful to admit that I have no marrow, and no wife will ever make a chronicle of my anatomy. No, it is positively clear: a bedfellow is a bailiff, a summons, a foreclosure, a pauper's oath and a hearse.

Lizzie was out of patience; she was determined that she would find out what were his views. That she scarcely knew him was not important, and that she might know him better was her corrosive predicament. After all, he had answered her matrimonial advertisement and his second visit, like the first, was already so prolix that again she realized she would be too tired after he left to take an enema.

She had gotten the pen and the ink from the dresser, but he had taken no notice of it. Did she have to command him again? Should she say: See here, Mister Tobias, I just don't have the constitution to wait any longer for you. If you're not old enough to know what you are doing, the situation is hopeless. Never mind your years—for which I forgive you—but speak to the point; are you here for a wedding, or to trifle with my valuable time? You cannot expect me to wait on you—and your brother and sister—without making some reasonable marriage settlement upon me.

Yet he was such a suspicious soul that he might take her for a pickpurse or a hard, scheming woman. At this point she did speak to him: "Can't you see that I don't mean any harm to you, and that I wouldn't hurt a fly unless it fell into the soup? Why don't we settle matters and come to an understanding? I don't care to be disrespectful, but if you're not a good seventy-two, and you should be grateful . . ."

But this was an impure remark, and he interrupted her: "Well, is that the way to address a guest? Do you think I'm such an inexperienced bookkeeper that I don't realize that you're much older than you admit? I write down everything that people tell me. On Wednesday you hear that a woman is a grass widow, but Friday she tells you she never had a lover, and Saturday that her marriage was annulled, and on Monday she's a virgin. People are far more changeable than the weather; no matter what the season is, you know you can expect a storm, a hurricane, a tornado, rain, snow, sleet or hail. That's pretty constant—but can you anticipate what a human being is going to do or say?"

Lizzie looked at him; it was the severest glance she had ever given him. She had already had her secret revenge; taking a silent inventory of his ramshackle frame and habits was sufficient: he doesn't drink, he has no need of tobacco, he won't indulge in an innocent appetizer . . . what part of his body does he use?

True, she might not be forty-four. Well, she did not appear much older than that except when she was fatigued or discouraged. There could be no doubt that he was closer to eighty than seventy, and should she be collecting relics or picking up bones in alleys like a stray dog? This lucid and comfortable judgment assuaged her considerably, so that she was able to become very soothing: "Why don't you step out into the back yard and look at my chickens?"

Tobias Emeritch stated flatly that he did not relish the stench of poultry, and Lizzie, no less positive, claimed that her Rhode Island Reds and Plymouth Rocks were as good as a sedative to excitable people. Prompted by a gentle and good-natured push, he rose and accompanied her. When they were out in the yard, she picked up the bucket filled with chicken feed and cast the grain about the pen like a professional poulterer. Tobias gnawed his tongue, which caused her to reproach him: "Do you have to stare at the hens with your mouth open—and without any color in your face?"

"Is it necessary," he replied, "for me to observe your chickens with the blushing cheeks of a lover?"

The sight of poultry seemed to make him listless. If she were more hospitable, she might open this tomb. Actually, he appeared more somnolent in the open air than inside. She returned to the back porch and looked into the secondhand wooden icebox which contained at that moment a watery squib of butter in a chipped dish and a cup of cold string beans. Still brooding, Lizzie prayed that they could come to terms; she had no intention of pauperizing him, and the thought that anything ill might befall him dismayed her.

Who wants to ride in a limousine following a hearse? Obviously, nobody would marry him for his jocular disposition, and maybe he was not much of a companion, but he was an improvement over the four walls.

While she was busy on the porch, Tobias was at the dresser, picking through her receipts from the electric light company and inspecting a postcard or two; then he noiselessly opened the drawer, looking for love letters that she might be receiving from other correspondents. It was not simply avarice that consumed his skin; he was a profoundly jealous man. He pulled open the door to her clothes closet, where Lizzie stored many of her memorials, and found Captain Henry Smith's Stetson hat. He took it out and turning it upside down put his nose against the sweatband. When Lizzie caught him, she ran up to him with the most startling agility and snatched the hat from his hand.

"What are you doing in my private clothes closet?"

"This is a man's hat," he shouted, "your lover's, no doubt."

"Don't be a fool; it's my son's," she retorted.

He snorted: "It smells much older to me!"

Tobias was already resolved to make an unexpected appearance at her house in the close future. He was determined that although he had no inclination to cohabit with a woman, he was not going to be a cuckold either.

That Tobias Emeritch might be furtive did not surprise her, but who would expect the blackamoor's passion in this almost disembodied figure? She tempered her scolding with majestic courtesy: "Sir, since you are a bloodhound in my house, smelling my oldest receipts, postcards and letters from bygone friends, why are you so backward in other respects? You need not be bashful; please take the pen, and there's the tablet of paper, and write down in plain language just what provisions you intend to make for my security. Since you are a suspicious character and imagine I'm hiding a man in the dresser drawer, why do you want to be the husband of a woman in whom you have no confidence? People must have a certain amount of trust in one another."

Tobias Emeritch did not fail to hear that one. "That's fine," he remarked defiantly, "so why don't you start trusting me?"

But she was not behindhand herself and saw it was imperative to have a swift answer for such a sharper: "Mr. Tobias, you're not the type to have too much faith in; tell me, honestly, do you have any confidence in yourself?"

"Why should I have," was his own rapid response, "when I know I'm likely to change my mind before the day is over? So if I doubt my own word, should I believe that somebody else is any better than I am?"

Endeavoring to divert him, she dropped into her gentlest manner, almost cooing: "Look, the cabbage soup is excellent, and I have a sheep's stomach stuffed with roasted chestnuts, kidney beans, liver and cinnamon toast."

He sat down most unwillingly. Very gingerly she tied one of Popkin's gold-embroidered napkins around his neck. The sound of "sheep's stomach" did not improve his appetite, and he ate the meat with restrained disgust; at the same time he could not keep the napkin out of his mouth and he thought he was chewing moth balls. Beside herself with anguish and desperation, Lizzie did not know how to please him. He was spoiling the meal for her. She admonished him, doing her best to hold herself together and not shriek: "Excuse me a moment, and I can go to the hen yard and get a tender broiler or a fryer for you. In a quarter of an hour you will be the happiest man in Northmoor."

The blood ran out of Tobias' cheeks, and he wished to make a statement, but was unable to do so. Since Lizzie could not understand his mood, she imagined that what he actually wanted, but was too timorous to express himself so boldly in another's house, was a rich dessert. She enquired in a pleading tone, "What about a plate of strawberries with sour cream just to top everything off?"

Tobias Emeritch, in a helpless, queasy voice, beseeched her, "Don't mention food to me—it upsets my stomach."

That raised Lizzie's anger. "Well, you don't increase my appetite either!" she answered.

Apologizing to her, he sniveled and muttered, "Whatever I say is wrong; what kind of a couple will we make? Two persons together should be harmonious with one another. Though I don't get along very well with myself, I don't see how I could put up with two of me. Admittedly, you're different from me, but aren't we all the same?" In a louder voice he proceeded, "Has anybody got a lien on your properties? Are you in arrears? I sincerely hope you take care of the electric bill promptly. All these things count up and are genuine evidence of a person's sound judgment. Who needs an extravagant housekeeper? Frankly, it would pain me deeply to discover later on, when it's too late, that you buy ice in September, or that you put on the lights in the evening when you could save this unnecessary expense by retiring at six o'clock. You hear of people burning gas to take the chill out of a room when they could have gotten into their overcoats or thrown foot rugs over their shoulders. We live in a period of unimaginable waste. What sense is there in sending one's trousers to the tailor's to be pressed; what can you do with a crease? Think of having a suit cleaned; anybody with an ounce of intelligence knows that sooner or later it will pour."

This aimless conversation would never come to an end; it was impossible to relieve this old man of his monetary aches. "Oh, you make me tired," she told him, as though by now she wanted him to go home. "It's sure hard on a woman's nerves to be pestered by a man who is always under your feet, but you worry me sick because even after you arrive—and sit down in your coat—you don't seem to have enough strength to make an appearance. Never in my life and in all my experience did I ever see anybody fade away like you do. After all, this is a courtship, although I must say you're some dandy of the heart. Don't you think you ought to put yourself out a little, so that when you're present I don't feel that you're absent?" And she asked quite testily, "Where are the chocolates?"

Lizzie took him by the arm, pinching his sleeve, marched him out to the front porch, and they walked over to the grocer's. The skies were extremely low; the clouds were black and hilly. Lizzie had let go of him because he moved lethargically. She went on ahead, Tobias trailing behind her, and crying out, "My dear, Madam Lizzie, it's going to rain; let me hold the umbrella over your head."

Turning around, she called back to him, "Let it rain, it won't cost you anything," and she moved faster, while he bleated and begged her to wait for him.

At the grocer's, a wooden shanty down the road, Lizzie asked for three cans of Dutch Cleanser, two cakes of tar soap, five pounds of potatoes, a large sack of granulated sugar, a bag of flour, a box of black pepper, a loaf of rye bread, a package of macaroni, a pound of sweet butter and two quarts of milk. When Tobias Emeritch saw her handling the grapes and feeling the apples to see whether they were hard and had sturdy stems on them, he became extremely agitated and complained, "For heaven's sake, save a few articles in the store for the next customer; are you going into the wholesale grocery business?"

Lizzie moved about to face Tobias Emeritch, who was shaking. This was an ambush; he knew it—she would make him pay the bill. He started for the door but stumbled against his umbrella, and Lizzie pulled him back. She was most emphatic: "I forgot to bring my pocketbook; be so kind as not to keep the grocer waiting; I need a little change."

Pulling out his wallet that had been cooking in his trousers for a year, he cautiously held it and used his free hand to peck pennies, dimes and nickels from his pocket. He managed to lay only the loose change in the palm of her hand. While counting out 68 cents, he stuffed the wallet into his coat pocket. But Lizzie immediately plucked it from that crevice, took out three filthy one-dollar bills and paid the grocer. She kept the 68 cents and the small change the grocer returned.

As soon as they were outdoors Tobias Emeritch said, "Remember, you're a lady of honor, and I expect a receipt from you for $3.68; that's not chicken feed, you know." She was halfway home by then, but he went on, "Is it necessary to inform you that Jeremiah the prophet said we live in a land of robbers and thieves?"

Moving his head up and down ruefully, he paid no attention to the ruts in the road. A heavy storm was coming up, and Tobias stood still to conserve his energies and to gaze with wonderment at the emerald meadowland opposite the duplex, and at a bull of tremendous girth which was looking back at his offending, gaping face with ferocious hostility. The rain began to fall, quickly gathering into a puddle, and Tobias slipped and went down into it. The umbrella flew open and was blown over into the glistening grassy pasture; the bull pranced toward it as it descended to the ground, and butting it first with his head, then gored the cotton material, and after stamped on it.

Lizzie, far in advance, paused and caught a glimpse of Tobias, who was absolutely motionless. She became apprehensive, fearing that he had been struck by lightning or had had a stroke and was now paralyzed. With quick and sure steps she hurried back to his side; at first she searched his sagging and morbid face, and then as she raised her eyes, she saw the bull treading the umbrella. Lizzie took Tobias by the arm, turned him about and led him toward the porch.

Her clothes soaked and strands of her hair matted down, she pushed him up the steps; they entered the parlor and then went into the dining room adjacent to the rear porch. Removing his coat, and then his jacket and shirt, she took a towel out of the trunk and rubbed his shoulders and back;

after that she found an old shirt of her son's that she made him put on. It fitted him like a nightgown. Lizzie lighted the kerosene stove and made him sit down on a varnished kitchen chair in front of it.

Tobias slept, upright in the chair, for over two hours, and when he awakened he felt so tranquil that he parted his lips to smile—but then thought better of it. Quite conscious —which he found a most uncomfortable sensation—he remembered the $3.68 which he would probably never recover. His rheumatism began to bother him, and then he had a cramp in one foot. He whimpered, "You always want me to spend money." But he dropped this thought which unduly inflamed him and asked, "What does your son do?"

At that Lizzie braced her shoulders and standing erect before him as if she were delivering the valedictory at a commencement exercise, she cleared her throat and confided, "Oh, he's way up in the world; he writes books—and he gets so much praise for them."

Tobias Emeritch scowled and replied, "Does he put it in the bank?"

That made Lizzie indignant: "You call yourself an educated gentleman; tell me, would a cultured man go to a bank teller with a satchel full of praise and say to him that he would like to start a savings account with it?" Lizzie fetched a copy of Gautier's *Golden Fleece* and showed it to Tobias—who inspected it and pronounced that it was a French novel.

Tobias had no inclination to bruise himself further over the $3.68 and considered that it would be more convenient to mention something else: "What are your relations with your grocer?"

Fuming at this, Lizzie demanded that he take his coat, galoshes and hat and leave her courteous house at once. Tobias was in a grave quandary; where should he go? He searched the rooms for his umbrella until Lizzie reminded him of the bull.

When Lizzie said good-bye to him, he realized that after he had driven back he would have nobody to see but brother Ebner, who was entombed in his bed, and his sister, who would complain about the rattling windows. He was undecided, and that softened Lizzie; she told him to go home and think it over and, though she made it clear that he would not get back his $3.68, she would marry him if he would only show her a small amount of consideration.

At first she was about to let him go out by himself, but seeing how loosely he filled his shambly clothes, she took him by the arm; after he cranked the car and crept into it, she sorrowfully waved her hand at him.

Now it was February, the month of winds, freezing hopes and lamentations, and the rain gabbled against the windowpanes. Lizzie had not heard from Tobias for five months. Three times he had come to Lizzie's house to drive her to Kansas City to take out a marriage license, but on each occasion they quarreled. He had sworn that he would see his attorney and have him draw up papers so that Lizzie could have title to a little wooden cottage and $5,000 in cash, and though he would press his rigid, empurpled lip against the shoulder strap of her kitchen apron and apologize, he never did anything about it.

Claiming, as he put it, that he was "property-poor," he warned her that he could not afford to give her more than ten dollars a week for housekeeping expenses; after an altercation he increased that amount to twelve dollars . . . but a fortnight later alleged he had promised her only nine dollars as her allowance for seven days. Then he declared that only after she was his wife, would he sign over the bungalow and the cash to her, as a wedding present. She ought to take his word for it, he pronounced; but Lizzie averred that his promises were already overdone, and would be cold meat by that time. Haughtily he let her know that he had no intention of dying a pauper; to which she retorted that she could not see how he could die or live any poorer than he already did.

Then her son returned. By now he had come to understand that his mother was arrayed in broken and forlorn rags because her life was in tatters. When he was alone, or far from her, he vowed that he would never chide her again for her slovenly appearance. But when he peered into the icebox, or gaped at her sick, sniveling stockings, or examined a pile of dishes filled with the leftover carrion of several meals, he still railed at her.

How many times he had rebuked himself. What dotages of books had wasted his nature? Was he not tossed about from one book to another? And had he not strode through the pages of volumes as if he were in the drunken streets of Babylon and wallowed in the mire of novels and philosophy until his eyes were so muddied by vanity and custom that he could not see, hear or feel?

One day, out by himself in his mother's back yard, he was watching a straggling hen peck the rain as it splashed and wormed around in the ground.

He resolved that he would fall at his mother's feet and beg her to pardon him for all his sins. O, miserable, deformed son, your mother has long ago forgiven you; are you not the son of her afflictions, and of her dark, peopleless forests?

The son ate his remorse, but it was mouldy bread. His mother was grieving but near her tomb sat a Gadarene demon, his tongue. Was it not he, rather than his mother, whose days were the sluttish songs of habit, and who had a heart that had died? From the beginning he had been a guilty and fallen son.

Now if he were not bedewed with her sorrows, he would be sterile, and no fire, hail or snow could burn or melt him. At this instant he must go to her and kiss the latchets of her torn, grubby boots . . . but he did not. Worse than the paralysis of feeling would be some mock show of self-abasement, for it is a terrible sin to look or appear humble, or to adopt the lamb's meek visage, when one has not the gift for it.

He panted after kindness, but the waters of his brooks were dry. He said, "I love the good and hate the evil." But a flea sat in the corners of his mouth and it bit him, and when he scratched it, his virtues tickled like vices. And he roared like the bear and mourned as the dove: "That foul act which I have not yet done I have already committed in a wicked dream." Then he made a fell prophecy: all people have the automatic impulse to harm others, and while one is stroking the neck of the beloved he has an involuntary desire to break it.

He had been estranged from the womb and would injure whatever he loved. Having no water within him, he came upon a pool, and in it he saw the visage of Cain and knew that wherever he went, or whatever he did, he would be a wilderness.

Coming back into the dining room, he gently implored his mother to put on a fresh dress. She went to her trunk, which, aside from her meager possessions—papers, letters, a shirtwaist and a watch—was like the holy of holies in the temple, for it contained nothing but manna, which is the remembrance of hunger and past hopes.

She returned in a faded silk blouse and apron. She had pinned on the gold watch which she had given herself when she married Popkin. They sat down at the table in the dining room and played casino. The laughter had long since expired in her; it had been graved since the time that Captain Smith abandoned her. On the rarest occasions, when she heard a laugh rise from her crypt, she listened to the cock crow and it stalked away and vanished like an unclothed ghost. When a smile appeared on her face, it was the wan image of a former, carnal smile.

Although she seemed distracted, and to be paying slight

attention to the cards, Lizzie had already won two games from him. He began to watch her shuffle the deck and on a sudden he recalled that in both games his mother had gotten every point—the ten of diamonds, the four aces, the deuce of spades, and big and little casino. In the midst of their third game she shuttered the cards so nimbly that he reached over the table before she could deal them and turned up the ten of diamonds that she had cleverly put on the bottom of the deck. No matter how closely he watched her, she dealt either the aces or the deuce of spades to herself, and then the other points. Roaring at her, he stood up and denounced her as a cheat; as he rose, the morning newspaper fell from his coat pocket to the table. Lizzie adjusted her tortoise-shell glasses and picked up the paper—simply to do something else, so that she would not grieve over her son's sick temper. Motionless, she read: "Tobias Emeritch, aged 74, a prominent merchant and philanthropist, has died, leaving $50,000 to his brother, Ebner Emeritch, a wealthy retired manufacturer, and to his unmarried sister, Martha."

Her face was immutable, and when her son turned away from the window, she took her hand from her throat which looked as though it were pieces of threadbare woollens she had patched together. She whispered, "My son, I am an old woman."

He stood in her tears and placed his hand over her suffering wrinkles. Then he went out again into the rain. He cast his heart out of his mouth, and although he wept and wept, when he stared at the dirt into which his heart had fallen, it had grown into a stone. Suddenly a cry like a sword passed through his bowels, and he moaned, "Mother, mother, guard me from myself."

XII

"Abba, Abba, it is finished."

John

There are five trash towns in greater New York, five garbage heaps of Tofeth. A foul, thick wafer of iron and cement covers primeval America, beneath which cry the ghosts of the crane, the mallard, the gray and white brants, the elk and the fallow deer. A broken obelisk at Crocodopolis has stood in one position for thousands of years, but the United States is a transient Golgotha.

In 1926, my mother had decided to join me in Astoria, a cheap German borough with grum and gritty delicatessen and hardware stores and the dead bricks of tenements. But after a year in Astoria we moved to Bensonhurst, then a rheumy marshland. A low, squab mist hovers over the bay which damps the job-lot stucco houses. Many months later I found an apartment in a block about ten minutes by elevated train from Queens Plaza. Queens is an immense warehouse for New York cadavers, and I had taken the greatest care to find rooms that were remote from the graveyards. But after I had signed the lease and was standing at the window overlooking high, shaggy iodine-colored bushes, I found they concealed the cut-rate Virgin Marys and Christs of Calvary Cemetery.

My mother had become an old woman; her apron was much skinnier, and the sleeves of her underwear looked ill and starved. Now she seldom scrutinized her decayed skin. Could her lips really be as faded and sapless as they appeared to her when she thoughtlessly picked up her looking glass? And yet she continued to cling to one belief: others will die but I will not. At moments she could not believe that there was not one person noble enough to say to her: "Here is a morsel of a smile; you are not forsaken." But the world was Pilate who had washed his hands of her.

Too old now for barbering, Lizzie fancied she could become a matchmaker. After she had dismissed this chimera, she considered returning to Kansas City; she still had her houses amidst the chattering weeds and the antiseptic sunflowers of Northmoor. Away from the Midwest, she now imagined her days there had been good. How she hankered for the alder, the tender back yard and the Indian summer crickets.

Poring over the obituary notices in the papers had now become her daily pastime; it was also a specious consolation. When she read: "Samuel B. Forbes, importer of ceramics, deceased in his 91st year," she rejoiced; she was sure she had as many years, if not more, stored away for her in the Lord's garner. But when she examined another woeful piece of tidings: "Jezebel Mullen MacMahon, 47, dead of liver disease," she declared that the woman must have led a dissipated life and worn out her organs. Then she looked at the classified advertisement columns: *Help Wanted Female* was only good pasture for a typewriter chippy, so she turned to *Lost and Found*. Oliver Goodness offered a reward for a ring he had dropped in a Fifth Avenue coach. She could write to him and that might start a correspondence. Speculation of that sort might lead to a partnership in a small broker's office. Perhaps it would be better to go to Canal Street and track down Popkin. She knew his cousin had been a salesman in a haberdashery there. Popkin must now be at least sixty-nine, or more, a good seventy-two; that gave her confidence.

Having so little else to occupy her, my mother had begun to brood over the $3,000 Popkin had swindled from her in 1909. Whatever she deemed good or bad had occurred to her in the past. She preferred a galled memory to anything that was now happening to her.

She thought that maybe she did not look so seamy as she imagined; perhaps she could threaten to sue him for damages, whereupon he would remarry her. Had Popkin ever done her any wrong, and what effect had he had upon her life? Had he altered it one tittle? Popkin was weak rather than vicious, and weak people cannot trouble our depths; the heart is indifferent so long as it is not wounded.

One Saturday afternoon I returned to the flat and found there a man in a loose brown jacket; he wore a white shirt without a tie and a faded maroon vest that sagged comfortably below his navel. Bad food as well as a certain style of thinking had given him a lumpish appearance. Was he the same person I had known in 1909, or a dilapidated replica of him? What had happened to the sharp and well-trimmed pate of the jewelry salesman? Was he wearing a new face or a different experience? Obviously, he wished to convey the impression that he was natural and skeptical; his meals bulged confidently in his belly, but his face was seasoned with weariness. I learned that Popkin was now a salesman in a clothing store on Delancey Street.

What might Popkin's thoughts have been as he studied Lizzie after thirty years? He must have been glad that he had left Kansas City. How her throat had failed! What poulterer, he sighed, had plucked her hair? A man like himself could age yet be even more seductive than he was when he was a raw prentice among the ladies. When he sauntered in the evening along Second Avenue amidst the Jewish intelligentsia, it was not uncommon for a smartly rouged widow or a bored adulteress to look at his experienced nose and to appraise his mouth.

Lizzie sat on the metal cot opposite Popkin. She was rigid in the dated lace dress that he had bought for her in Palestine. That was the only concession she had made to him. Otherwise, she was formal and cold—far more than she intended to be. She wanted him to know that she was a prize, and believed that this would be made more plain if both behaved as if they had never been in the same bed together.

The two scrutinized one another and each shook his head. Popkin took a handkerchief from his pocket and flopped it about his face to dry a tear. He tried his utmost not to show that he was weeping a little for her as he mumbled to himself, "What a relic the poor thing is; anybody can see she is rapidly sinking."

Lizzie fastened her eyes on his pouchy neck and then she looked at his stomach. "Why does he eat rotten delicatessen food," she thought. "Look how much gas he shows; a man cannot afford to let himself go like that. If old Popkin had not once been my husband, I would not have recognized the slob. Could you believe it, he used to be as neat as a pin."

Popkin folded one lip over the other and he made some sounds, but she did not catch his remark: "Where did the old girl get that costume? Does she still think it's 1895?"

Lizzie was rancorous; she could hardly keep from blurting out, "You old fool, did you come to pay me a visit or to talk to yourself?" But reconsidering her diatribe, she added to herself; "Maybe he's so advanced in years that his mind's weak; you can't fool nature. Still there's no excuse for acting like a boor; he could at least pay me a compliment for putting on the dress he bought me with my money."

Before Popkin had arrived, Lizzie had been crowing; no mistake about it, she had Popkin right where she wanted him. She would now settle with him—but in a ladylike manner. He had spent the savings account that had come from years of sweating over her scissors and comb.

Their conversation was not going well. The deliberate

aloofness of Popkin nettled her, and she pushed her skirts more closely around her. "What kind of a bargain does he imagine he is? Does he think I am going to chase him?" She stirred a little, moving her nostrils—she was not positive but believed she could smell another woman on him. Maybe, she speculated, she had better pump him and see just where she stood.

"You know," she began, "eating in restaurants will give you a nervous stomach, Louis. It makes a man look pasty and sour. Don't tell me—I'm still from Missouri—that you've become a housekeeper." At this Lizzie let out a small, forced giggle.

Her remarks had such a disagreeable effect upon Popkin that he commenced to taste his mouth and he made a face. This was a furtive attack and most ill-mannered. He knew that he should not have accepted her invitation; he had grown old in one visit. Well, he would have to deal with her in a more candid way.

"Lizzie," he said, "I don't believe in marriage anymore. I admit a man needs a companion, and I've got one—a Lucy Stoner. She carries her own name, and I take care of mine. We're a pair of free lovers."

Smarting from this outrageous disclosure, Lizzie could scarcely control her nerves. What impudence this sloppy codger had! Did he come here to boast about a chippy, a low common-law wife? She wiped her face which was smeared with perspiration and held her throat so that she would not snivel. Then she snorted, "You can't fool me, Louis, love is never free; I guess I've had the experience and ought to know!" And she gave Popkin such a strong and passionate glance that he lost most of his mundane slouch.

Popkin was ready to leave, and when he took out his watch Lizzie stumbled toward the kitchen sink to get a glass of water. She removed her glasses and wiped her eyes with a stale dishcloth. She had been patient and noble long enough. Either he would have to make a cash settlement with her out of court, or she might marry him, but she would be quite outspoken. A woman would have no picnic with such a bilious rounder. But should he be unreasonable, she would be strict and sue him for breach of promise, heart balm and damages. With interest on the money he had swindled from her, and an additional lump sum she was entitled to for the grief he had caused her, she would have about $10,000. When she came back from the sink, she was about to tell him that she had had brain fever after he had gone to Jerusalem and that her hair had fallen out, and not all of it had grown back again, but she restrained herself. It was poor business for a woman to call a man's attention to her defects. Show the average man a few gray hairs or a wart he has never observed before, and he becomes listless and stays out nights.

That Popkin looked like small change did not concern Lizzie; she craved her imaginary advantage. Popkin was still glancing at the doorknob and wondering how he could reach it. Before he had come, he could not wait to air his radical opinions about marriage. He had expected a large glass of Russian tea with lemon, but looking about the room he was puzzled because he could not see a samovar. How differently everything had fallen out. He had wanted to talk about Kansas City—about Delaware and Wyandotte Streets, the Paseo, and Fountain Place, where they had had a six-room flat when they were married.

He got up and went over to Lizzie and, taking hold of her hand, said, "Lizzie, why don't I buy the boy a suit? You know he's like my own flesh and blood." He desired to show himself to be a man who could never forget the obligations he owed to a kinsman.

But Lizzie did not like his hand. "He sweats so much," she said half-aloud, pulling her fingers away from his. Besides, she had no intention of accepting a $25 Delancey Street suit as payment for the $3000 he owed her, and for which she had received only a hand-embroidered bedspread with two pillowcases to match, a table cover with six napkins, a lace dress and a Hebrew parrot that cocked his beak and shouted: *"Aleph, Beth, Gimel!"* Lizzie was certain that Popkin had handed over most of the money to his former wife, as she had never seen any of the diamonds he was supposed to have bought in the Holy Land and smuggled into America.

Giving Popkin a cool face Lizzie announced, "If you want to be a gentleman, Popkin, and do what is right, you could give up that chippy." She stopped short; she realized that she had made a narrow-minded remark, and what was worse, she had lowered herself by pleading with him. When her glance fell to the floor, she noticed that his socks had dropped down about his heels. It was hardly refined for a lady to be gaping at a man's nude skin, and what interest could she have in Popkin's leg; still she was so repelled by the sock that dangled and hung over his shoe, and the gray, nasty flesh that he showed, that she was unable to take her eyes from that part of his body. Popkin became so uncomfortable that first he crossed his legs and then he pulled down his trousers and sat bolt upright and prim. This upset her and she detested Popkin the more because he acted as if she had been looking at him. Lizzie had always known how to keep her place, and no one could say she was not polite; but what sort of new fashion was this? By now her indignation was most agreeable, and she felt she had a real advantage over Popkin; she was quite elated and remarked to herself, "That ugly rounder has no garters on; he's half undressed, just like a woman in a sporting house. In all my experience I never knew a gentleman to show his bare ankle in a public place."

As she glanced up again, Popkin was at the door. She could no longer repress her wrath and, as she wrung her hands, she exclaimed, "I've handled you with kid gloves long enough, Louis. I just can't afford to be noble-hearted; it's too much of a strain on my nerves."

Popkin crept out, and Lizzie sat down again on the cot. She took her revenge and rocked it in her arms. It was finished; what strength had she for a court case? Are there no triumphs? What can one do against a bad act? She always had chagrins which were supposed to be lessons in experience but which never prevented her from suffering another humiliation. Whatever made her think she could overcome anybody? Had she ever won an argument? Besides she had never had the skin for a quarrel; the least commotion boiled her veins.

If I have said little about myself, it has been too much; but I had far less intelligence than the fossil remains of the Testacea. Besides, what is more boring than the sensitive young man who desperately wants to have feelings? I looked everywhere for a Buddha, and found several lizards, foxes and the small rodentia on our venal and barren Patagonia. As for her whom St. Augustine calls the shake-rag goddess Pecunia, I had no luck with her at all. I dreaded useless and brutal drudgery; work that is bad and vulgar warps the hands and the human affections. Sir Thomas More speaks of those "silly poor wretches" who are "tormented with barren and unfruitful labor . . . [which] killeth them up."

I had resolved to be a writer and to clean out the Augean Stables of society, but there is no meat, bread or potatoes for Hercules the stableboy. After I had written three novels my plight was no better than that of the niata which starves to death when there is nothing on the pampas but a few twigs and reeds. Nor was I any more apt with a good book merely because I was in the world. Santa Teresa has said that she read many books without understanding any of them. Reading Plato's *Timaeus* was as squalid a pleasure as the bite of a louse; no matter how I studied the *Dialogues* I was still covered with the vermin of ignorance. And how men love to scratch themselves. After poring over the works of the sages I had no less spleen, bile or vanity, and I was just as vacant as I had been. The crow says: "Give me more life that I may be ever eating dung." In what way was I different from the crow in the *Mathnawi?*

The distance between my mother and me had grown. My life was now so hopeless that I wrote a book. All day I scribbled while listening to Beethoven's *Moonlight Sonata* on the phonograph. My mother staggered about, dropping a kettle or a fry-pan, and finally turned to me, begging, "Please turn that funeral song off. I just can't stand it, my son."

Was there some piteous ancestor wailing in my ribs? What I heard was the hymn of lineage: Ham begat Cush, and Teraḥ bore Abraham . . . but where is Saul? I tried to piece together the image I had had when I was six years old of the man I believed to be my father and I collected his separate features—the licentious locks, the vulpine white teeth and the agile nose—even as the men at Jabesh-gilead had gathered together the bones of Saul, King in Israel, son of Kish. I pined for that other Saul, Paul of Tarsus, and I wept for every Saul that had lived. But Saul the barber was my anointed Anthropos.

On days when nothing filled my sore, raw spirit I went to Hebrew orthodox cemeteries in search of his headstone; could I find his name in an epitaph, maybe I would not be so broken and separated from all flesh. Every burial ground whispered to me, "Waif, stand before the Cave of Mach-pelah and mourn for the FATHER. The perverse son tells his soul that he abhors Abraham, Isaac and Jacob, but all flesh owes the price to the seed that begat it. If you curse your seed, who will quicken your tomb?"

Was I to be a castaway all my days? And could I only plant my ghost in the wilderness and eat my manna in waste places? Each time I have dropped a thought a dark forest has sprung up around me.

One night as I lay in bed, I heard a maggot wail, and it was torn into many parts, and it was Saul. It was separated from other groaning worms that were twined together and who recited: ". . . the sons of Levi were Gershon, Kehath and Merari, and the sons of Judah were ʿEr and Onan and Shelah and Perez and Koraḥ."

I asked, "Am I of their stock?" But Saul did not answer me.

When I bent over to caress the worm, it was piecemeal, and I turned my eyes against my breast and watched the various bits of myself crawling into the ground. Then I heard it say: "I am Saul your father. Though I have sinned much, do not renounce me lest you mangle your own worms; no man can flee from his own worms and not be an evil to himself."

Now in my dream I saw that many maggots were clinging to me, which I thought were Enoch, Noah, Shem and Abraham, and then I beheld Jesus the paraclete. He had a lump on his neck that galled his whole back; the sensual auburn curls of Saul crowned his head, but the face was dominated by the long Nazarene nose of my mother. It was a wild, prophetic nose, and like the olive, the seer of the trees that grow in the vales of Schechem and on the plains of Gilead.

I looked in vain for the hands that were said to have made the oxgoads and the ploughs, but in the place of a rough workingman's hands were trembling feelings out of which he had fashioned the sayings and parables.

I asked the spectre, "Art thou Jesus?"

And he answered, "I am Yeshu of Nazareth."

Then I said, "Was Joseph the carpenter your father?"

His foot shook. I paused, fearing to vex the ghost. But I could not hold back the words from my hungry lips: "Was your mother Miriam the adulteress? Did she lie with Joseph's groomsman?"

The Nazarene spoke: "I think my mother was a natural woman; I always preferred the women who sinned to the foolish virgins who had no oil in their vessels. Tell me, is it not a rumor throughout all Judea that the women of Nazareth are lovely wantons? Have the Pharisees forgotten that the daughter of Lamech was called Na'amah, which means beautiful pleasure, and was she ever denounced in Israel as a transgressor? My real mother must have been Miriam Megaddela Neshaya, Mary Magdalene, the women's hairdresser, because I loved her more than anyone in the earth."

These words were nails in my eyes, and they pained me so bitterly that I could not see the voluptuous ringlets of Saul. Did Miriam Megaddela Neshaya, the lady barber who had dressed Yeshu's locks also shave and manicure customers in Memphis, Louisville, New Orleans and Dallas? Now I saw her standing at her regular chair, holding the comb and scissors in her hands, and when she laid them down for a moment, she folded the curls that hung over my forehead. Who was sitting in her chair—the Nazarene or I? There were large seals of bastardy on his chest and loins, and the gore fell at his feet, and I bent down to kiss the illegitimate blood.

I could hardly perceive his emaciated and nameless stem, unfilled by the Father. Had he invented the genealogical tables in the Four Gospels? Was he the descendant of David? Does not every bastard allege that he is of royal seed and of the stock of Jesse? Who was his father? Saul? Or God? Not once did he call for Joseph.

My cheeks shook because Jesus of Nazareth had no lawful ancestors. "He has no spermal parent," I wept.

And I was bitter when I heard him address God in his Aramaic tongue: "Father, Father, it is finished!"

In my dream the Galilean lake continued to pour its waters through me as I repeated, "Abba, Father," and I said, "I will walk the rest of my days over the Brook Kidron until I find Saul."

He spoke again: "I was conceived in a lawless bed, but I am a Jew of Nazareth, and the pure blood of Israel flows through my veins. Since I was illegitimate, I was considered as defiled as one who has a clubfoot or is blind in an eye, and therefore unfit to stand in holy places. But take heed lest you forget that the law is never the heart."

"But you were not alone," I said, pondering my own deserts. Then I added with a wry mouth, "I don't believe you had twelve friends, or even five as the rabbin claim."

He replied, "I pretended there were twelve disciples because Jacob, the father of Israel, had twelve sons, though not one of them was Yeshu of Nazareth. A waif, I was despised by everyone and taken for an uncouth fellow; for is it not asked, 'Can anything good come out of Nazareth?'

"A beggar in Bethany and at Capernaum, imprisoned in Tiberias, wretched in dissolute and simpering Tyre and Sidon, I was in exile everywhere. When I returned to Galilee, it no longer existed, because one cannot go back to anything. Were it possible to recapture the incident in Jerusalem and to drink the same evening at Gethsemane, I could believe that I had lived rather than died. Do you really think there is a world?

"You have a right to wonder if there were twelve beloved ones who trembled when I was ailing and who were as sudden as the aspens upon my pulses. You have not forgotten that he who warmed himself by the fire and swore that he did not know me went by the name of Shim'on Kefa, Simon Peter or Petros, the Rock!"

"Who are you, then?" I pleaded, and I heard the echo: "No-place, no-time, no-body."

"Are you Jesus Balaam the sorcerer?"

"Why call ye me Balaam? Am I he who knew not even when his ass perceived the angel? Was I so callow in the arts of contemplation?"

"Is it true," I continued, "that with the aid of Beelzebub, who only performs his subtle craft in the dark, you were able to cast out unclean spirits? Did you not go to the land of the Gadarenes to learn how to expel the devils that make swine of men?"

His retort was so waspish that I was certain that he was not spectral: "You are making a mock of my anguish and feigning that you do not know what I meant when I claimed that I walked on the sea. Surely you know that there can be no trance without water; nor are you so ignorant of hydromancy that you have not yet discovered why I am referred to as Jesus Piscis. Call me Balaam, if you like, but the only magic I ever practiced was the sorcery of the dream. When a man slumbers, he can perform miracles. At Caesarea Philippi I did not deny that I was The Messiah, or that I could hypnotize the leper and the palsied; when I raised the dead I only resurrected Lazarus' demons."

I took a drop of compassionate spittle from my mouth to wipe away his illegitimacy . . . and then the vision changed, and I saw a boy standing underneath the viaduct in Kansas City in front of the Star Lady Barbershop. The hot, smutty July pavement was holy ground; and as the flies began to swarm and hum around the barber pole, the boy heard the wings of angels. He could not turn his sun-baked face away from the thick plate glass on which was enameled: *16 East 8*. He started to chant aloud: "16 East 8," and he knew that this was his song of Jehovah, for both the address and the name Jehovah are made up of seven characters.

"Yeshu! Yeshu!" I cried, clinging to the curls of Saul, but before I could open my eyes, I saw that my lips were on my mother's long, Galilean nose, and I whispered in her ear, "Miriam Megaddela Neshaya, the lady barber, oh my mother!"

Then I awakened and sat up on my cot, but the vision of Miriam was still before my eyes, and in my ears I heard the refrain "16 East 8," those seven letters of the dream which were the Kabbala of my childhood. Why was it impossible for me to let go of the misery of my boyhood? I hugged close to my breast the scene of the skinny, narrow shop containing the five barber chairs and the pair of brass cuspidors bespattered with tobacco juice which was as pungent and

brown as the saliva of grasshoppers. The two scurvy electric
fans hanging from the ceiling and the mahogany settees on
which waiting customers sprawled in their workingmen's
blue-denim overalls would never disappear from my mind.
Did I not also cherish the back room, where the water closet
stood no more than a yard or so from the rusted, cockroachy
gas range? Would I ever break the terrible image of that
table covered with cracked and spotty linoleum, beneath
which were two deep, bow-shaped drawers where my
mother kept her flour and in which six newborn mice once
nested? Even though I swooned with nausea as I remembered this, why was it that I could not part with the recollection?

There was the black, filthy alley behind the shop, fes-
tered with four-footed creatures that mangle the imagination. The rear of an umbrella factory gave onto the alley,
and there one could find and collect a sheaf of tin spokes, or
come upon a whole frame; two doors away was the shop of
a wagonmaker, where a child could pick up axle grease with
a stick and put it in a tin can. And nearby were large wooden
cases that one might sit on and contemplate the steep hill of
mustard-colored clay that ran away from Phineas Levi's
pawnbroker's establishment. What sticky, amorous secrets
there were in the prostitute's rooms above Basket's Quick
Lunch counter: the odor of Lysol and potassium permanga-
nate and the sweat of venery came from there, stinging my
nostrils. When I saw Tisha, whose mother ran the place—
and advertised it as light housekeeping—I thought all the
rough, emerald pimples and pouchy boils on her cheeks and
neck were the marvelous, occult sores and scabs of Venus.

Would I walk past the shanty commission houses on
broken-down lower Walnut Street or loiter about the penny
arcade on Main Street all my days? Would I always be looking for a large, pondy mudhole in a vacant lot, hidden behind a signboard, where one could make a raft to float on
the water?

What purity there had been in the anguish over a lost orange; how round and carnal was the fruit, and after I had peeled it and was making ready to slice and put it into my mouth, I had dropped the orange in the gutter. And how I wept.

Is there no real revelation after childhood? Can we learn only by remembering what we felt then? Why do we love our vermin? Do our souls need dirt, lice, rats, mud puddles and woe? The sweetest fennel makes us indolent and gives us antiseptic memories. We caress and stroke our rotten, starved years because the dream requires it. You who have pondered Joseph's interpretation of Pharaoh's dream consider this: the seven lean kine that stand in the hot river Nile will always devour the seven fat ones—aye, seven again; it is the sign of pestilence and famine—but there is more food here for the despairing, niggard heart than in the tenderest grass and herbs.

I sat on the bed, holding my head between my hands. With a weary glance, I swept up our penury; there were the narrow iron cot and the mealy bed upon which my mother slept, two chairs, with spindly, sick legs, a secondhand deal table and her steamer trunk which she used as a dresser and on which she set her jars of rejuvenating face and hand creams. A famished cotton sheet served as a curtain between her couch and my sleeping space.

This was in a cold-water flat we had taken at $24 a month in a slum tenement on East 96th Street in Manhattan after leaving Queens. My mother was still determined to occupy herself. Speaking Polish and German enabled her to get a few customers for her violet ray treatments. She still had enough strength in her hands to massage a fatigued woman or a young wife who was agitated because she had not menstruated; she kneaded the flesh of her back, and sometimes she pared the calluses of a patient to relieve her of a toothache or a neuralgic jaw.

The cold-water flat on 96th Street was our desert of

Paran. My mother was a Hagarene daughter from the beginning, and I had inherited her wilderness. I was already as gray as Ephraim. Canoes that are filled with stones to sink them have a pensive quiet at the bottom of a river which every man craves. Would that our thoughts were heavy enough to push us down to our depths and hold us there. "Behold, he drinketh up a river and hasteth not," says Job.

My mother had little left to keep her going but her will. She had made up her mind to live; dreading to make a grave of her belly, she hardly ate any food. She avoided salt, pepper, ketchup, sugar, fats, meats and milk. If she were fatigued, she nibbled two carrots and chewed half-cooked porridge. And she had become more absent-minded; after she had taken a sooty, dented pot and boiled a little water in it, she poured parched cereal over the simmering water, and then forgot about it; by the time she remembered, the pasty oatmeal or farina was spoilt. Often, if she caught herself rushing about, she would suddenly stand still and beseech herself not to hurry, which would only increase her high blood pressure, or, God forbid, irreparably damage her heart.

Aside from other tormenting ailments she had prolapsus, a dropping bladder; she feared to lift a pound of potatoes, as she thought it might be too great a strain on her. Because she was short, she always maintained she had gotten a hernia from standing on her feet for fourteen hours a day while holding her scissors and comb above the heads of customers.

Despite her resolution to remain alive, every new day was a terror to her. By two o'clock in the afternoon she had gained a part of her battle against the morning; then she would snatch the remnant of a petticoat from the floor of the clothes closet and wipe the scum of lotion from her cheeks. If she happened to step upon an old corset cover she would pick it up and clean her shoes with it. She could not part with anything; she hoarded buttons, a piece of a chemise, a smutty chamois or powder puff, a hair switch, half of a razorstrop. They represented her life which was over.

Sometimes she took the pincushion she had had since she was in Memphis and held it in her lap while she rocked to and fro. She cringed whenever she thought of the present; what a hideous, massive heap it was, and where would she get the strength to struggle with it?

Late in the day, if she was not drained raw by her nerves, she might search for a copy of Smollett's *Humphrey Clinker* or Le Sage's *Gil Blas* and read a few pages. Since she seldom recalled where she had left off the previous day, she often reread the same chapter. Once she came upon a musty receipt, dated January 31, 1911, for the rent of the Star Lady Barbershop at 16 East 8th, and she took off her sweaty glasses and dabbed her eyes with a clout she had ripped from a worn-out window curtain. Then wandering among the junk heap of scarred saucepans, a rusted skillet, a broken meat grinder, the old Yale lock from the barbershop door, a pair of keys for the front door at 710 A East 8th, and sticky dishes that lay on the floor, atop the gas range or under the table, she suddenly pressed her hand against her heart to see whether she could feel it beating. After slumping into a chair, she staggered toward the steamer trunk where she had hidden the alarm clock, the crystal of which had fallen out. Clutching it, and pressing one thumb against the hands that were like a mangled fly, she took deep breaths and counted her pulse. When she felt quieter she threw the clock back into the trunk and locked it. Ever since she had come to New York, she regarded the clock with hatred. If she thought about it, and then reminded herself that sixty minutes had passed, she would groan, "I am one hour closer to the grave."

The only relief Lizzie had from her worries was to go back to her memories. A postcard view of Swope or Fairmount Parks gave her more hope than any lawn she now saw; nothing was green any longer except the grass in Kansas City. On occasion she recaptured a glimpse of Captain Henry Smith's jolly, bloated neck; she could see him sitting opposite her at the table on the deck of his boat, the *Chester*. Had she ever eaten anything with relish since they had had clam chowder with oyster crackers and a bottle of Bud- weiser? And there was gray Cromwell, wearing his moral gold-rimmed glasses, and his gray suit was as plain as his principles. When she had the ill luck to awaken from these reveries and remember that somehow or other she had to get through Monday or Wednesday, and then thought of Thursday morning, she rose and stumbled against the metal leg of the cot, bruising her ankle. As for the future, O dear, merciful Lord, let me have one, she begged, pouring alcohol on her wound. She dropped a large grievous sigh and shook her dense neck. Making a gothic arch with her hard-working fingers, she asked God for several more years; no, she was not greedy—had she ever demanded much? Just the sun and more of the summer grass. Could He not give her ten years more of autumn nights? All that she wanted was to walk quiet and slow among soft dusks; how blessed it would be to have one more decade beneath the moon, and to be able to hear the Troost Avenue streetcar growing on the tracks as it approached the 8th Street flat. If the Lord God would only take into consideration all her misfortunes and give her credit for them, perhaps she could live until she was ninety- one or ninety-three, maybe even ninety-seven—was that so excessive, especially considering all her struggles? Then she would ask for nothing else but a few scattered raindrops of hope.

Her face was bitten by anguish and the uninterrupted warfare against hunger, and the dread of it. The character of the woman was as ineradicable as the parched pomegranates, dates, nuts, beans, grapes and bread that lie whole in the mummy chambers of Memphis. Could it be that because she was so worn out she was now closer to her origins? Ameri- can in almost every detail of habit, speech and dress, she was an admixture of Missouri and Babel. Could her neighbors have understood this, they might have swarmed about her. She was already a relic in a new world.

Meanwhile, I had taught for a semester at James Madison High School. But I was not asked to return because I suggested that pupils read the tales of Chekov, Tolstoi, Gorki, and the novels of George Gissing and Gogol instead of the prescribed rubbish by Zane Grey, Dickens, Thackeray and Jack London.

I was ashamed because I could do little or nothing to appease our plight; we had to live as best we could on the meager rentals from my mother's houses in Kansas City. Worse, I could not handle her pain, and I was unable to think because I could not feel. My mother's face had become dim, but I did my utmost to grasp her image. However, my sight was as diseased as that of Tobias, in whose eyes the dung of sparrows had fallen and settled. That this was the impotence of the spirit made it no less intolerable. We cannot live, sorrow or die for somebody else, for suffering is too precious to be shared.

Since I was useless, I began to sleep late; I craved to be the four-footed beast in the darkness, for the sun confused and punished me. The long shoots of evening were the tapers that gave off the light the day had denied me. I already began to doubt that my mother lived, though I dreaded that she would die, and I would lose her image. After we go down into the pit of night, when we are in our beds, we smell the fish of Oceanus, and when we awaken our palates are brackish, and the odor of Leviathan is in our mouths.

Unable to drive out of my bones that one dirge: "My mother will disappear," I fled from her. I eschewed her cruel, Gehenna mornings, and I sank deeper into the darkness. I saw that man was born to be deceived and that he is a wan image roaming an orbed plain in the Void. Sleep is death, and death is sleep because we are never alive. Strindberg said: "I dream, therefore I exist," but I dreamt, and did not live.

Each day I failed to take up her old age that fluttered like the feathers of a small wren, and gently stroke it. Why could I not be lowly and fall down before her feet? But I had always rejected my mother's countenance; in my vanity I had crowned my head with the auburn curls of Saul, and when I smiled I showed the fleece that shone so white between his profligate lips. A real physiognomy is an antique crypt, and at the age of forty my face was dominated by my mother's, as well as the thousand devils that I had come by from Saul. Though I said, I will walk all my days over the Brook Kidron until I find Saul, I was also searching for my mother. But I was plagued by the herd of swine at Gadarene; if I believed I was not evil, or dared to assume that I could be good, a demon graved in me would come up and sit on my mouth and scoff at me, and though my spirit fell out of my body whenever I noticed this, my demons grew harder in me.

I groped for understanding, knowing that the miracle of perception is involved with the miracle of love, and yet I did not know what I imagined I knew, for my acts were bad and loveless ones. Both my mother and I were the unloved ones, and the unleavened bread in the desert. This is what I said to myself, but saying it is not knowing it.

I avoided my mother's face and did not go to kiss her, and the more motionless and lethargic I became, the harder it was for me to recognize her. Many times she was in the room and I neither heard nor saw her, and so she grew fainter. When we fail to see the phantoms near us they vanish from our sight.

One night I slept and dreamt I saw a woman who was only two empty udders; I imagined I beheld her, but there was no mouth or chin or cheeks in her. As I grieved for her, water grew around me. It was neap tide, and my sleep was shoaly, and sour and dyspeptic, and I endeavored to walk in the water toward her to give her a filial kiss to restore the mouth, the cheeks and chin that were missing—but the

227

waves held me back so that I could not reach her. Then I saw a cruse of water and a loaf of bread, and I awoke and moaned, "She is dead, and the bottle of water and the bread she has left me are for my hunger." I sat there on the bed, and the vision clung to me like the fog bank that gathers around one's eyes after a migraine. I looked about for my mother; then I hurried over to her small casket, the iron cot into which she descended every night. A skinny sheet lay awry over the pallet, but the shabby becrumbed coat was gone. I threw on a jacket and rushed out into the street, which was painted with sleet. There I saw coming toward me a woman whose back was lumped by her unforgiving hopes; she walked with unsteady feet on the ice, carrying two milk bottles under her arm. Relieved when I saw her knobby chin and the nose that fell over her deflowered mouth, I upbraided her: "O my mother, why are you so stupid? Do you wish to fall on the ice? What are you doing with those two empty udders?" Startled when I heard these words, I grasped the bottles from her and ran back to the flat. The dream would not let go of me, and I tried to shape the face I could not collect. I had resolved to kiss her hands when I saw her, but as she came through the door the devils grinned at me, and I could not forgive her—but for what I did not know. I believed I saw a forsaken and palsied heap of rags go to that accursed cot and lie down.

At forty years of age I thought that the bulls of Apis and Mnevis had expired in my loins, though Lilith, the angel of lust, visited me more often than she had. My dreams were round and wombed, but as soon as I awakened my day was a bunch of hyssop.

At this time I was thinking of marriage, but as I had not known the woman long, I was most uneasy. Would not marriage be a laudanum? I needed sensuality as others require alcohol, tobacco, gossip, loose chatter, opium or faith. Then I vaguely hoped that after I had become her husband I would no longer wander in the Hagarene forest. Were disreputable houses available and cheap, I should have relinquished all thoughts of wedlock.

When I told my mother about this woman, she promptly wrote the agent in Missouri to sell her houses so that her son might have the money to provide for a wife.

And so I was married. And at the same time I obtained a temporary appointment to teach at a university. But how long could I heed the sounding of the trumpet for the asses to come to the pragmatic donkey-prayer at daybreak? Could I be the gross Caliban, wallowing in the academic mire, while feigning to be the intransigent Ariel?

My wife and I stayed with my mother in the cold-water flat for a while. One afternoon, when my wife was absent, my mother threw open the door and ran into the room. Her shoulders were still muscular and her legs nervous and agile. Was she in some acute pain? Sitting next to her, I did not look at her or take up into my eyes the few ulcered mementos of our past—the steamer trunk, the two chairs with peeled, starved legs, those white jars of face cream and the black violet ray box. I waited to see what she would do. Removing her glasses—which she always did when she was exalted or in a desponding mood—she took off her heavy black shoes and her hat that looked like a dilapidated bird's nest. A sharp rapture seized her, and I saw her for a moment wearing nothing but her ecstasy. She was feverish, not jubilant as she had been when she stepped out of her cold bath at 710 A East 8th and rubbed her stout loins with the rough bath towel. I turned a little to contemplate the spare flesh sitting at my side, and seeing what was left of her, I bent my gaze toward myself. She was holding herself in her arms, cradling her bosom in her hands. Suddenly she dropped to the floor, pressed her lips to my feet and began to weep: "Edward, your mother's life has not been a complete mockery. Son of all my miseries and disappointments that swarmed like flies around the honey of your mother's short youth, look, I have overcome bad luck—God has not made me a beggar to my own child!"

Then she drew from the depths of her breast a sheaf of hundred-dollar bills and she placed them in my hands. I sat there regarding this kneeling woman with stupefaction, but held fast to the money. What will she do if I keep it, I asked myself, choking the green papers between my fingers. I stuffed my pockets with these grassy maggots; then I got up and moved away from her as though I hoped that distance might lessen my disgrace. Abruptly, although no one else was at home, I looked around me to see whether anybody had noticed me pocketing the money. In less than three minutes I had made a pauper of her, and how could I cure her indigence? Other thoughts smote me: "Does this most unfortunate woman expect to die? Is she insane?" Plagued by so many ailments, where had she gotten the strength to think of anything else but her own fate? For those who are sick love themselves passionately.

Standing on the one rug bitten by a generation of want, I still clung to all her drudgery in the Star Lady Barbershop. Then she took more money from her bosom and, imagining I was standing next to her, she put it in my hands which were not there, and the winged lucre flew to the floor. Crooking my back, I stooped over to pick it up. Instead of bowing to her I made a low leg to the bills scattered and crawling over the floor. All my life I have committed one of the worst of the seven cardinal sins: I had not the strength to overcome the average in myself. When we are ordinary, we do not amount to anything: our everyday life is our vermin. All that I had done for so long was to scratch the lice of my indolent sensibilities and imagine that I was showing a great deal of emotion for my mother. Now when I regarded this pile of palsied spirit and tatters before me, a shrewd, cold feeling came over me; the demon sat on my lips and smirked at me: "Will she die before she becomes a burden to you?" When I heard his leering whisper, I

230

groaned. Where had this sin been interred? And why had it come now to make its diabolical grimace at me? Can anybody doubt that it is the malice we have towards ourselves that is our real foe? And I thought, who can behold his own worms and not shrink from himself?

Shortly after this ecstasy my mother began to decline more rapidly. Her temples burned when she lay down at night; she kept a cold compress on her head, which made her nose look rabbinic. She knew what ailed her and said in a most woeful tone, "My son, I have hardening of the arteries. Oh, my poor Edward."

The doctor told me she could live another eighteen or twenty years, and when I heard this I rejoiced and I thought of King Hezekiah, and how grateful he was when Isaiah said that God would give him fifteen more years of life. But when I informed her what the physician had said, she fell into a deeper melancholy, and I was angry with her because she was not content to have these years before her. I admonished her, "Mother, we can no longer live as many years as Enoch or Jared. Why don't you be quiet? You are so nervous, always running in the streets with that lunatic violet ray machine."

One evening I saw her staggering about in the room, jostling against the sink and the steamer trunk. She turned to me, throwing out her hands; the tears hung upon her sagging face, and I saw there all the rivers of sorrow which are of as many colors as there are precious stones in paradise. She said to me, "I am going to die, Edward. Let me sign over to you what I still have left."

I stood there, incapable of moving. Had it come, the void, the awful and irrevocable chasm between us? What should I do? Instead of taking this shrunken heap of suffering into my arms, I only shook my head. I had already stolen too much from her; I had not the strength either to lift up my guilt or to say more.

Every night after that when she lay on the cot, she continued to grease her face and arms and neck with her lotions, and before going to sleep, I came to her and knelt on the floor beside her cot and kissed her, and then I arose and went to my own bed.

With the money she had given me I purchased an old house on Cape Cod and a secondhand car, and one night my wife and I sat in the car outside the flat saying good-bye to my mother. Then I watched this shamble of loneliness, less than five feet of it, covered with a begrimed and nibbled coat, walk away from me.

For the next two years letters came from her twice a week, always beginning with "My beloved Son." Once as my eyes crawled down to the bottom of the last page, over-run with her strong, gothic script, I read: "You know, my dearest one on earth to me, what a good future we have. . . ." I took the *future* and cast it violently to the ground, and pressed my heel against it until it hissed and crept away. Had not Jehovah made enough tragic sport of her life? Now I sank beneath all her hopes and even her endearments crushed me.

On the 15th of February, 1946, I lay in my bed, going to and fro in it and unable to seal the wandering scenes that passed through my head. Again a river arose and a cruse of water and a loaf of bread grew out of it, but stare as hard as I could, there was nothing else, and when I awakened, I shrieked, "Mother, your wicked, fallen son will come to your side; you will not die alone." Shaking the sleep from me, I prodded my wife, saying, "Let us go to my mother be-fore she dies." Her face was a stranger to me and she gave me no answer.

On the 18th of February there came another letter from my mother, but I would not open it. Had I had a hammer, I could not have broken this envelope made of black basalt. On that night in the month known as Shebat in Hebrew, which is a time of tears and lamentations, she died. She was alone, and her body lay on the cot for five days before a neighbor found her.

It is hideous and coarse to assume that we can do something for others—and it is vile not to endeavor to do it. I had not the strength to handle her tragedy, for my will has failed me every hour of each day. It is said that a wise man falls down seven times a day and rises; I have fallen and never gotten up.

My mother was born unfortunate, and she was pursued until her end by that evil genius, ill luck. The Psalmist says, "No one can keep his own soul alive"—nor anybody else's either. We despair because we are no better and are not consoled that we can be no worse. A life is a single folly, but two lives would be countless ones, for nobody profits by his mistakes.

I do not go to her grave because it would do her no good. Though everything in the earth has feeling—the granite mourns, the turf sleeps and has fitful nights, and the syenite chants as melodiously as Orpheus and Musaeus—it would be idle to say that Lizzie Dalberg, whose bones still have sentience, is what she was. She is and she is not, and that is the difference between the trance we call being and the other immense experience we name death.

Who was Lizzie Dalberg? I wish to God I knew, but it is my infamy that I do not. How often had she pleaded with heaven to lead her out of the peopleless desert of Beersheba, but to what avail? She only questioned God in anger once: "Why am I miserable, while others who are pitiless and contemptible are so fortunate?"

But she never received an answer. Not God, but gibing Pilate came to her and asked, "What is Truth?"

And I knew not why until I had heard her quiet reply: "My life."

When the image of her comes up on a sudden—just as my bad demons do—and I see again her dyed henna hair, the eyes dwarfed by the electric lights in the Star Lady Barbershop, and the dear, broken wing of her mouth, and when I regard her wild tatters, I know that not even Solomon in his lilied raiment was so glorious as my mother in her rags. *Selah.*